SUPPORTING SPECTACULAR GIRLS™

of related interest

Aspergirls
Empowering Females with Asperger Syndrome
Rudy Simone
ISBN 978 1 84905 826 1
eISBN 978 0 85700 289 1

The Spectrum Girl's Survival Guide
How to Grow Up Awesome and Autistic
Siena Castellon
Foreword by Temple Grandin
Illustrated by Rebecca Burgess
ISBN 978 1 78775 183 5
eISBN 978 1 78775 184 2

A Guide to Mental Health Issues in Girls and Young Women on the Autism Spectrum
Diagnosis, Intervention and Family Support
Dr Judy Eaton
ISBN 978 1 78592 092 9
eISBN 978 1 78450 355 0

Inclusive Education for Autistic Children
Helping Children and Young People to Learn and Flourish in the Classroom
Dr Rebecca Wood
Foreword by Dr Wenn. B Lawson
ISBN 978 1 78592 321 0
eISBN 978 1 78450 634 6

SUPPORTING SPECTACULAR GIRLS™

A PRACTICAL GUIDE TO DEVELOPING AUTISTIC GIRLS' WELL-BEING AND SELF-ESTEEM

HELEN CLARKE

FOREWORD BY DR REBECCA WOOD

Jessica Kingsley Publishers
London and Philadelphia

First published in Great Britain in 2022 by Jessica Kingsley Publishers
An Hachette Company

6

Front cover image source: Helen Clarke/Mike Elgie

A CIP catalogue record for this title is available from
the British Library and the Library of Congress

ISBN 978 1 78775 548 2
eISBN 978 1 78775 549 9

Printed and bound by CPI Group (UK) Ltd, Croydon, CR0 4YY

Jessica Kingsley Publishers' policy is to use papers that are natural,
renewable and recyclable products and made from wood grown in
sustainable forests. The logging and manufacturing processes are expected
to conform to the environmental regulations of the country of origin.

Jessica Kingsley Publishers
Carmelite House
50 Victoria Embankment
London EC4Y 0DZ

www.jkp.com

For Mum, who always intuitively did the right thing for me,
regardless of what other people said or thought,
and for Dad, for passing his love of learning on to me.

Contents

Disclaimer and Notes on the Text

Though this book contains information about autism diagnosis, speech and language therapy and occupational therapy, the information provided is not intended to be a substitute for medical advice.

I purposely do not provide a checklist as to how autistic girls may 'present', as although some autistic girls might fit a particular 'profile', I believe this would create further unhelpful stereotypes. All autistic people are individuals. What I seek to show throughout this book are the challenges that affect autistic girls and women, and the strengths of many of the girls I have worked with. I have drawn on my own and other people's observations and experiences, and how these are reflected in research and data. I present many of the challenges experienced by autistic girls which relate to other people's expectations of them, how society forces them to adapt themselves and the difficulties that arise as a result, making suggestions as to how these issues can be addressed through increased understanding.

Many issues regarding safeguarding and safety are discussed throughout this book. Each school, service or organization will have its own guidelines in relation to how it safeguards children and adults.

Foreword

It can sometimes seem like the more that we talk about autism, the more that large swathes of the autistic population disappear from view. This particularly applies to autistic people who do not communicate primarily through speech, those with high support needs (especially if they live in residential care), older autistic people, those with co-occurring conditions and autistic professionals outside of the tech industry or office spaces.

As far as girls and women are concerned, there has been, in recent years, a growing recognition that far more are autistic than previously thought, and the perception that autistic people are predominantly male is increasingly rejected. This in turn leads to more complexities, however, as uncertainties remain as to whether autistic women continue to be viewed through a male lens, or if understanding autistic women on their own terms could, and should, lead us all to understand autism better. Not only this, but as our conceptualization of gender shifts with the recognition that many people do not identify in binary terms, the impact of these understandings on how we value, relate to and support autistic people is still poorly appreciated.

One issue is clear, however, and that is we are still falling short in our education system in terms of enabling positive participation and outcomes for autistic children and young people in school. Far too many autistic young people experience multiple forms of exclusion, as well as acute anxiety and stress in the school environment when they do attend. Notwithstanding an appreciation of the complexities of gender, we still have a limited understanding of how these issues impact on autistic girls in particular, as the predominance of the 'male model' of autism stubbornly perpetuates.

Helen Clarke's detailed and empathetic book addresses this gap in our knowledge, as she provides information and clear strategies on how to understand, support and appreciate autistic girls aged 11–15. Underpinned by a wealth of research evidence, as well as her own experiences as an autistic woman and a teacher, Helen offers invaluable insights and advice on different aspects of the lifeworld of autistic girls, while being careful to not over-generalize and to signpost to further sources of information when needed.

Each of the seven chapters has an imperative as its title, such as 'Be Healthy', underscoring the emphasis Helen places on the rights autistic girls have to be happy, safe and well, and in so doing, to be themselves. In this, the author has neatly eschewed the typical emphasis in our schools on using interventions to somehow remediate the presumed impairments associated with autism, focusing instead on their unique and individual qualities, and how autistic girls can be helped to flourish in school. For example, while acknowledging fully that autistic girls may well require support in a number of areas, Helen underlines the importance of autistic role models, a topic dear to my own heart due to the Autistic School Staff Project which I lead (Wood 2020).[1]

This carefully researched book has been written in an accessible manner and could be enjoyed as a single read-through or dipped into for information and strategies. Interwoven with examples from the author's own personal and professional experiences, this book is full of insights and practical tips which would be of great benefit to all who work with autistic girls, particularly in school settings. Above all, this

1 Wood, R. (2020) Autistic School Staff Project. Available at https://autisticschoolstaffproject.com.

book has been written with sensitivity and warmth, and so I hope that some autistic girls read it too, as this excellent resource would surely reassure them that they are no longer invisible, but instead understood and appreciated, and by extension empowered, through its contents.

Dr Rebecca Wood

Dr Rebecca Wood is a Senior Lecturer in Special Education at the University of East London who leads the Autistic School Staff Project.

Acknowledgements

I am grateful to everyone who has generously found the time in their own busy lives to contribute to this book, sharing their work, thoughts, experiences, knowledge and opinions.

As a former teacher who values the impact that research can have, it is a privilege for me that Dr Rebecca Wood has provided the Foreword to this book, and I would like to offer her my thanks. Dr Wood's research and writing focus on the education of autistic children, encouraging the reader to question their own perceptions, their own practices and approaches, and what the education system has to offer autistic children. Dr Rebecca Wood is, herself, proactive about bringing about positive change through her work.

I would like to acknowledge the researchers and authors I have referenced in this book. Their work can improve the well-being of autistic people, reflects the priorities of the autistic community, uses respectful language, highlights many of the issues that autistic people experience and provides 'evidence' about what needs to change for autistic people across health and education. I would like to thank Dr Alex Sturrock from The University of Manchester, who works with many autistic girls, for her contribution; thanks also to Kathy Leadbitter for her support and encouragement, and to Dr Craig Goodall, who has provided many practical suggestions to support autistic children in the classroom.

Thanks also to Dr Rachel Moseley for her contributions to this book that are very much valued.

Health and education both impact the well-being of autistic children and I am grateful to those working in health services who have been able to share their expertise. I am extremely grateful to Helen Murphy, occupational therapist, and to Karen Henry, midwife. I thank you for your time, generosity and support.

I would like to acknowledge the autistic and non-autistic parents who have contributed their thoughts and experiences. I am grateful to you for your honesty and trust, for providing me with insights into your lives and for allowing me to work with your children. I would like to express my gratitude to Hayley Morgan for sharing her experiences of motherhood from the perspective of being an autistic mother. In addition, I am grateful to Jodie Smitten, who is a parent and autism specialist who works to increase understanding to improve the lives of autistic children. Jodie has kindly shared one of her poems about her perspectives as a parent. Thanks also to Eliza Fricker of 'Missing The Mark' for your kindness and humour and for sharing your experiences as a parent.

Thank you to all those working at The Women's Organization and The School for Social Entrepreneurs, and to Marie Hall of Empowerment House, Liverpool, for supporting me.

I am extremely grateful to Nicola Beattie and Julie McKnight for sharing their wisdom and expertise in mental health and well-being, for their endless support, advice, ideas and encouragement, and for their contribution to *Spectacular Girls*. You are both true allies.

I am grateful to all the people who have generously contributed their thoughts and opinions and who have shared their experiences so that other people can experience better mental and physical health and well-being. These include Florence Neville, co-founder of Autism Health and Wellbeing (Autism HWB), who set up 'a space for autistic people to share the things they have found helpful and healing', Sarah

Boon, and others who wish to remain anonymous. I would also like to thank ARFID Awareness UK, and Hope Virgo, for sharing their knowledge in relation to eating disorders. I would likc to offer my thanks to Mike Elgie for his graphic design expertise, creativity, kindness and patience. I acknowledge Stephen O'Toole, of Victor Walsh, Liverpool, for providing me with sound advice as well as support and encouragement. It has been a pleasure to work with someone who is also creative.

I am grateful to Lynda, Emily, Karina and the team at Jessica Kingsley Publishers for providing the opportunity to write this book and for their support, patience and understanding. For those of us who may find it difficult to communicate for numerous reasons, writing can help us to share our thoughts.

Thank you to my family for allowing me the time to write.

Finally, thank you to all the people who have chosen to read this book who believe that all autistic girls and women should be able to lead happy, safe, healthy, long and fulfilled lives. Your well-being matters too.

Preface

I have written this book from the perspective of being autistic, a teacher and a parent. Being autistic, I have faced numerous barriers in writing this book, including burnout, perfectionism and anxiety; many of the issues that I write about I have experienced first-hand. Ironically, whilst writing a book about well-being, I have had to take my own advice on numerous occasions! I only discovered in my mid-20s that I was autistic, thanks to the autistic children I was working with and through reading research articles whilst studying for further qualifications. I continue to learn from other autistic people and am aware that the more I learn the more there is to know, and that my own understanding is constantly evolving as other people offer new insights.

For 20 years I had the privilege of teaching autistic children and the pleasure of seeing these children succeed in education, but reluctantly I had to make the difficult decision to leave a fulfilling job that I enjoyed (that was my routine and structure) when my autistic daughter could no longer access mainstream education due to the detrimental impact this was having on her health, despite the best efforts of those who worked with hers. Prioritizing her well-being, I removed her from the system, but it was also during this time, whilst she was being assessed for an autism diagnosis, that I also found myself having to question other people's perceptions of her as a girl, as well as the diagnostic process itself. I was also aware of other autistic girls, out of education, experiencing mental and physical health issues and struggling to receive appropriate support.

Research and health statistics highlight that autistic girls and women are being affected by a significant number of challenges across the lifespan. Through exploring these issues and why these disparities might occur, it is hoped that autistic girls will experience better mental and physical health, will be more able to understand themselves, will be better understood by others, and will be more able to lead happy, healthy and fulfilling lives.

The word 'Spectacular' in the title of the book represents the many positive qualities and strengths that autistic girls have. Spectacular is reminiscent of the word 'spectrum', which suggests that all girls are unique.

CHAPTER 1

Introduction

I was born in the 1970s when little was known about autism, especially about autistic girls. Prior to this date autism research was primarily focused on autistic boys (Asperger, 1944). From an early age I remember feeling different to my peers but growing up I knew of no other autistic girls or women, nor saw any representation of autistic people in the media that I could relate to.

At school, I was often labelled as 'shy', a word that is sometimes still used to 'explain away' autism, especially when girls are spoken about. Teachers assumed that because I was quiet I lacked confidence. It was only me who knew that I had 'inner confidence', but I was never assertive enough to say so! I spent a lot of time observing others, using as many strategies as I could (without realizing it) to blend in. Being quiet and smiling seemed to work. Teachers got the impression that I understood more than I did, which resulted in me being left alone. School was a confusing and stressful place for me in the early years, although I was fortunate to attend a small school with an inclusive ethos, where teachers really valued children for being their unique selves, and this helped me to feel good about myself. However, I did not understand why other children did not follow the rules (I was polite and compliant), or why changes to my usual routine caused me so much anxiety (everyone else seemed to look forward to school trips and birthday parties at the weekend, whereas these events filled me with dread and could make me physically ill), or why I found the environment so overwhelming due to having sensory needs that I was unaware of at the time.

I made my way through school, finding change and transition difficult (especially the move from primary to secondary school). I found examinations caused huge pressure, particularly so because of the uncertainty and change that followed. I made it on to university, even though I was discouraged from applying by a tutor who was sure I wouldn't get in. With the full support of my parents, I ignored my tutor's advice and was successful. People focus too much on what they perceive autistic children cannot do, rather than focusing on what they can. As a result, these children are often underestimated or are not provided with the opportunities they deserve. This applies not only in schools but later in life in the workplace.

Moving away from home to an unfamiliar place and living with unfamiliar people was a difficult transition. There have been many times in life when I know I could have benefited from knowing earlier that I was autistic and why certain aspects of life were different or challenging – job interviews, working life, friendships and relationships, emotions, pregnancy, childbirth and motherhood.

I knew little about being autistic until my mid-20s when working as a teacher. Although I began my teaching career in a mainstream school, I have taught in several schools and have been fortunate to work with a considerable number of autistic children, of all abilities, from nursery through to the post-16 age group. I was only when working with secondary-age pupils (in a special school) that I began to consider the possibility that I might be autistic too. Whilst completing further qualifications alongside my teaching role, I became interested in autism research and found that I could relate to the experiences of other autistic people that I had read about. I could also see many similarities between the children I was teaching and myself.

Working with autistic children has broadened my own knowledge of what being autistic means and has made me question what the education system has to offer autistic children (and what it should be providing), the advantages and disadvantages of different types of provision (such as specialist and mainstream schools), the curriculum and what autistic children would benefit from learning, how autistic children are being taught, how the physical environment can impact on learning, and why it is important that every member of staff working with autistic pupils should receive training if the needs of autistic children are to be met. According to the teachers' trade union NASUWT (2013), 60 percent of teachers do not believe they have adequate training to teach autistic children, and yet 70 percent of autistic children (in England) are taught in mainstream schools. A whole school approach is needed for autistic children to really benefit. Autistic children can be academically able, and many excel, but for them to achieve their potential, their social and emotional needs also need to be considered.

As a former teacher, I know that teacher well-being must become a priority and I understand the demands placed on those working in schools. Wood (2019) acknowledges that 'teachers are under a lot of pressure to be able to accommodate and understand how to teach a diversity of pupils who might have varying ways of processing information and learning'. The challenges that schools have in meeting the needs of autistic pupils are appreciated (lack of training, lack of resources, budgetary constraints); however, autistic children deserve an education equal to their non-autistic peers. When autistic children are supported by people who value them, understand them, have high expectations of them, are willing to adapt **themselves** and **their** approaches, autistic children are more likely to succeed in education and experience improved health. The needs of autistic pupils are no less important than those of non-autistic pupils; but for autistic children to be fully included in the education system, the curriculum needs to be adapted to meet their specific needs (without making them stand out), the environment requires careful consideration (and may also need to be adapted) and attitudes towards autistic pupils need to be positive.

When autistic children are expected to cope in noisy, crowded school environments that overstimulate, when they have to suppress their feelings and self-stimulatory behaviours (stims) that help them to regulate themselves, when they have to change themselves by masking and camouflaging, when they are misunderstood, when they aren't provided with routine and structure, and when they are expected to adapt how **they** communicate rather than other people adapting to them, it can result in some autistic children – often girls – having to seek mental health support. Unfortunately, this is not always available as services can be overstretched and are sometimes not tailored to the needs of autistic children, though it would be preferable to prevent such difficulties in the first place. With greater acceptance and understanding of autistic children, and the onus being on the adults to adapt to the child, autistic children would experience better educational outcomes and improved health. Ideally, schools and health services would work together to improve the well-being of autistic children. Research highlights that autistic people experience many inequalities in life compared to non-autistic people in relation to education, employment, health, well-being, lifespan and mortality. Autistic girls face additional issues and can experience 'double discrimination'. Other minorities within the autistic community can face many of the same issues.

The challenges and inequalities that autistic people experience are as follows:

- difficulties in gaining a diagnosis, being misdiagnosed
- feeling different to peers
- having no or few role models
- mental health issues (due to unmet needs, having to adapt, camouflaging feelings)
- physical health issues
- difficulties gaining an appropriate education, absenteeism, un-elective home education
- high levels of self-harm amongst adolescent girls
- the stigma of being autistic within communities
- suicide ideation (there are higher rates of suicide amongst autistic women)
- not having a support network, being socially isolated, not knowing how or where to access support
- bullying
- having difficulty accessing health services, being misunderstood, communication issues, others who lack understanding of autism being 'gatekeepers' to services

- problems accessing education, absenteeism, school exclusion
- concerns regarding safeguarding (exploitation and abuse)
- friendship and relationship difficulties, relational conflict
- myths and stereotypes regarding autistic people (in particular, autistic girls and women)
- being underemployed
- inaccessible environments
- not being able to disclose autism diagnosis for fear of mistreatment, being treated unfairly or differently, being infantilized.

What are the aims of this book?

This book highlights both the strengths and challenges of autistic girls (undiagnosed, awaiting diagnosis or diagnosed) aged approximately 11–15 years, and seeks to raise awareness of many of the issues affecting them in relation to education, health and well-being. With a focus on autistic adolescent girls, it explores six areas, 'Be Unique', 'Be Safe', 'Be Calm', 'Be Healthy', 'Be Expressive' and 'Be Independent', as shown in the 'Model of Well-Being for Autistic Children in Mainstream Schools' (Figure 1.1). Other relevant and significant issues affecting autistic girls and women across the lifespan are discussed. Although the book focuses specifically on autistic girls and women, it is appreciated that other autistic children (for example, those who are non-binary or gender fluid), each being equally important, may experience some of the same issues and challenges. This book aims to show that a greater appreciation of how autistic girls think, learn and experience life from a different perspective, can improve their well-being, in contrast to approaches or expectations that the autistic girl should adapt.

It puts a spotlight on:

The child: What each autistic child might benefit from knowing (or exploring) that may improve their self-esteem, health and well-being, aiding their access to education.

Other people: The impact that other people can have on an autistic child's health and education (exploring how other people's expectations, perceptions, knowledge, understanding, attitudes, approaches and practices can have an impact on the child, and how other people communicate with the child).

The environment: The impact of the environment (whether it can be adjusted, sensory considerations, how the environment can overstimulate or provide calm).

The additional issues that autistic adolescent girls encounter are explored (including the demands and pressures of school, friendships and relationships, emotions, misunderstandings in relation to communication and behaviour, coping with change and transition) as well as their own expectations of themselves and other people's expectations of them. As Lawson (2017) says:

> How do these females who society expects to be socially competent, cope in a world that expects them to be able to read body language, be friendly, sociable, and happy in a group, understand the hidden curriculum (the unspoken rules of human interaction) and perform in society at the expected level, manage their daily lives?

This book explores what inclusion really means for autistic girls in the mainstream education system, suggests how the curriculum can be made more relevant to autistic children by reflecting their needs, and how practices and approaches can be adapted to make learning more accessible and enjoyable, leading to improved well-being. It has been compiled to promote positive self-identity and self-esteem, and focuses on the qualities, strengths and interests of autistic girls, as well as giving consideration to what makes each individual happy to improve well-being. It is hoped that autistic girls will become easier to identify, that the challenges they face will be better understood and that many of the inequalities they experience can be addressed or prevented.

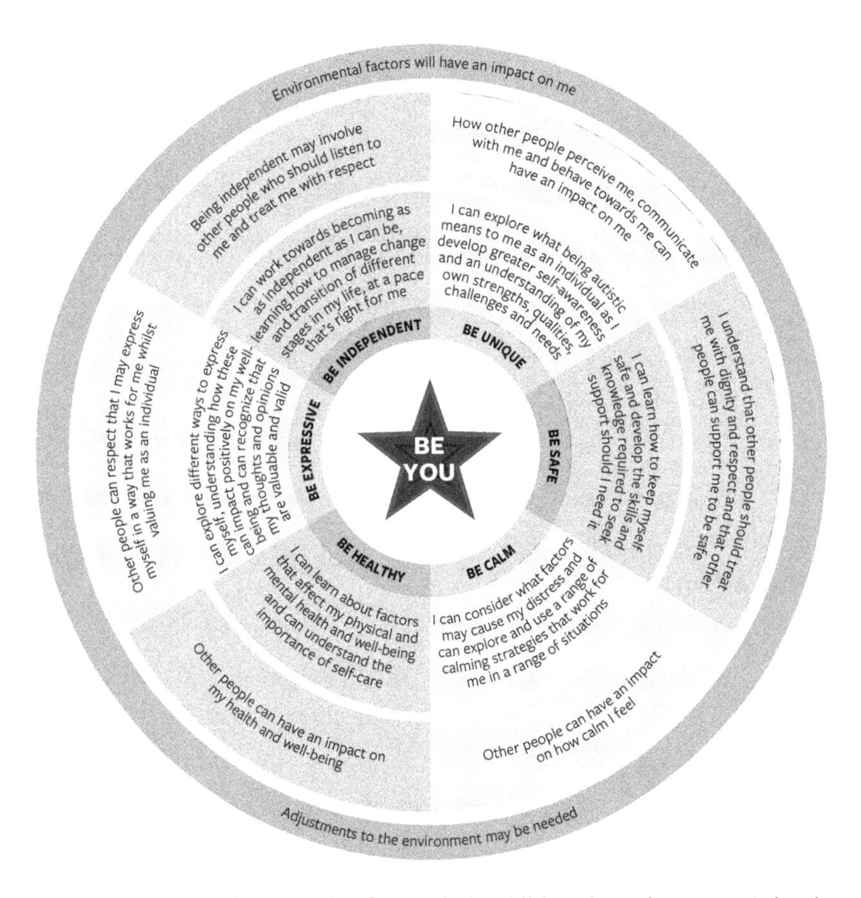

Figure 1.1: Model of Well-Being for Autistic Children in Mainstream Schools and Other Settings

Who is this book for?

This book has been compiled for those with an interest in the education, health and well-being of autistic girls including autistic people and their families, professionals working in health or education, social workers, students, therapists, counsellors, charities, organizations, and those with an interest in autism research.

Terminology

Identity-first language is used throughout this book as it is the preferred terminology of the autistic community (Kenny *et al.* 2016; Sinclair 2013). I refer to 'autistic people' (identity-first language) rather than 'people with autism' (person-first language). However, I am respectful that there is no single way of describing autism that is universally accepted and that autistic people have the right to use language that best suits them when talking about themselves.

Throughout the book I refer to 'parents'. This also includes carers of autistic children.

I respectfully use the words 'autism' and 'autistic' when writing. However, when quoting other people's thoughts, opinions or work, other terms may be used such as ASD [Autism Spectrum Disorder] and ASC [Autism Spectrum Condition].

Trigger warning

Some of the topics in this book may be triggering for some people. There is reference to self-harm, suicide ideation, suicide, exploitation, and abuse. Elevated mortality rates for autistic women are also mentioned, which some readers may find distressing. I respectfully include these issues to raise awareness of them in order to bring about positive change.

What this book is not

This book is not intended as a social skills programme, nor is it a resource providing a 'gendered curriculum' or 'intervention' (see

Milton 2014). Instead, it seeks to show the impact on autistic children when they are expected to adapt in systems and environments designed with the needs of the non-autistic majority in mind. South, Costa and McMorris (2021) refer to the 'double empathy problem' coined by Milton (2012) and state: 'Increased acceptance of autistic youth and adults into schools, workplaces, and social groups cannot depend only on changing autistic people; greater awareness and flexibility is likewise needed for neurotypical partners.'

Limitations of this book

The information and suggestions provided throughout this book provide general advice. As every autistic girl is unique, the content may need to be adapted to meet the needs of the individual. A broad overview of what autistic girls may need in order to thrive is provided, rather than specialist 'one to one' guidance. To improve well-being, autistic girls can benefit from having supportive parents who understand them and who listen to them, and practitioners (such as speech and language therapists, teachers, teaching assistants, occupational therapists) who can work collaboratively with the child and their family, sharing valuable insights and information, whilst accepting and valuing the child as they already are. It is acknowledged that a personalized approach (a person-centred approach) to any type of learning is always required as each person is an individual. The child's own views should always be sought, where possible, in a way that works best for them. What is provided in this book is contextual information and suggestions about what might be taught – and importantly why and how – so that it can be relevant and personalized to the child/children you know or work with. It is not intended to be a formulaic approach to supporting **all** autistic children in the same way.

What is well-being?

Improving the health and well-being of autistic people should be a priority for research. As Vermeulen (2014) says: 'It is remarkable that emotional well-being and the pursuit of it, although being highly valued for every human being, have received so little attention in research on the autism spectrum.' Many of the issues affecting well-being are discussed in greater detail throughout each chapter of this book.

This book focuses on improving the well-being of autistic girls. Well-being, according to the *Oxford English Dictionary*, is the 'state of being comfortable, happy or healthy'. Although well-being can relate to how autistic girls think and feel about themselves, it is also dependent on the relationships they have with others – how accepted, understood and included they feel, and how others communicate with them. This will have a direct impact on their mental and physical health.

To help autistic girls build confidence and self-esteem, it is important that the many strengths and skills (and positive personality traits) they have are recognized and that girls are accepted for who they are. Strengths might include: having an eye for detail, being highly creative, being hyper-focused, being skilled in a specific area of interest and being able to experience the world in a different way to other people. Autistic girls too, can have many positive personal qualities: they can be honest, caring, considerate or highly empathic, witty and determined, in addition to many other qualities. Having worked with many autistic girls over the years, I have noticed that many share a strong sense of justice because they care deeply for others, despite myths suggesting otherwise. Many are goal-driven and passionate, with a determination to change the world for the better. Greta Thunberg is a perfect example.

Helping autistic girls to grow in confidence means valuing them for their differences and accepting them as they already are – how they think, communicate, express themselves and experience the world differently. Autistic girls should not feel they have to change but they are often expected to adapt themselves. Sometimes it can seem that society places higher value on, and provides greater opportunities for, people who are outgoing, who are vocal or who are perceived to have 'better social skills'. This means that autistic girls who appear more introverted, those who may find social situations difficult, or those who may communicate in ways other than through speech, can sometimes be under-valued. Everyone matters and everyone should be valued.

People have different skills and abilities, learn at different rates, and in different ways. (I learned to play the guitar in three weeks, aged eight, but it took me until I was 30 to learn to drive!) Autistic girls should not be under-estimated. Everyone has worth, whatever their capabilities. Focusing on strengths and interests, and positive qualities, can improve well-being, and all autistic girls should be celebrated for being themselves! Some autistic girls may lack confidence in themselves if they compare themselves to their non-autistic peers, and their well-being can be affected by what they think they can and cannot do. These girls should know that when you are autistic easy things can be difficult and difficult things can be easy!

The well-being of autistic girls can be affected by their relationships with others, so it is important that girls feel connected in a way that suits them and is manageable. There are many ways to 'connect' with others, such as in person, and in digital or other spaces. Autistic girls can experience a sense of belonging by reading, or hearing about, the experiences of other autistic girls and women or by spending time in the company of others who are like them. As well as having good relationships with others, autistic girls need to feel safe and secure with people, and in their surroundings. Unfamiliar people and places can sometimes cause stress. Feeling connected to the environment, to nature and the world around them can enhance well-being as nature can provide calm and be restorative. Not all girls will have access to open spaces, and some may need support to access them, so it is important that all girls, whatever their circumstances and needs, are able to find calm whoever and wherever they are.

Being able to access the right level of support at the right time can improve well-being. Too little support can lead to exclusion and too much can be viewed as ableism. Ensuring that autistic girls are involved in decisions that affect them, however they communicate, will help them to have greater control over their own lives. Opportunities to develop their knowledge and skills, as well as time to pursue their own interests and passions, can help girls to feel fulfilled. The things that make them happy will help them to navigate the challenges they face and will help them to manage adversity. Being understood and accepted by others will help to improve their well-being. Self-acceptance is also important.

CHAPTER 2

Be Unique

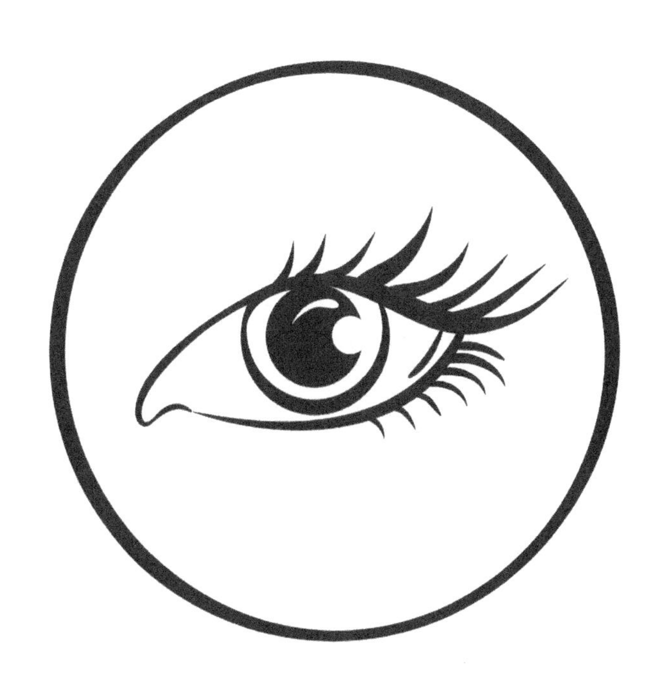

'Be Unique' focuses on what autism is, and how language used about autistic people and portrayals of autistic people in the media can affect the self-esteem of autistic children. This chapter highlights the strengths, qualities, challenges and needs of autistic children and suggests why autistic children can benefit from seeing themselves represented by autistic and neurodivergent role models. It explores how the well-being of autistic children can be affected by other people's perceptions, knowledge, attitudes and the environment. The focus is on the issues that autistic girls face, including other people's expectations of them as girls, and what can be done to address these challenges.

Be unique – context

How we each view autism is highly personal and will depend on our own experiences. How individuals, groups and organizations define autism is constantly evolving as knowledge grows and opinions change. There will be people who describe autism as a disorder, a difference, a disability, a hidden disability, a condition or an identity. The National Autistic Society (2020) defines autism as 'a lifelong, developmental disability that affects how a person communicates with and relates to other people, and how they experience the world around them'.

The *Diagnostic and Statistical Manual of Mental Disorders, 5th edition* (*DSM-5*; American Psychiatric Association 2013) states that for a diagnosis of autism to be made, the person seeking a diagnosis would need to demonstrate 'difficulties' in social communication and interaction (framed as deficits and impairments); they would also have narrow interests and repetitive behaviours, be over- or under-responsive (hyper- and hypo-responsive) to the sensory environment all of which would be present from birth, regardless of the age at which the person sought a diagnosis.

Although the prevalence of autism is thought to be approximately 1 percent of the population (meaning that in the UK there are approximately 700,000 autistic people), it is possible that this figure is underestimated as many people remain undiagnosed. According to the Parliamentary Office of Science and Technology (UK Parliament 2020):

> Researchers have suggested that autism may be under-diagnosed in adults, females, gender-fluid and non-binary people, and those from ethnic minorities. (George and Stokes 2018; Hull and Mandy 2017; Hussein, Pellicano and Crane 2019; Kapp, Gillespie-Lynch, Sherman and Hutman 2013).

Whichever way you view autism, your own views and beliefs and the way that you use language when talking about autistic people will have an impact on how an autistic person experiences the world. Dr Julia Leatherland (2018) provides a respectful definition of autism in contrast to the diagnostic criteria:

> Autistic individuals share a neurological type, which is qualitatively different from that of non-autistics and which will necessarily impact, both positively and negatively, on: aspects of their thinking and learning; sensory processing; social relational experiences; and communicative style, abilities and preferences. An autistic person's experience of and ability to be successful in the world, will be dependent on the closeness of compatibility between their individual profile of skills and difficulties and their physical and social environment. Levels of sensitivity to environmental factors vary between individuals, and within the same individual over time, so that the presentation of autism is ever changing. A person's neurological type, however, remains constant, and being autistic is a lifelong identity.

Notice that Leatherland describes autistic people without using words that portray autistic people negatively, that is, without reference to 'deficits', 'impairments' or 'disorders'.

Language matters, as Milton (2017) explains:

> For philosophers the way we talk about something 'is more than just words' but frames the way we think about ourselves and one another. By viewing the 'autistic person' as the 'disordered other', it can reduce an individual's sense of self-worth and self-esteem.'

Hull, Petrides and Mandy (2020) recognize that 'some members of the autism community feel the label "disorder" produces stigma and emphasizes the difficulties associated with autism while minimizing the strengths'. Again, notice that Leatherland's description above contains no mention of functioning labels, of 'high' or 'low functioning', or terms that lead to misunderstandings about autistic people. When the term 'low functioning' is used, there is the possibility that a person will be underestimated. The term 'high functioning' can lead people to believe that a person may not experience challenges.

How autism is diagnosed

Usually a parent considers that their child is developing differently to other children. They may notice that their child's language development is different to that of other children or they may notice that their child has sensory sensitivities. Sometimes parents recognize that their child seems to prefer playing on their own, though at a young age this may be viewed as typical development as children play in parallel before playing with others. In addition, parents may notice that their child becomes distressed at change and seems to need routine. Professionals working in schools may also notice differences and will share this information with parents. Usually, a class teacher will discuss this with the Special Educational Needs and Disabilities Co-ordinator (SENCo or SENDCo), but sometimes parents may liaise with a school nurse and ask for their child to be referred. Alternatively, a parent may choose to contact their General Practitioner (GP) before being referred to an autism specialist or paediatrician for an initial assessment of their child.

There are various diagnostic tools used by professionals to diagnose autistic children, including the Autism Diagnostic Observation Schedule (ADOS) and the Diagnostic Interview for Social and Communication Disorders (DISCO), and to gain a diagnosis a person must meet certain criteria (see the *International Statistical Classification of Diseases and Related Health Problems* [ICD 10/11; World Health Organization 2004, 2020] and *DSM-5* [American Psychiatric Association 2013). A multidisciplinary team of professionals will often provide 'evidence' towards a diagnosis. A paediatrician, for example, might seek information from other professionals such as an educational psychologist, clinical psychologist, speech and language therapist and/or occupational therapist to help build a broader picture of the child and their needs. Headteachers, SENDCos, teachers and teaching/support assistants are often asked to contribute information towards a diagnosis, and parents are also consulted. For older people seeking an autism diagnosis, a clinician will gather together information relating to their childhood and early development, abilities in relation to social communication and interaction, sensory needs and sensitivities, interests, and their need for routine and predictability. A family member may also be asked to contribute information to this process.

Autistic girls and diagnosis

Whether to seek autism diagnosis is a difficult and personal decision. For younger autistic girls, it is the parents who decide whether to seek a diagnosis, sometimes following discussions with their child or with health or education professionals. For some parents, seeking a diagnosis can be a positive step towards helping their daughter to understand herself or helping her to gain access to services or educational provision, although there is no guarantee of this and it's important to note that there are many girls *without* a formal diagnosis doing well in schools. Being diagnosed can help some autistic girls to feel part of a group, a wider network of people with whom they can connect and share experiences with, which can help her to develop a positive identity.

In contrast, there are also those who choose not to seek a diagnosis as they do not want their daughter to be labelled or for others to have lower expectations of her due to their lack of understanding. With respect, a small minority of parents can find it difficult to accept that their daughter might be autistic so do not wish to pursue a diagnosis. This can be due to fear about their daughter's future, due to lack of understanding of autism, from being misinformed by available literature and resources, or because of stereotypes of autistic people. Other parents may reason that the difficulties and challenges their daughter experiences may be due to other factors rather than being autistic. It is understandable that parents will experience a range of emotions and conflicting thoughts when first considering that their daughter might be autistic. Some parents reach out to the autistic community for advice. Others seek support from health and education professionals.

Some parents report that they choose not to seek an assessment for fear of not being believed, that they may be blamed for their child's difficulties (their parenting skills are questioned) or that they may be accused of fabricating difficulties. Others may not want to pursue a diagnosis because of stigma.

Some parents may not have the privilege of being able to seek support, disclose that their child is autistic, or seek a diagnosis for them. Some parents have concerns about the safety of their child where problems might arise from lack of understanding of autism by a particular service such as the police, health, education, or social services. Sometimes autistic people are misjudged by others and suffer due to lack of awareness and understanding.

There are organisations working to rectify this such as the 'National Police Autism Association' in the UK who are working to bring about positive change who support autistic people and their families, by sharing "... best practices for working with the autistic community..." and who work "... alongside the Disabled Police Association, which represents disability in policing at national level..." to "... support the DPA's goal of ending all forms of discrimination and ill-treatment of people with disabilities."

Some believe that the diagnostic process may erode a girl's sense of self-worth if the language used has negative connotations (for example, 'impaired', 'disordered', 'deficits'). However, there are many highly skilled and sensitive professionals who use respectful language making note of each girl's strengths and positive qualities whilst recognising the challenges she faces during the diagnostic process.

Even when the decision has been made to seek a diagnosis, it is apparent that girls and women can face numerous barriers to obtaining a diagnosis.

Barriers to obtaining a diagnosis

Although some autistic girls do not experience any barriers to obtaining a diagnosis and the process is straightforward, others can face numerous difficulties that can also impact on their health and their education.

Long waiting times for assessment and diagnosis

National Health Service waiting times for referral and diagnosis of autism (known as the 'ASD Pathway') can be considerable (NHS Digital 2020) and it appears that autistic girls are generally diagnosed later than autistic boys (Begeer *et al.* 2013; Kirkovski, Enticott and Fitzgerald 2013; Rutherford *et al.* 2016). Some people, who have the financial means, choose to avoid long NHS waiting times and seek a diagnosis privately.

A survey by the Autistic Girls Network in the UK found that 43 percent of approximately 700 respondents waited up to two years for diagnosis, and 24 percent waited more than three years. Having to wait a long time for an assessment and a subsequent diagnosis can have a detrimental impact not only on girls but also on their families. Not having a diagnosis can have an impact on *where* and *how* an autistic girl is educated, the provision and services that she can access, but it can also affect the family financially. (For example, parents having to leave their jobs to care for, and educate, their autistic daughter if out of education.) it can also mean that some autistic girls are not receiving the support they need early enough.

> The waiting list was very long. We were told it could be a year or two, and even then, the generic autism assessment is biased towards boys because autism in girls isn't widely understood.

Diagnostic tools and criteria

As Hull, Petrides and Mandy (2020) point out, "A fundamental issue with the current diagnostic procedure is that behavioural markers used as diagnostic criteria are established based on pre-existing conceptions of what autistic behaviours look like. These criteria have been developed based on the predominantly male populations previously identified as autistic". (Kirkovski et al. 2013; Kopp and Gillberg 2011; Mattila et al. 2011).

This review by Hull, Mandy and Petrides discusses female typical autism presentation, the 'Female Autism Phenotype' or 'FAP'. Samantha Craft and Ruby Simone 'Aspergirls'(JKP) have both compiled their own lists and many people will identify with these female presentations of autism. This cannot be ignored as it means that more girls and women recognised as being autistic. However, it is important to recognise that difficulties may also arise from presenting autism as 'male' or 'female' because not only does this ignore many other autistic people, but because it may lead further stereotyping or misdiagnosis when people don't fit into a particular category. It may be more helpful to view people as individuals and for clinicians to view autism more broadly.

Gender bias

In recent years, the male to female ratio has become more equally balanced at 3:1, according to Loomes, Hull and Mandy (2017) yet 'There appears to be a diagnostic gender bias, meaning that girls who meet the criteria for ASD are at disproportionate risk of not receiving a clinical diagnosis.'

Reasons why autistic girls are not being recognised

Being more aware of the reasons why girls and women are not being recognised as autistic should help to address some of the barriers that they face. Clinical studies often involve more males than females and more males than females are referred for diagnosis. This means that in research, there are gender data gaps. More research is needed to fill these gaps. We know that more older women are now stepping out, having not been recognised as children. (Professor Francesca Happé's work focusses on under-researched subgroups such as autistic women and the elderly.)

There are many other reasons why girls and women are not being recognised.

Strengths can overshadow difficulties

Some autistic girls are especially likely to remain undiagnosed if they have good expressive language ability as there can be an assumption that they will be capable in other areas. This can overshadow other communication difficulties such as difficulties understanding non-verbal communication or being literal. Not all girls and women who are referred, gain a diagnosis as sometimes girls do not appear to be 'autistic enough' (i.e. there is not enough evidence to conclude a diagnosis). The challenges that some girls experience, are not viewed as being significant enough.

Camouflaging

Some autistic girls may have high social motivation and may (unknowingly) camouflage and mask aspects of themselves, including suppressing self-stimulatory behaviours (stimming) and sensory sensitivities. This helps them to fit in, but as a result, may mean that others don't recognize them as being autistic.

Internalising difficulties

The challenges that autistic girls experience can sometimes be internalized so they are not always apparent to others. Autistic girls can put great effort into appearing competent and capable whilst others are not aware of the effort and mental strain that has been invested. They also do not witness the after-effects of this which can affect the mind, body, or both. It may appear to some professionals working in schools that girls are doing well, but the pressures and stresses a girl experiences are only observed by parents in the home, after school, as this is the girl's safe space where she can offload.

Lack of awareness across services (e.g health and education)

Some professionals may not be able to recognize autistic girls because they may not have received specialist training. Autistic girls are difficult to identify especially to 'untrained observers' says Gould (2017), referring to a study by Dean, Harwood and Kasari (2017). This is because some girls display more subtle signs of autism, which may be one of the reasons 'highly intelligent girls are being diagnosed late' (Russo 2018). Hull et al. (2020) state that 'there is also substantial evidence [Russell, Steer and Golding 2011] suggesting that diagnostic processes are less likely to identify females, particularly those without intellectual disability.' As signs of autism can be more subtle in some girls, it can understandably be difficult for some educational professionals to recognize autistic girls in their classrooms. But also, professionals in schools are being expected to contribute 'evidence' towards the diagnosis but may not know what 'it' is they are supposed to be looking for! Unfortunately, this can stall and hinder an autistic girl from gaining a diagnosis, though it should be mentioned that several professional opinions are gained to conclude a diagnosis (for example, that of a speech and language therapist or an occupational therapist). Some girls are not diagnosed as they are not considered 'autistic enough' to receive the diagnosis, but it is important to note that girls who internalize emotions or whose challenges go unseen, are no less autistic. Respectfully, sometimes even professionals need to be challenged though I am aware that much evidence and information is considered prior to making a professional judgement.

Misdiagnosis

Sometimes girls are misdiagnosed with other conditions such as anxiety or bipolar disorder rather than autism (Gould and Ashton Smith, 2011). Misdiagnosis can lead to confusion and anguish for autistic girls and women, as well as their families. Some autistic girls report to having been at crisis point before being diagnosed.

A doctor came to see me. He said to me that he didn't think I was autistic, he thought I had high social anxiety. I accepted that and the topic was forgotten about. It wasn't until I was discharged from the unit and I started at community CAMHS [Child and Adolescent Mental Health Services] appointments that it was brought up again. A locum consultant saw me and then spoke to my mum, asking if I had been assessed for autism. My parents wanted to pursue it further, but the NHS waiting list was very long. I was struggling with suicidal ideation and self-harm, and the possibility of hospitalization was never far out of sight. I was only 18 months

The difficulty is that girls who mask or internalize difficulties, who imitate or mimic others are seen to be coping but are often not.

Another view is that females may be less likely to be autistic due to what is known as the female protective effect or 'FPE'. Hull and Mandy (2017) explain this in greater detail.

Reasons for not seeking a diagnosis

Not all girls and women who are autistic want to seek a diagnosis and some people self-diagnose. Not all parents choose to seek a diagnosis for their daughters. There are a variety of reasons for this amongst different individuals:

- They may self-diagnose because of the long waiting time for an autism assessment on the NHS.
- They do not have the financial means to seek a diagnosis privately.
- They may believe they will not be able to get a diagnosis.
- They may not know how to get a diagnosis or may need support to do so.
- They may not want to put themselves through the diagnostic process.
- They may believe they will not be able to get a diagnosis. They may not agree with the diagnostic process itself as they may consider that autism is viewed through a non-autistic lens.
- Some people may think that gaining a diagnosis will not make a difference to their life.
- Others may be concerned that having a clinical record might limit job and other opportunities.

Many autistic women 'self-identify', 'self-recognize' or 'self-realize' often later in life, sometimes because professionals have failed to identify them as being autistic when younger.

The positive aspects of gaining a diagnosis

Some girls view being autistic as part of their identity, something to feel proud of. Having a formal diagnosis can help some girls to better understand themselves, helps some girls to be kinder to themselves and helps girls to understand that they don't have to conform. Knowing that there are other people who think like them and who have similar experiences to them can be empowering. Other positive aspects to being diagnosed formally are that; some girls can access greater support in school, that they have certain rights, that adjustments and accommodations can be made to help them reach their potential. In health services, greater support and adjustments may also be made. Being diagnosed can help some girls feel a sense of belonging (to the autistic community) that they may not have previously experienced if they haven't known anyone else who is autistic. Some girls may need confirmation through a formal diagnosis. Some girls may need this to access certain types of school provision. They may not be able to go to a specialist school without a formal diagnosis for example. Girls can appreciate themselves for who they already are.

What positive change needs to occur?

Greater access to accurate information and training for professionals may lead to improved awareness so that autistic girls can be referred for an assessment earlier if necessary, so that misdiagnosis can be prevented and so that those seeking a diagnosis later in life can receive support should they need it. Ensuring that health and education professionals receive training should enable girls and women to gain better access to services and the right support at different times throughout their lives. Reduced waiting times are also needed. Some women are waiting seven years to access an autism assessment. The media can also play a part in eradicating stereotypes of autistic people by considering how autistic people are portrayed and the language that is used when referring to autistic people. Stereotypes can cause confusion but being able to communicate with other autistic girls and women can help them to understand themselves better:

She challenged the stereotypes in my head and explained to me that autism in girls can present differently.

What can be done to help prevent mental health issues in autistic girls and women?

Whilst having high expectations of what autistic girls can achieve, the academic curriculum must be balanced by a greater focus on well-being and self-care, along with an appreciation of diversity. Although the well-being of all children is equally important, it appears that girls in particular are experiencing difficulties. Statistics from Public Health England (2019) reveal that it is adolescent girls who are self-harming in the greatest numbers. Maddox, Trubanova and White (2017) state: 'Almost 75% of the women with ASD reported a history of NSSI [non-suicidal self-injury], compared to only 33% of the men with ASD.' Research by Sedgewick, Hill and Pellicano (2018) also highlight self-harm as an issue for autistic adolescent girls. In addition, they recognize:

> In the context of a growing body of research about the female phenotype of ASD (e.g. Mandy *et al.* 2012; Solomon *et al.* 2012), it is possible that the gender difference in NSSI prevalence is associated with unique challenges that females with ASD face as they transition into adulthood (Halladay *et al.* 2015).

Research also informs us that 'gender is another possible moderator of excess mortality in ASD. Relative to males, females with ASD have been reported to have an elevated mortality risk' (Hirvikoski *et al.* 2015). Therefore, it is imperative that autistic people are better understood, and that well-being and health are prioritized.

Signs of autism can be more subtle in some girls, so it can be challenging for educational professionals to recognize autistic girls in their classrooms. Even so, professionals are being expected to contribute 'evidence' towards the diagnosis but may not know what 'it' is they are supposed to be looking for. Unfortunately, this can stall and hinder an autistic girl from gaining a diagnosis. It should be mentioned that several professional opinions are gained to conclude a diagnosis (for example, that of a speech and language therapist or an occupational therapist), but even then, not all professionals receive specialist autism training, which is why some decisions and opinions need to be challenged. Autistic girls who are not considered 'autistic enough' to receive a diagnosis, who may internalize emotions or whose challenges go unseen, are no less autistic.

As we have seen, obtaining a diagnosis can be problematic for some girls and women, and many are misdiagnosed with other conditions such as anxiety or bipolar disorder rather than autism (Gould and Ashton Smith, 2011). This can lead to confusion and anguish for autistic girls and women, as well as their families. Some autistic girls report to having been at crisis point before being diagnosed.

> A doctor came to see me. He said to me that he didn't think I was autistic, he thought I had high social anxiety. I accepted that and the topic was forgotten about. It wasn't until I was discharged from the unit and I started at community CAMHS [Child and Adolescent Mental Health Services] appointments that it was brought up again. A locum consultant saw me and then spoke to my mum, asking if I had been assessed for autism. My parents wanted to pursue it further, but the NHS waiting list was very long. I was struggling with suicidal ideation and self-harm, and the possibility of hospitalization was never far out of sight. I was only 18 months from starting uni. We went private to a

> place specializing in autism in girls. At the end...they thought one thing described the reasons for everything: 'autism'. I left feeling relieved. Finding out I am autistic gave me a deep understanding of myself I would never have found elsewhere.

Bargiela *et al.* (2016) explain that the 'stereotype that people with ASC [autism spectrum condition] all have very severe and overt social and communication problems added to professionals' reluctance to diagnose females who showed some capacity, albeit superficial, to socialize with others' and that 'young women also felt that Rain Man stereotypes, which incorrectly assume that ASC is always associated with savant skills and with an interest in mathematics and science, had delayed their diagnoses'. Greater access to accurate information and training for professionals may lead to improved awareness so that autistic girls can be referred for an assessment earlier if necessary, so that misdiagnosis can be prevented and so that those seeking a diagnosis later in life can receive support. Reduced waiting times are also needed.

The media can also play a part in eradicating stereotypes of autistic people by considering how autistic people are portrayed and the language that is used when referring to them. Ensuring that health and education professionals receive training will enable girls and women to gain better access to services and the right support at different times throughout their lives. Some women are confused by stereotypes, but meeting other autistic girls can help them to understand themselves better:

> She challenged the stereotypes in my head and explained to me that autism in girls can present differently.

Developing a 'sense of self' and why this is important for the well-being of autistic girls

Hodge, Rice and Reidy (2019) describe a sense of self as 'how people might describe themselves and the value that they attribute to who and how they are as a person'. So how do autistic girls develop a sense of self, especially when being in the minority? How do autistic girls learn to understand themselves and with whom? How do they develop confidence and self-esteem when amongst peers and professionals who are predominantly non-autistic?

First, it is necessary to determine how the girl perceives herself and why. How autistic girls perceive themselves can depend on many factors and every girl has the right to draw her own conclusion. How she views herself might depend on:

- whether she knows she is autistic (and her views about this)
- her life experiences
- her relationships with peers and family, professionals, and others
- her interests, strengths and how she manages challenges
- whether she feels listened to
- her level of self-awareness and whether she understands herself
- whether she feels understood by others
- how able she is to make decisions for herself (with support, if necessary)
- the language she hears about herself and about other people who are neurodivergent
- whether she feels included (and able to be herself) or excluded (which may be unintentional but will have an impact on how she feels) either by other people's behaviour, practices or by the environment
- the 'messages' she picks up from around her about autistic people (for example, representations of autistic people in the media)
- to what extent she feels able to 'be herself'
- whether she feels 'different' and what her thoughts are about being 'different' to other people.

Many autistic girls and women say that they knew from an early age that they were 'different' (that is, before knowing that they were autistic). They will have differing views about autism. Each girl will react differently to the diagnosis (or figuring out for themselves) that they are autistic. Some girls may find it irrelevant to their identity. Others may see it as a relief, an explanation for why they feel 'different'. Some view being autistic as a positive thing. In contrast, some girls do not feel ready to accept this, sometimes because they do not want to feel different to their non-autistic peers. For some girls it can take time to accept that they are autistic. Some girls and women may have mixed feelings (both positive and negative) about being autistic throughout their lifetime, depending on what they have learnt about autism and themselves (sometimes through study) and depending on their circumstances and what stage of life they are at.

> [Being autistic] definitely comes with its challenges and obstacles. In the past I have not coped well at all and found some really unhelpful coping strategies. I do feel a lot more positive now but I still can feel down about it because my social anxiety really makes doing things outside of the house difficult. But I have much better things I can do to make myself feel better and I don't feel down for as long.

Girls develop a sense of self through what they see and hear, so being more conscious of how we speak about autistic people and the language we use can help girls to feel more positive about themselves. Words and phrases such as 'suffering with autism', 'disorder' and 'impairments' may suggest that being autistic is wrong, however unintentional this may be, and imagery used in relation to autism can also reinforce negative ideas about autistic people; it may suggest that autistic people are lacking something, that they are not 'whole', that they are less, as opposed to having strengths, capabilities and positive qualities.

How autistic girls perceive themselves can depend on whether they think their relationships with others (including peers, professionals and family members) are 'successful' and how understood and accepted they feel. Autistic girls can be led to believe that who and how they are is wrong or not enough if they are expected to adapt, change aspects of themselves or modify themselves to fit in. Sometimes autistic children are expected to change themselves to appear more non-autistic, or what some people might consider more 'normal', as though this is preferable to being autistic. Accepting an autistic girl for who she is, and valuing her, will help her to build a positive identity. Expecting autistic girls to modify, adapt or hide aspects of themselves, hour after hour, day after day, month after month, year after year, can be harmful and suggests to them that they are not accepted. Can you imagine a non-autistic person being expected to adapt themselves to be more autistic?

If other people can adapt their language to be more respectful, adapt how they communicate, better understand how autistic girls experience the world, be flexible and adjust their expectations (without underestimating the child), girls can feel more included. Making the environment (for example, the classroom) more accessible can also have a positive impact – making the necessary adjustments, taking into consideration sensory needs and sensitivities can mean a child feels accepted. This can include providing a well-organized, well-structured, low-arousal environment that maximizes independence.

Role models

As autistic girls grow up, they shape their own identities by observing other people in real life. Many will observe or 'research' other people in the media. Autistic girls can benefit from seeing themselves represented in the media, and in society, but sometimes there are few role models and little representation. Fortunately, this is slowly changing. Autistic people who could be considered to be role models include;

Greta Thunberg, Siena Castellon, Barb Cook and the 14 autistic women in *Spectrum Women* (see 'Further Reading'), Dr Camilla Pang, Shadia Hancock, Hannah Gadsby and Chloe Hayden, known as 'Princess Aspien'. Girls often learn about themselves through reading about others. Books whose characters are autistic can help them to realize that other people have similarities to them, and this can be extremely validating and important for children in the minority.

Helping autistic girls to recognize and value their strengths

Autistic girls can benefit from opportunities to explore who they are, how they perceive themselves and why. Knowing **when** and **how** to talk to a girl about being autistic can be difficult for some parents and professionals. How this should be approached depends on the individual. Raising awareness of autism can be done both indirectly and directly, but without self-knowledge many autistic girls will be at a disadvantage, as lack of self-awareness and self-understanding can lead to confusion or stress, and in some cases mental health issues. Helping girls to build self-esteem through considering their strengths can be helpful, but equally, autistic girls can benefit from a greater understanding of what challenges they face, how to manage these and what the causes are. Working with autistic girls to address challenges requires sensitivity and a non-judgemental approach. Having a trusting relationship is vital.

Focusing on strengths can help autistic girls to build self-esteem and self-worth. Although there is the stereotype of the autistic savant – a person who displays one or more exceptional abilities – only a small proportion of autistic people fit this profile. Autistic people are individuals who have different strengths and qualities, in the same way as non-autistic people do. Some autistic people attribute certain strengths to being autistic. Some of the strengths that autistic girls have might relate to their abilities but may also relate to their personalities.

> This is something that I really struggle with, but I am getting better at noticing my strengths. Art is something that I have loved since being small and most of my spare time is art-based. I am specializing in Fine Art – portraits and animation – and am hoping to develop my own characters and drawing style. I guess I am also good at determining how someone is feeling and helping them to fix it.

The strengths that autistic people have can include:

- having a highly developed musical ability
- being extremely creative
- being excellent problem solvers
- having a strong visual memory
- having incredible mathematical ability
- being able to remember large amounts of information or specific facts
- being spiritual and intuitive
- being able to recognize patterns and make connections
- being methodical, logical or analytical
- being precise
- having an in-depth knowledge of a topic (so can become experts in their field)
- showing great attention to detail
- having sporting skills or abilities (including those relating to balance or accuracy)
- having an ability to categorize
- having hyper-focus
- being able to persevere with difficult or detailed tasks
- being hard-working, loyal and honest
- being able to connect with others in different, sometimes unconventional, ways (including through shared interests)
- sharing their knowledge

- being able to notice and correct errors
- being determined to change the world for the better for other people.

Having worked with many autistic children and young people for over twenty years, I have noticed how common it is to dislike unfairness and injustice, something I feel strongly about too. It is possible that many autistic children have such a strong sense of justice because they have experienced injustice and inequality themselves. Because of this, they become great advocates for others. Seeing the world from an alternative and unique perspective – either because of different sensory perceptions or thinking differently – are other very positive aspects of being autistic.

Encouraging girls to focus on their personal strengths and pursue their interests can help them to build confidence and improve well-being. Although intense interests might appear to some people as obsessive behaviour, 'repetitive behaviour' can be a 'protective factor' and a form of self-preservation. Wood (2019) recognizes the many benefits that autistic children gain from pursuing strong interests in schools:

> Enabling autistic children to engage with their strong interests has been found to be predominantly advantageous, rather than deleterious, in school environments (Gunn and Delafield-Butt 2016). Positive effects include improved learning and curriculum access (Hesmondhalgh and Breakey 2001; Wittemeyer *et al.* 2011), better cooperativity and social skills (Gunn and Delafield-Butt 2016), increased participation in after-school clubs (Jones *et al.* 2008) and improved fine motor skills and social and communication abilities (Winter-Messiers 2007). Furthermore, such an approach enables autistic children 'to relax, overcome anxiety, experience pleasure, and make better sense of the physical world' (Gunn and Delafield-Butt 2016), and to moderate their levels of arousal, thus impacting positively on their emotional well-being

> too (Winter-Messiers 2007). Furthermore, such an approach enables autistic children 'to relax, overcome anxiety, experience pleasure, and make better sense of the physical world' (Gunn and Delafield-Butt 2016), and to moderate their levels of arousal, thus impacting positively on their emotional well-being too (Winter-Messiers 2007).

When feeling overloaded or burnt out from having to process too much language, having to adapt in social situations or because of the impact of the environment, being able to engage in interests repetitively (or for long periods of time) can provide recovery time, allowing the brain and body to recharge. Being fully immersed in a voluntary activity of choice that provides challenge and fulfilment can be referred to as a 'flow state' (Csikszentmihalyi 1990; McDonnell and Milton 2014). Self-stimulatory behaviour ('stimming' or 'stims') is also classed as 'repetitive behaviour' and can have a calming or self-soothing effect, though the purpose can be misunderstood. Kapp *et al.* (2019) explain:

> Stimming was identified as a repetitive, usually rhythmic behaviour that was commonly expressed through body movements (variously described as hand flapping, finger flicking, hair pulling or pinching, feet flexing, spinning, necklace playing) but also vocalizations (e.g. muttering, grunting, stuttering, whistling, singing). Many participants said they experienced it as involuntary and unconscious, at least at the beginning of the behaviour. Although many described stimming as automatic and uncontrollable, no participants consistently and inherently disliked their stims (as opposed to their social consequences). Indeed, most participants described stimming itself as comfortable or calming, suggesting a self-regulatory function (which some participants explicitly identified).

When autistic children understand themselves, they no longer need to measure themselves against other people's capabilities but can value themselves as they already are.

Things to consider when working with autistic girls

Find out about them

All autistic girls are unique, so it will be necessary to gather as much information as possible before working with them, especially if they are not previously known to you. How you choose to use the contents of this book will depend on the needs and abilities of the girls you are working with, what staff and resources are available, the time you have available and the environment you are working in. Some people may work on a one-to-one basis with an autistic girl (at home, in an educational setting or an alternative setting); others will be working with a whole class – either with a group of autistic children or with groups of children, some autistic and others non-autistic. So it's important to consider when working with a particular girl, what her communication needs are, what her communication preferences are and be aware of how these may differ in different situations or environments (when under stress or under pressure).

You might also consider whether she has any co-occurring conditions such as dyspraxia, dyslexia, or ADHD, and whether she has any additional needs relating to mobility (and if so, how the child be accommodated and fully included). You may also take into consideration what level she is working at so that all activities you plan can be accessible and differentiated. Some autistic girls have difficulties with memory, so providing additional material can be helpful (for example, visual reminders). Some girls will need additional time to process spoken language as well as extra time to reply. (In busy schools or in healthcare settings people are often rushed, through no fault of their own, but it's important to remember to give the child enough time to process and answer). Knowing a girl's strengths and interests can be useful as these can boost her self-esteem and confidence. It is important to be aware of whether she has an autism diagnosis, is in the process of being assessed, or is undiagnosed; also, what she knows about autism and her feelings about this.

Tell them what to expect

Letting autistic children know who will be working with them, what their names are and, if possible, providing a picture of what they look like (if the person/people working with the child is unfamiliar) can reduce anxiety. Including a short 'bio' explaining a little about the person's interests can also help them to seem more familiar. This will help to put her at ease. A friendly approach will help girls to feel more comfortable in your company. This is important as it can take time to get to know some girls who keep themselves to themselves to protect themselves. They may keep aspects of themselves back from you until they know you will not judge them. It can take time to develop trust so being understanding, sensitive and considerate will help to build good relationships. Change of any kind can be stressful. Therefore it is important for those working with to be consistent. Autistic girls can benefit from working with the same person. Although it is not always possible to have the same person working with a child, if several people are familiar with them, then this can address that issue. Where changes are going to occur, preparing her in advance can help her to adjust; explaining why the changes are happening can also help her to manage better. Keeping girls informed in advance about where and when you will be working with them can help them feel more comfortable too.

Providing a picture of the room (and a picture of the building) will help them become more familiar with being in that environment. Letting them know, in a way that they can understand, how long activities, sessions or lessons will last will help girls to feel safe, secure and comfortable. Routine and predictability can help girls to feel more relaxed. Keeping the format of any lessons (or sessions) the same will help a girl know what to expect. It can be helpful to know in advance, or at the beginning of any lesson or session, what is going to take place. This might be in the form of a schedule – a visual and/or written list of what activities will happen and in what order. This might be on paper or in digital form. Encouraging girls to ask questions in ways other than through speech (for example, by writing them down) can be an inclusive approach. Not all autistic girls will be able to ask questions aloud or will want to. It can sometimes be assumed that if a child is in mainstream education they will want to answer questions, or make choices, using speech. This is often not the preferred means of communication for some autistic girls, so it can be worth considering how alternatives such as visuals, colours, music or gestures can be used to communicate thoughts, answers and preferences.

Help them to feel comfortable

Providing choice can help autistic girls to feel more in control. Being able to opt in or out of an activity, depending on how comfortable they feel, promotes trust. This helps them to step further outside of their comfort zones, knowing they will be safe, and teaches them that their own boundaries should be respected.

Sometimes it helps them to feel comfortable enough to take part in a task or activity if they can observe it first. Providing a safe space to go to nearby if they choose to opt out shows the child that their choices are respected. Many girls can still benefit from listening and observing from a distance if they are not taking part initially. They are more likely to opt in, when ready, if given options. Giving autistic girls the choice of whether to share their work (or thoughts), or keep them private, shows respect. Some girls may want to share their work but might not want to speak in front of others, if they are able to do so. Some may prefer you to do this for them. Consider using a clear, visual system for an autistic child to opt in or out of activities if they need to (for example, a colour-coded system, with one colour meaning 'I'm happy to take part', another colour meaning 'I don't want to join in'). This feels less intrusive and less judgemental and can help a child feel more comfortable.

Whilst maintaining a professional boundary, I am often open and honest about my own challenges and find that this can be validating.

Quite often, autistic girls can feel alone in their experiences and thoughts, especially if they are surrounded by non-autistic peers.

When working with autistic girls it is helpful to provide some information about what is going to happen during the next lesson or session (making the unfamiliar more familiar should reduce worry and help children to feel more comfortable and well prepared). Sometimes it can be difficult for girls to imagine what other people expect from them, so providing examples (of work) can help them to better understand. Modelling or demonstrating an activity can be helpful.

Listen to the girl's feedback and adapt to accommodate her further

When working with autistic girls it is important to provide opportunities for them to provide you with honest feedback in a format that suits the individual. Whereas some autistic girls might like to provide written or verbal feedback, some might prefer a visual system (for example, happy/sad faces, thumbs up or down, or a colour-coded system) to show you what worked well or what did not. This information can then be used to adapt future sessions and personalize learning further. As it can take time for some autistic girls to process language and information, some may not ask questions immediately but may want to ask questions at a later stage and it is important that they are given an opportunity to do so. Autistic girls, and their families, can provide valuable insights through feedback. Being able to adapt yourself and your approaches means that the girl isn't forced to adapt herself.

Communicating with autistic girls about autism

Ideally, autistic people would be spoken about respectfully, and in positive terms in and around schools and in other environments and spaces, including online. In schools, children would learn about autistic people and their strengths, in all subjects, across the curriculum. Autistic girls would see themselves represented by strong role models and would come across autistic people with whom they could relate to within their communities. Unfortunately, sometimes this does not happen, due to stigma, discrimination and stereotyped media portrayals of autistic people. This means that some autistic people cannot openly disclose that they are autistic. Due to internalized ableism, being led to believe that being autistic is negative, because of what they have seen and heard, some autistic girls feel that being autistic is something they must hide. Instead, autistic girls should feel proud to be themselves.

When talking to autistic girls about being autistic, there is not one best way to approach it as everyone is different and each girl will have had different prior experiences and knowledge. How this is explored, and the language used, will depend on the individual and what they already know. This requires sensitivity, and how this is approached will depend on each girl and her needs. Some girls will benefit from one-to-one sessions so they can communicate freely whereas others will be happy to work as part of a group with other people. If working with a group, some find it helpful to establish a 'group contract' between all those taking part to ensure trust and respect. Some people will speak more openly about autism when working in a class group of children who are neurodiverse (both autistic and non-autistic children) and this can benefit non-autistic children and autistic children alike. Non-autistic children need to be aware of, and respectful of, autistic children and the different ways they learn, communicate and experience the world, as well as their strengths.

Group discussions

If it's necessary to set up a group to discuss autism with children, it is important to consider the following prior to this:

- Autistic girls can choose whether they want to be involved, know what the benefits might be and have time to think about this.

- Parents are engaged and informed about what is going to be discussed and how.
- Parents give permission for their children to be involved.
- Parents are provided with an opportunity to ask questions as their own knowledge (and opinions) about autism will be varied. Some parents will be autistic themselves, whether diagnosed or not, whereas others will not be.
- Autistic girls are prepared in advance for any sessions and should view these as a positive opportunity to explore their prior knowledge about autism and what being autistic means to them.

Autistic children themselves can be supported to decide how they want the group to be run and what they might expect from each other. This might include:

- They may have differences of opinion but are tolerant of each other.
- They can be open, honest and able to trust each other.
- They can be supportive of each other. Children can show support for each other by appreciating that some people might find it difficult to speak or communicate at different times so might want to communicate thoughts in other ways or may need time out.
- Children and those working with them may appreciate that what one person might find easy, another person may find difficult. Everyone is unique and everyone experiences challenges and has strengths.

Topics to discuss might include:

- Prior knowledge of autism (what children know, how they have gained that information, where and who from).

- Thoughts about themselves (age diagnosed, experiences, feelings in relation to being autistic).
- How autistic people are portrayed in the media and how this might have an impact on autistic young people (for example, masking aspects of themselves due to internalized ableism or, in contrast, increased confidence when seeing positive role models).
- The many strengths that autistic people have and the challenges that autistic people can experience (they may consider their own strengths and challenges and share helpful strategies about how to manage such challenges).
- Communication differences between autistic and non-autistic people (for example, directness, honesty, being literal, trying to figure out the context of a conversation, taking time to process language) and learning that though autistic people communicate differently to the majority of people, that the way they think and communicate is not inferior.
- Exploring each child's understanding of feelings (self and others) and their own ways of expressing these.
- How intense interests or passions can be positive and serve a purpose: they can aid relaxation and self-preservation if the person feels overloaded or overwhelmed as they allow the body and brain to relax; they can also help autistic people develop a high level of skill or knowledge, which can be a strength.
- How, for some people, engaging in intense interests or doing things repetitively can be a sign of overload so might mean that the causes of overwhelm need to be addressed. (For example, it could be a sign that more routine or structure is needed, or that they are having to process too much language and therefore other people should reduce the amount of language used, or that they are feeling overloaded by the sensory environment.)
- Exploring their own sensory needs and sensitivities.

- Thinking about their current goals and aspirations (including barriers to achieving them and how these can be addressed).
- Mental and physical health issues are important as there are many inequalities that need to be addressed. Children and young people can benefit from knowing about autism disclosure (the advantages and disadvantages of sharing with others their diagnosis) and how to deal with other people's differing responses to disclosure.
- Talking about well-known and lesser-known autistic people, all of whom are important, regardless of 'social status' or how 'successful' they are judged as being by others. It's important for children to understand that everyone has worth and that success should not be judged by how productive a person is. They should know that self-care and well-being should be a priority and that they deserve to be treated with dignity and respect.
- Autistic girls should have opportunities to learn more about autism, using resources that are adapted and differentiated for them, and they should be able to ask any questions in a way that suits them. Girls may have mixed feelings about being autistic and may need time to process what they have learnt. Self-understanding is preferable to feeling confused and can improve self-esteem and wellbeing.

Supporting autistic girls in schools

Dr Craig Goodall, advisory teacher and author of *Understanding the Voices and Educational Experiences of Autistic Young People: From Research to Practice*, provides additional advice regarding autistic girls.

From my experience as a classroom and advisory teacher, I have found that parents of girls more readily report that their daughters externalize the internalized build-up of stress from their school day when at home. This is often to the surprise of their teachers, who see a child who is managing well in school. As educators, we must start by being cognizant of this. We must begin by appreciating that because the child is not necessarily externalizing their anxiety – or the impact of stressors in school – this does not mean that they are not struggling with navigating the school day. Girls are described as good imitators (Hebron and Bond 2019) and are reported to expend considerable cognitive effort to camouflage (consciously or subconsciously) or mask their struggles with the school environment to fit in and develop a façade of coping, which can lead to poorer mental health, including increased levels of stress, anxiety and depression compared to autistic boys and non-autistic girls (see Livingston *et al.* 2019). Ro, an autistic female aged 16 years, said in Goodall (2020, p.92): 'I was isolated and separate in like a bubble of depression and anxiety.'

How can we help?

Build routine, structure and support to proactively counteract unpredictability. This will help reduce anxiety by giving the child some control in a world that at times may seem chaotic or overwhelming (see Beardon 2020). We must consider the entire day: what happens before school, what happens during and what comes after the school day. There are many transitions (some small, some large), many different routines (some imposed by adults, some child-led), processes and expectations across the entire day that bring multiple sensory, social, organizational and academic demands. Reducing anxiety levels before school and providing supportive strategies and opportunities to relieve stress during the school day will hopefully limit internalizing and externalizing of stress.

1. Prepare the night before for the next school day – provide home with a visual timetable to help the child pack her school bag and know if she needs additional equipment or items such as her P.E. kit. Autistic children do not like being rushed, and mornings can be a point of conflict between parent and child as time is limited to get them to school on time. Develop a morning routine, thinking back from the time the child needs to leave the house to arrive at school on time – this can be displayed visually and be ticked off as each step is completed.

2. Begin the day with a clear routine, such as time spent using a busy tray of activities, a period of independent reading or a maths challenge book. This may also be a good time for the anxious autistic girl in the class to check-in with a key adult to discuss the day ahead, acknowledge any potential areas of stress (for example, a change of teacher or classroom for a subject) and reinforce the support strategies they have available (for example, calm zones in the classroom/school, emotional toolbox, exit cards, regulation exercises). We can tackle any potential worries they have in order to reduce the chances of them ruminating on these issues throughout the day. For example, we could use a worry jars technique which allows the child and teacher to discuss potential worries and categorize them into 'sizes', allowing the child to offload these worries and help to manage and resolve these. Have three different-sized jars (or images of jars to write on), listen and acknowledge each worry and decide if it is

a small, medium or large worry. The child may be catastrophizing what is a seemingly small worry (such as forgetting a schoolbook) and this can be dealt with before the school day begins. The teacher can provide the resolution (for example, providing a copy of the book for the child to use) and the child can then rip this worry up to provide closure. Some larger worries may need more work and can be kept in the large jar to be tackled later, hopefully removing them from the child's mind. This technique could also be used at home.

3. Reduce demands by increasing physical and visual structure. Consistently use whole-class timetables (or colour-coded timetables for secondary pupils) and prepare the pupils in advance for any upcoming changes (and visually show these on the class timetable). Straightforward routines, such as having a green tray for finished work, orange for work in progress, or red for work not started can help build independence and reduce the need to 'work out' what to do. Clearly demarcate areas within the classroom (for example, a calm zone or spots to sit on at carpet time), have resources clearly labelled and reduce clutter (particularly around focal points such as the interactive whiteboard). To minimize direct attention on the individual child, have whole-class brain or movement breaks. Perhaps allow time for the child to focus on an area of interest after busy social periods such as lunch time, or at the end of the school day, to allow her to relax and be ready for the transition home. Build structure into tasks by providing concise and chunked instructions given visually as well as orally – this will help remove that feeling of 'not knowing what to do next'. Keep a set format for worksheets. For example, a rectangle for the child's name

and a line for the date at the top of each brings a sense of the familiar so she can get started easily; perhaps have a green dot for where to begin and a red dot for where to stop. Build in activities that play to the child's strengths, such as allowing her to present her learning on a given topic in the way she feels best (this may be a poster, a poem, a play or a video of her discussing the topic, and so on).

4. Consider the learning environment from the child's point of view. Carry out a sensory audit with the child to step into their shoes and understand how she experiences the classroom. There may be aspects of the classroom that could be adjusted to support her – such as decluttering around the interactive whiteboard area or providing an alternative seating position due to too much distracting visual stimuli.

5. I have found that some autistic children, particularly those who appear shy, are unwilling or less keen to ask for help in the traditional way (by raising their hand or orally asking for help). We can provide the child alternative ways to express or ask for help in class, such as reversible two-coloured bracelets which the child simply flips to indicate they need help. After all, and from my experience, developing the confidence to ask for help is an important skill for autistic girls who can find themselves vulnerable (see Sedgewick *et al.* 2018).

6. Provide break and lunch time routines and alternative activities. Perhaps consider a quiet hub for autistic girls to eat lunch and be with others like them, and facilitate alternative activities, such as reading a book if they wish or using outdoor whiteboards. Ro discussed her experiences of the school cafeteria in Goodall (2020, pp.88–89):

> ...the noise and business and if you don't have a clique to sit with, people in your class would be like 'what are you doing here?' and it was so full of people. You had to find somewhere to sit every time. It was a new piece of pressure each time going in. I went through whole days without eating to avoid it.

7. Consider end-of-day routines. You could provide time at the end of the school day for transitioning to home – use a visual 5, 4, 3, 2, 1 countdown, with each number representing a certain amount of time, such as one minute, and move an arrow down the numbers to visually display the transition process. Consider allowing the autistic child more time to pack her belongings by letting her begin a little earlier (say at the 5 of the countdown) and try not to give an important verbal instruction when the class is bustling and the school bell is ringing. Also consider allowing the child to move on to her next class, or leave at the end of school day, a few moments prior to others to avoid the chaos of the corridor.

8. The school day is over, but homework still remains. Supporting parents to develop a post-school routine is important. The child may require some down time before tackling homework, or they may want to complete it immediately. Either way, have a routine for homework. For instance, a schedule could read: 'Homework task one (yellow folder), check in with parent, brain break for 5 minutes, homework task two (red folder), check in with parent, place folders in bag, tablet time for 30 minutes.' Then again check the schedule for the following day and prepare as required.

9. Autistic girls are more likely to have one or two good friends, and sometimes appear on the periphery of larger social groups. From experience, they also have interests typical of their non-autistic female peers, so the impacts of this can go undetected. It is reported that autistic girls may have greater difficulty understanding and navigating conflict within relationships and therefore may be impacted more greatly by this (see Sedgewick, Hill and Pellicano 2019) – again, being able to discuss these worries and have support and guidance from the teacher or a classroom assistant will help the child steer their way. Teachers can utilize the small number of intense friendships the child may have via structured pair work rather than larger group work, in order to reduce demands, pressure and the need to mask to fit into the group (and the drain on energy levels this may bring). Be aware of social 'hangovers' (social classroom activities, for example, or the child having had a family social gathering at the weekend may require some recovery time, no matter how much they enjoyed the social activity). 'Hangovers' can be managed with some time dedicated to a high-interest activity. Be aware that on a Monday morning the child may need recovery time from a busy weekend. Be mindful that they may be seeking 'alone time' at break, so perhaps give them this time to have a proper social break. Try not to conflate a child spending some time alone as them being lonely (and sad) and in need of the teacher trying to orchestrate social interactions.

10. Be prepared to support a girl with developmental transitions such as menstruation (see 'Further Reading' for Robyn Steward's book *The Autism-Friendly Guide to Periods*, which provides a detailed guide for 9–16-year-olds).

11. Be aware that seemingly harmless approaches, such as asking children to find a partner, can have an impact. Sarah-Jane, aged 17, in Goodall (2020, pp.92–93) describes this:

    > As usual, I had no one and I was made to pair up with the teacher. I felt so little having to stand there waiting to pair up with the teacher. It was awful. It kind of scars you. Mentally it didn't help me.

12. Despite more boys having a diagnosis, autistic girls are certainly not alone and should be made aware of autistic female role models such as Siena Castellon (see 'Further Reading' for *The Spectrum Girl's Survival Guide: How to Grow Up Awesome and Autistic*, which is targeted at girls aged age 12–18 to help them build confidence to be their autistic self and reduce the need to camouflage).

13. Above all, listen to the child, help her develop their toolbox of strategies, discuss with her why you feel a strategy you want to implement may support her, consider how small changes could impact her (a change of seating arrangements, or changing a display board without advance warning can impact majorly on autistic children).

14. Listen to parents, seek their advice on what strategies work for them at home (sometimes children are engaging in work with external agencies without school being aware), share strategies and co-produce solutions to help the autistic girl navigate the entire cycle of the school day.

What can autistic girls benefit from knowing or exploring, and what should parents and professionals be aware of?

Children should have opportunities to consider their own identity (being autistic, their gender, their sexuality, and so on) and recognize and value their own individuality whilst appreciating their own differences. Every girl is a unique individual and has their own personality (whether they are autistic or non-autistic), so autistic girls need opportunities to consider what their own values are. They should think about what and who is important in their life (sometimes possessions, such as an item or toy, may have significant meaning to an autistic person and this should be respected) and be encouraged to consider their own strengths (including personal qualities or strengths that may relate to being autistic such as hyper-focus, having an eye for detail, being highly creative, seeing connections/relationships/themes between things that other people do not).

Autistic girls should also have opportunities to consider their personal likes and dislikes, their 'passions' or intense interests, and how these affect their life. They can also benefit from knowing how their own interests and experiences can positively impact on their quality of life (see Figure 1 in Vermeulen 2014).

Intense interests

Autistic girls may explore what is meant by an 'intense interest' (i.e. pursuing an interest in detail or for long periods of time) and the reasons why they might engage in their interests. It can be useful to understand how intense interests can affect well-being in a positive way (becoming highly knowledgeable and skilled in a particular area, boosting self-esteem and self-confidence, providing enjoyment, relaxation and alone time or escapism, and enabling them to connect with others in a way that works for them without pressure). The possible disadvantages should also be explored (when focused on interests, other needs or responsibilities might be neglected or forgotten), together with ways that these aspects might be managed to aid well-being.

Ways to boost positive feelings

The differences and similarities autistic children have with others (including both strengths and challenges, differences in communication, thinking, perceptions and how they experience the world) may be explored and appreciated. To aid well-being, autistic girls can benefit from understanding what is meant by self-care is and why it is important. In addition, they should be aware of the factors that may affect self-care as well as the practical ways that they can show themselves kindness (through positive self-talk, sleep, relaxation, spending time doing things they enjoy, sensory strategies).

Exploring what is meant by 'self-esteem' and what might affect it (for example, role models who they can identify with, reading about autistic people and their experiences, misunderstandings and misperceptions about autistic people, stigma, being infantilized on disclosure, communication differences, how autistic people are portrayed in the media) can help autistic children to develop self-understanding. Considering what motivates them, what their own goals and aspirations are, and what is meaningful to them personally can help them to feel happy. Other people may support autistic girls by presuming competence but also by understanding what barriers a child might experience in achieving their own personal goals and by thinking about how these can be addressed.

It can be validating to know that other people experience the same challenges and that other people feel the same way. It can be important for girls to understand that many of the challenges they face may be due to inaccessibility, other people's perceptions, the environment not being adapted, sensory sensitivities or communication differences.

Recognizing what strategies are currently being used to manage challenges, and exploring others that might be helpful, can be beneficial.

Learning about 'neurodiversity' (Singer 1998), 'the neurodivcrsity paradigm' and associated terminology, such as 'neurodiverse' and 'neurodivergent', can enable girls to develop a positive identity. Judy Singer and Steve Silberman write about neurodiversity, and Siena Castellon actively works to promote greater understanding of neurodivergent children in schools. People think, communicate, perceive and experience the world in different ways. Therefore, autistic girls can learn about a wide range of role models who are neurodivergent, the skills and abilities people have, and how these can be of benefit (in employment, for example). They may also become more aware of the challenges that neurodivergent people might face in society (stigma, lack of opportunities, being undervalued due to myths and stereotypes) and what can be done to address these issues. They may explore their own thoughts and opinions about being neurodivergent and consider what representations there are of neurodivergent people in the media and how this might impact on the lives of neurodivergent people (whether positive or negative). Autism can be viewed differently by different people, and opinions can change over time (diagnostic criteria is concerned with deficits and impairments, but some autistic people might not view being autistic in this way and may view themselves as having strengths). These strengths can include creativity and being detail-focused, honest and trusting.

Communicating with others

Helping autistic girls to understand their own communication needs, strengths and challenges can build self-esteem. Girls are less likely to be critical of themselves if they understand that it is okay to think and communicate differently to others and know that this is not wrong or inferior. Girls can benefit from gaining greater self-understanding.

This can include exploring with parents and/or professionals what is meant by social communication and social interaction. They may explore what communication strengths and challenges they have and why. These might relate to the girl's understanding, how other people communicate with them, and the environment. Girls should be aware that their ability to communicate might fluctuate, depending on:

- who they are talking to and how they relate to the person (if a person feels accepted, they are more likely to be a 'better' communicator)
- the situation
- sensory needs and sensitivities
- the environment they are in
- whether they feel safe
- how their body feels
- their feelings
- accessibility (they may communicate well by writing/typing rather than by speaking)
- what accommodations are made for them
- other people's expectations of them and whether these are reasonable.

Many autistic girls have difficulty understanding certain aspects of language so it can be helpful to teach these. During communication, autistic girls will often have to put in extra effort to figure out context so building up their understanding of language will help. Some examples of what you might teach could include for example, idioms and homophones. What they have not been taught, they will not know or be able to pick up in the same way as some other children might. Communication difficulties often arise due to lack of context and having to constantly figure out context to understand language requires additional effort. Building up understanding of language can be useful. Often what we say is not what we mean, 'take a seat'.

It's helpful to reflect on our own use of language as difficulties can arise due to 'the conversation partner' or other person not saying what they mean, not being clear or direct, or using too much language rather than being concise.

Sometimes autistic girls may be perceived wrongly because they express themselves differently to a non-autistic child. This is not wrong and should be respected and understood. Some girls, who have speech, can find it difficult to express their feelings in words but should be able to express them in a way they feel comfortable with (visuals, symbols, gestures, or any other way that works for them). Communication is affected by the amount of pressure they feel, social anxiety, specific situations (for example, having difficulty using the phone, whereas other ways to communicate might be more suitable), not being sufficiently prepared for discussions (not knowing what will be discussed, for how long, or in what order, whereas having this knowledge in advance would be helpful) and communication differences (when the communication partner to an autistic person is non-autistic). (See Milton (2012), Crompton et al. (2020).) Not having sufficient time to process information or being overloaded by too much information (too many requests, too much information, too many questions) can adversely affect communication. The environment can also have an impact on the girl's ability to communicate (crowded or noisy environments, background noise that cannot be filtered out) as can sensory sensitivities. Communication will be more 'successful' when she can communicate in her preferred way (at a particular time or in a particular situation), when she is not feeling pressured (by herself or others), when she feels comfortable with whom she is communicating with, when she is in a low-arousal, comfortable environment and when alternative ways of communicating are made accessible to her.

Sensory needs and sensitivities

Sensory needs and sensitivities and how these may affect learning and everyday life should be considered. Sometimes reactions to the sensory environment can be misinterpreted by others, so this should also be explored. Autistic girls should be aware of how the sensory environment can be calming or soothing. Sensory experiences can be positive and can aid well-being. Sensory experiences tailored to each girl can be incorporated into all areas of the curriculum. More information relating to the sensory needs of autistic children can be found in Chapter 4.

Routine and coping with change

Routine and predictability are often needed. Some girls can be more flexible whereas others need a high level of routine and structure and can be extremely distressed by small changes. Autistic girls and others around them may benefit from knowing or exploring why some people need sameness, predictability and routine. It helps to build self-awareness and understanding.

Girls may consider what their own needs are in relation to needing sameness and routine and why these are needed. This can relate to what some people call 'repetitive behaviour', such as pursuing special interests and doing the same enjoyable things repeatedly (watching or listening to something, reading the same book, etc.), or sameness in terms of routine, foods, places, how things are done, and self-stimulatory behaviours (stimming for self-regulation, when happy, when anxious, etc.). Some children are echolalic (i.e. they might repeat words or phrases). There are various reasons for this: some girls do it because they need time to process what has been said or to clarify what has been said; others may use a specific phrase with a specific person as it is familiar.

Girls can benefit from learning to understand what a comfort zone is (being with familiar people, doing familiar things, being in places they know well), when to step out of the comfort zone and when to retreat for self-preservation and self-care. Sometimes, for some girls, changes to routine can be difficult, so having a greater awareness of this can be beneficial as it can affect everyday life and plans. However, moving out of the comfort zone and experiencing something new can be a positive thing for some children (though should be approached with caution). A young person that is supported in the right way may discover a new interest or talent. This will involve lots of trust. Autistic girls should understand why moving out of the comfort zone (doing things that are not familiar) requires self-understanding and self-care as doing new and unfamiliar things can be exhausting and may use up energy. Autistic girls and others should be aware that recovery time might need to be factored in when doing something new. It can be difficult to do things that are unfamiliar (for example, being with unfamiliar people, going to unfamiliar places or taking part in unfamiliar activities), but they can exploring strategies that may help **before**, **during** and **after** stepping out of their comfort zone can be useful: before – preparation, photos of the place or person, a schedule; during – being given visual supports, a structured environment, someone to speak to; after – time out, a calming activity, time to recuperate by doing an activity of choice, no demands from others, a quiet environment.

Understanding context

If an autistic girl has not been taught something, or has no previous knowledge of it, or it does not relate to their life experiences, it can be difficult for them to imagine it. There is no 'context'. Opportunities to broaden experiences will be helpful but it can be difficult for some autistic girls to generalize across situations.

Autistic girls and others may benefit from knowing that some people may have difficulty imagining and predicting what might happen (for example, they may have difficulties foreseeing the consequences of their actions). It helps to build self-awareness and understanding.

- Some people may have difficulty predicting other people's behaviour or understanding how other people may think or feel. This can be misunderstood as the autistic child not having empathy, which is not the case as the child may simply need further information to understand a particular situation.

Hyper-focus and monotropism

Autistic children may **appear** to have difficulty listening to others when focused on a task and can seem to be 'in a world of their own'. This is because it can be difficult to shift attention from one task to another quickly, especially if they are interested in what they are doing and in the flow. When taking in lots of information, or when hyper-focused on a task or interest, it can sometimes take longer for them to respond to questions or requests from others and it feels uncomfortable being distracted from that. Please be aware that this is not rudeness, it is just the child's way of thinking and processing, which is not wrong, just different to many non-autistic children. This is known as monotropic thinking, focussing on one or a small number of interests rather than lots of different things at the same time. For an in-depth explanation of this important theory, I would urge you to read the work of Dr. Dinah Murray, whose life's work has been highly significant in our understanding of autism. Fergus Murray's work too, will also be of particular interest to many teachers because it is concerned with the thinking processes of autistic young people and how this relates to education. In `Craft, Flow and Cognitive Styles' Fergus refers to "autism pioneer" Dr. Dinah Murray, and explains monotropism, flow states and hyperfocus. Fergus says,

So my mum was born in 1946; she had me in 1978, the youngest of three kids. She's said that if she was growing up in the 2000s she would undoubtedly have attracted a diagnosis of autism; I'm sure she's right, but as things worked out, she only came to think of herself as autistic some time around 2010, after many years of working with autistic people and thinking about autism. I was seeking out an autism diagnosis myself at around the same time. By that time she had already published and lectured quite a lot on her theory of autism: Monotropism, part of her conception of the mind as a system of interests that are effectively competing for our attention. Her basic idea about autism - a simple one, really, but powerful - is that autistic minds have a tendency to focus their attention and other processing resources on a small number of things at once, with little left over for things that are outside of our immediate attention tunnel. In other words, autistic people tend to have only one interest aroused at a time, or a small number compared with most of people. Those interests have a strong stream of processing resources directed towards them, often leading to intense experiences, inertia (difficulty starting, stopping or changing course), looping back to well-trod paths, and feelings of deep discombobulation when we are thrown off track.

Fergus explains how this relates to autistic children in schools, What's important to realise is that the intensity and frequency of such experiences vary wildly from person to person. If you imagine that an autistic kid at school is likely to be wrenched out of their attention tunnel multiple times every day, each time leading to disorientation and deep discomfort, you are on your way to understanding why school environments can be so stressful for many autistic students. If you can avoid contributing to that, you may find that you have an easier time with your autistic students: try entering into their attention tunnel when you can, rather than tugging them out of it. Parallel play is one powerful tool for this; start where the child is, show interest in what they're focused on. If you do need to pull them out of whatever they're focusing on, it's best to give them a bit of time.

Being able to study one or a few subjects of interest in greater detail plays to the strengths of autistic young people in contrast to having to study a wider range of subjects in lesser detail, some of which are of no interest and seem meaningless.

Organization

Autistic children and others may benefit from knowing that:

- Some people find planning ahead, organizing themselves and seeing things through to completion more difficult than others. This should not be viewed as laziness, nor should it be seen as procrastination. It can be better described as what is known as inertia. 'Autistic inertia' is something that a person will be more likely to experience if they feel overloaded or overwhelmed. It could even be viewed as a form of self-preservation. For girls who feel overwhelmed, relaxation is key. Taking the pressure off young people is important too and supporting children to manage and complete tasks will be helpful. Sometimes some girls prefer larger tasks being broken down into smaller tasks.
- Each girl may have preferred strategies in relation to self-organization (for example, writing lists, setting reminders on an alarm, written reminders, digital schedules), whereas some girls may prefer or need some level of support from others.
- Some people have greater difficulty starting a task (in this cases, visual or verbal prompts can be helpful, as can cueing the child in by name rather than addressing the whole class).
- The physical environment can provide structure and autistic children can benefit from having a clutter-free, well-organized environment.
- Remembering to complete a task may be difficult, especially if it is of little interest or if there is no time limit in which to do it.
- Some girls may find it difficult to end a task, especially without warning. They may need to know how long a task is likely to last but also need preparation for when a task is coming to an end.
- Some girls may have difficulty if they are prevented from finishing a task, so solutions must be agreed. For example, the work/task can be put somewhere safe and the child can finish it later,

or they can finish it now but be aware of the implications of that choice, such as being late for another lesson. Being disrupted when in the flow of something can be upsetting and is to be avoided. Preparing a child for change can really help. Where this is necessary, preparing autistic girls for change can really help. Providing her with options is a helpful solution as it gives her control. Ideally, the child's `flow' wouldn't be broken but being adaptable and flexible and understanding that autistic children think differently and that it is not wrong will help the child.

- An autistic girl will not lack motivation to start a task and continue with a task, when it relates to her interests and provides the right level of challenge.

Key points

- Autistic girls have many strengths and positive personal qualities.
- Identity can be shaped by what autistic girls see and hear around them and how autistic people are portrayed in the media.
- A sense of belonging can aid well-being.
- Autistic girls can benefit from knowing about autistic role models.
- Understanding themselves (how they think, communicate and experience the world) is important for autistic girls' well-being.
- Where others adapt to the child and adapt the environment, autistic girls will be less likely to suppress aspects of themselves and will feel more included. This will improve their well-being and help them feel accepted.

CHAPTER 3

Be Safe

This chapter sensitively explores the safety of autistic girls and women and discusses a variety of issues, including social motivation, the oversharing of personal information, reading other people's intentions, body language, conflict and confrontation, and communication differences, such as being literal. Also discussed are the challenges autistic girls may experience in recognizing, communicating and reporting incidences of inappropriate behaviour towards them, exploitation, and abuse. In addition, the chapter focuses on trust, honesty, friendships, relationships and consent. It is hoped that through greater awareness of the issues affecting autistic girls and women, they may experience improved well-being throughout their lives. The chapter also explains how other people can have an impact on an autistic girl's safety (either positively or negatively), and how the physical environmental and other factors (for example, sensory issues) can affect safety and well-being. Although many issues relating to the safety of autistic girls are raised in this chapter, it is important to remember that the support of caring family members and professionals can have a positive impact on safety and well-being.

Be safe

Autistic girls deserve to be treated with respect and dignity; however, worryingly, they can be at risk of exploitation and abuse. Therefore, keeping them safe and teaching them how to keep themselves safe is a priority and one of the most important things we can do to ensure their well-being. There are many reasons why autistic girls are at increased risk of exploitation. Understanding the reasons why can enable us to safeguard them, prevent them from coming to harm and, importantly, help them to understand and protect themselves (as far as they are able) at various stages of their lives. Sedgewick *et al.* (2019) report:

> While our sample of neurotypical women reported experiencing sexual

> assault and domestic violence at similar rates (26.3%) to the most recent official statistics on the topic (20.2%), the proportion of autistic women experiencing such events (79%) was alarming...and renders this an especially important – and urgent – issue to address both in research and practice.

They rightly recognize that there is 'an urgent need for specific and tailored personal safety training and support for autistic women – and, by extension, autistic girls – to ensure that they can enjoy a safe transition to adulthood and positive adult relationships'. Sedgewick, Hill and Pellicano (2018) highlight the importance of 'having open and frank discussions at home and in schools, around consent and healthy relationships to protect autistic girls'.

To benefit this group, we should also consider **when** and **how** this is taught, as research tells us that autistic children are being provided with sex education later than non-autistic children, yet children with disabilities are at much higher risk of abuse. 'The rates of sexual abuse for children with developmental disabilities are nearly two times greater than for typical children,' says Edelson (2010), referencing the work of Mansell, Sobsey and Moskal (1998). Krishnarathi, Dharma Raja and Sundaravalli (2018) also state: 'Women and girls with disabilities face double discrimination, which places them at higher risk of gender-based violence, sexual abuse, neglect, maltreatment and exploitation.'

Social isolation

Autistic girls can often have one 'best' friend or find themselves on the edges of group, blending in. Autistic girls can be at risk of social isolation. They are underdiagnosed, diagnosed later in life than boys and may not be aware that they are autistic until later in life. This can lead to confusion for some girls. They may be the only autistic girl in their class, whether they are educated in specialist or mainstream provision.

Having friends and being part of a group can be a protective factor against exploitation and abuse. Many non-autistic children will have a social network of peers who they can talk to about friendships and relationships, but autistic girls have fewer (but more intense) friendships. Having supportive friends to confide in enables children and adolescents to broaden their understanding of social situations, helping them to judge other people's behaviour towards them. Sedgewick *et al.* (2019) acknowledge that autistic girls lack wider social networks and, without this social support, they can be at a disadvantage. Therefore, building protective networks for autistic girls is crucial; these must be 'autism-friendly' and must take into consideration social preferences.

As girls grow up and become more self-aware, the differences between them and their non-autistic peers can become more apparent. Being autistic, they have different needs (as well as different strengths) and if they are not aware of these differences, autistic girls can unfairly compare themselves to their non-autistic peers and put pressure on themselves to be like others. It is important that girls understand that they have their own unique strengths and abilities that non-autistic girls may not have, and vice versa. These girls are just experiencing the world differently and are no less important than their peers. They can benefit from gaining greater self-awareness and self-acceptance. Equally, peers may be more accepting and understanding if they are taught to appreciate others who are neurodivergent.

Being isolated and appearing to be different can make some autistic girls stand out. Sedgewick *et al.* (2019) state that 'research has shown that neurotypical participants judge autistic people as more socially awkward in short videos. This rapid impression forming may mark these women as easier targets for predatory men'. However, it is important to note that it is not only some men who can be predatory. Edelson (2010) reiterates this view, recognizing that 'although not an issue for all individuals with autism, certain social-emotional and communication challenges, when present, may be interpreted by sexual offenders as vulnerabilities that they can exploit'.

In addition to teaching autistic girls what is meant by 'sexual exploitation', we must also ensure that we teach them about financial exploitation as some girls will be taken advantage of because they are keen to help others but need to be aware that not everyone will be as honest as they are. They may be more willing to give to others because they want to be a good friend. Autistic girls need time to think decisions through. It can be difficult to make decisions when approached 'off-guard'.

Mandy and Tchanturia (2015) recognize the difficulties that autistic women experience, saying that one of the participants in their study 'seems to be rather socially naive, and this has left her vulnerable to exploitation, as she lent a large sum of money to her friend, who has since become difficult to contact and has not paid the money back'. Being a considerate friend is a positive quality that unfortunately some people take advantage of.

Understanding other people's intentions

Sometimes what people **say** and what people **do** do not correlate, making it difficult for children with lack of life experience to understand other people's intentions. Autistic girls should be taught about healthy friendships and relationships to help them understand how they should be treated and how to treat others.

Teaching autistic children to judge the **behaviour** of others (not just their words) can be useful in helping them to protect themselves, but we must also encourage them to ask for help (and teach them how to, providing the phrases or scripts) when they experience difficulties or are uncertain about people and situations. How people treat others is a good indicator of their trustworthiness, though autistic girls need to be cautious and should take time to get to know people.

Being unable to read the intentions of others and finding it difficult to generalize across situations can lead to difficulties as Sedgewick *et al.* (2019) explain:

> Autistic women described how they generally assumed 'the best [in] people'. Some participants therefore repeatedly found themselves in situations where they had been taken advantage of because 'there's that whole ulterior motive thing that I end up missing'. Some women also struggled to know when to leave situations they didn't like: 'I just didn't know how to avoid once it had started.' They also struggled to generalize from one incident to the next situation, with one participant reporting, 'I'm surprised every time.'

It can be assumed that autistic girls (especially those with good expressive language abilities) can understand and express their feelings similarly to their non-autistic peers, but this is often not the case in my experience. Even amongst a small group of autistic girls, there is a great variability in how able they are to understand and to gauge their own and other people's feelings. In contrast, there are some autistic girls who are very in tune with their own feelings and can articulate these well. There are also those who experience emotions so intensely that they literally soak up other people's emotions. This is due to 'hyperarousal of the empathic system', explains Dr Michelle Garnett (Cook and Garnett 2018, p.189). However, this consideration for others, which is a strength, can leave these girls at risk of exploitation by those who take advantage of their kind-heartedness and naivety.

Some autistic girls may have difficulty in reading other people. According to Edelson (2010), it can be 'difficult for individuals with autism to understand the emotions of others when the emotions expressed are deceptive'. She says:

> Offenders attempt to gain trust from potential victims and often do so

> by being deceptive. Therefore, they may display deceptive emotions that may not be recognized by some children with autism. In addition to difficulty with emotional processing, children with autism may encounter communication challenges that may make them particularly desirable targets of sexual offenders because of the perception that they would be unable to disclose the abuse.
>
> ... [Autistic children] may encounter communication challenges that may make them particularly desirable targets of sexual offenders because of the perception that they would be unable to disclose the abuse. (Edelson 2010)

We must therefore ensure that we support girls to understand the inappropriate behaviour of other people and be able to communicate their concerns to others. Communication differences can mean that some autistic children can be literal in their understanding of language and may misunderstand what is being said. Lawson (2017) says:

> Then there's the issue of sexuality and keeping safe. For some females this is a major issue. Some have little understanding of sexual etiquette, even if they have a normal IQ. The literal, black and white thinking processes in autism might mean if someone says, 'Can you have sex with me?' the person may reply, 'Yes,' because they perceive the question to mean 'Is it possible for you to have sex with me?' This is literal thinking that fails to negotiate the bigger picture.

Some autistic girls will be unaware of risk or danger because they cannot predict or imagine what might happen in a situation. Making them aware of other people's motives and helping them to forsee what *might* happen can help girls protect themselves from potential danger. Role playing can be a good way to help them know what to say and do.

Phobias and safety

A large percentage of autistic children have one or more phobias: 41 percent have unusual fears compared to '5 percent of typical children' (Mayes *et al.* 2012). To some extent, phobias can affect safety if a child reacts by trying to 'escape'. Much research appears to show that although autistic children are more likely to have phobias compared to non-autistic children. Gaigg, Crawford and Cottell (2018) also acknowledge that 'autistic individuals may experience excessive fear of unusual and highly idiosyncratic objects or events'.

Dickerson Mayes and Calhoun (2013) recognize that 'what is tolerable for most children...might be terrifying, distressing or infuriating for a child with autism', but acknowledged that as autistic children are unique, the things that 'terrified' some, 'fascinated' others. It is possible that some phobias can relate to negative sensory experiences (vacuum cleaners, hand dryers, balloons, lights, walking on surfaces), yet others are unexplained. Whether phobias are considered common or 'unusual' is subjective, but they can cause a child to feel frightened and unsafe. Examples of phobias include fears relating to the weather (rain, wind, hurricanes, thunderstorms), heights, escalators, elevators, machinery, vehicles, crowds, toilets, steps, people and colours. Schools can help to safeguard autistic children by compiling risk assessments that include an outline of a child's specific phobia and how best to help them to manage it. The first step is to ask the child what might help. For those who might find it difficult to imagine what might help, solutions can be offered visually and/or in writing (if the child can read) as a list on a wipe board so that the child can tick their preferences. It is important that children are involved in deciding what will help them so that they know they are in control, rather than being exposed to something that is distressing.

Providing a safe space

Many different factors can place an autistic girl on high alert. Things that seem trivial to others can cause extreme anxiety for her and should not be underestimated. Sometimes the reactions of autistic children can be misunderstood and misinterpreted. They can be thought of as being intolerant, overly dramatic or displaying 'challenging behaviour', but this is the child reacting to what they sense as a threat. Some children experience being in this heightened state numerous times throughout the day, day after day. This can take a toll on mental and physical health unless they understand what is happening (in their minds and bodies and why) and learn to develop strategies to avoid and counteract stress.

The way that girls react to stressful situations will vary. Some will express this outwardly by being verbal, having emotional outbursts or running away to 'escape'. This is not a girl having a tantrum but what is known as 'meltdown', a sign that a girl is overloaded. This could be considered as the equivalent of the fight or flight response.

Creating 'safe spaces' in homes (and in schools and other environments) can enable autistic girls to retreat to a safe place should they be likely to run away. This 'safe place' or 'zone' can be a quiet area of the home where they will not be disturbed – for example, their room or a place in their garden if they have one. In schools, it could be a quiet area where the child can be supervised, from a distance, allowing her dignity, away from prying eyes. Within that space could be items and resources that help the individual child to calm herself: comfortable chairs, soft blankets to wrap herself in or to hide under, sensory toys, access to music, ear defenders, colouring books to distract and calm, and paper and writing equipment for drawing, expressing feelings or communicating with. Some 'safe spaces' can be more sensory focused, depending on the child/children using it (and dependent on the budget), and might include bubble tubes, projectors, lighting effects and music, for example. Other 'safe spaces' can be low-arousal: a bare, low-stimulus area or room.

If an autistic child knows that an area is available for her to go to that feels safe, she is more likely to use it. Adults can provide support and understanding to resolve any difficulties without judgement in this calming space. Ideally, if we provide resources that help children to understand their feelings and express them safely, then these can be used to ensure that they are less likely to behave impulsively as they have a structure to follow. If you sense that a child is heading for meltdown, provide her with a visual reminder showing what to do before she reaches that point. Symbol keyrings showing visual prompts (for example, 'use sensory toys', 'go to your quiet space', 'listen to music', 'do breathing exercises') work well.

> I can struggle with managing my emotions when I am disappointed or embarrassed by making a mistake. When this first happens, it's okay to feel upset and to find a safe way to release negative emotions. I often like to spend some time alone to calm down in private, as I find people often say the wrong things to me in these situations, which can make me feel worse. I also like to engage in my interests when I am disappointed, as it helps me to release negative energy and remind me of the positive things in my life. It may take time to recover from disappointment. Still, I found it has become easier over time now I know what helps me in these situations.

Some children experience 'shutdown', the freeze response, which limits functional ability, including the ability to speak in some cases, where they would normally communicate using words. Attempting to resolve the problem at this stage can cause overload so is often best avoided. However, some children will benefit from gentle reassurance – knowing who you are, that you are there to help, that you will give them space and help them when they are ready – then providing them with the space they need, whilst making sure they are safe. Maintaining a low-arousal environment, without any demands being made, will help a child to recover. When able, some children may use alternative methods to communicate (technology, aids or visuals) until they regain the ability to use words again (if they normally use words to communicate). Some children may use a visual to show you whether they are ready to talk or not.

Using visuals

Autistic girls are often visual thinkers so can benefit from using *Comic Strip Conversations*™. Devised by Carol Gray (1994), the Conversations work well for many autistic girls because they allow them to express their thoughts, feelings and perceptions of situations through drawings, thought and speech bubbles, and the use of colour, to gain the perspective of others. *Comic Strip Conversations*™ can be used to resolve difficulties and explore solutions; they can also provide children with a better understanding of what to do in future. Some autistic girls will better understand concepts when presented as images. No speech is needed (but can be used) when communicating through *Comic Strip Conversations*™. There is also the benefit that you and the child can both communicate quickly (without providing eye contact, which can feel uncomfortable for some autistic girls) through images and writing where necessary, depending on the child's ability level. The Conversations can be used to help a child feel that a situation has been resolved satisfactorily and that there is a definite end to the issue, something that is important to an autistic girl who may otherwise spend vast amounts of time over-thinking situations.

Even if an autistic child has been shown where to go or what to do in any given situation, she may not remember, or may not be able to apply what she has learnt straight away. Autistic girls may find it difficult to generalize across situations (and different places), so a visual prompt can be a helpful reminder. Pictures feel less harsh than words.

Educating autistic girls about safety

Autistic girls and young women need to know how to protect themselves. Being assertive can be difficult. We must also consider to what extent the school curriculum is equipping autistic children with the knowledge, understanding and skills **they** need for life. With the focus on academic learning in many schools, and little time for life skills, autistic children can miss out – they need to be explicitly taught about the 'hidden curriculum' (i.e. the knowledge and skills that non-autistic children intuitively pick up, which autistic children might struggle to do). Autistic children need to learn these unwritten rules to keep themselves safe, to be more independent and to help themselves manage the challenges of life.

Whether they are being educated at home (electively or unelectively) or in mainstream, specialist or alternative provision, autistic girls need to be taught **how** to keep themselves safe (as far as they are able), **how** to seek help and know **where** to seek help from. Autistic girls will not be able to pick up some skills intuitively in the way that non-autistic girls might, so they will need to be taught these explicitly. Language may also need to be adapted as some girls will be very literal. Autistic girls are unique, so approaches will vary depending on the child's strengths, needs and preferred learning styles. The aim should not be for the child to appear more non-autistic; instead, approaches should be adapted so that what is taught can help a child to keep herself as safe as possible.

The following can be useful to aid understanding of topics relating to safety:

- Visual and written materials. Seeing pictures and sequences can aid understanding of concepts and can be tailored to the girl's age/stage.

- Role play, drama lessons or classes (acting out scenarios, watching others) and learning from real-life scenarios.
- Audio-visual materials. Watching clips and discussing them is less intrusive than talking about an individual.
- Independent work (self-study) is a good option for some children. Providing reading materials and learning resources can be useful (but it's important to ensure understanding).
- Anonymous questions can help children to feel less embarrassment and feel comfortable asking questions. (In groups, children can write questions for the adult to answer either verbally or in writing.)
- Cards/images showing difficult scenarios can help children to explore different scenarios – for example, 'What would you do in this situation? Discuss'.
- Modelling (demonstrating a skill, an action, or a way of communicating something to others) can help some children who may not understand the impact of voice, tone and volume, and what this shows to others (assertiveness). This is not about teaching children social skills but more about teaching them how to protect themselves when necessary.
- Discussing current affairs (using visuals, discuss current events to gauge views and thoughts) can link to real-life experiences.

As 'Be Safe' covers many topics of a sensitive nature, how these are delivered and differentiated for different girls will vary as some girls will be easily alarmed or may be very literal in their understanding. Careful consideration will be needed when selecting appropriate images to ensure they are appropriate to the age/stage/level of understanding of the girls being taught. Language will also need to be adapted. Girls need to be aware that if any information is disclosed that suggests that they are at risk of harm, then this information will need to be shared with people whose job it is to keep them safe. As building trust is important when working with autistic girls, helping them to feel comfortable when learning about safety is a priority. Ways that this can be achieved include letting girls know that they can choose to keep their work private or share it with others, and they can choose whether or not to take part in discussions. In addition, they can alert you to when they may feel the need to opt out. Girls should know that if there are any questions that come to mind **after** a session has ended, they can still share these directly or can ask questions anonymously. This is important because it can take time for autistic children to process information. Girls should be encouraged to ask any questions they want to, without judgement.

Safeguarding

The safeguarding of autistic children is paramount. All those working with autistic children should be aware that disabled children are at greater risk of exploitation and abuse. This should be reflected in their school policies and safeguarding documents. Parents, carers, professionals and others should work collaboratively to ensure the safety of autistic children, and those working in schools should be aware of the reasons why autistic children might be at greater risk. Fortunately, having a supportive family, approachable professionals and good friends are all protective factors against any form of mistreatment.

The curriculum

The curriculum should also reflect the differing needs of autistic pupils, and lessons should be delivered in a way that shows an appreciation of the way that autistic pupils learn. Autistic children can find it difficult to imagine something that they have no experience or prior knowledge of, so multi-sensory learning, providing visuals, models, audio-visual materials, and even self-study should all be considered, as well as linking lessons to real life where possible. Language might also need to be adapted so that autistic children – when learning about sex education, for example – understand what peers are referring to. It is also important, however, to use correct terminology.

School policies

The needs of autistic children should be reflected in all school policies, but policies must also be put into practice. Any 'Behaviour Policy' should be flexible enough to accommodate the differing needs of autistic children and should reflect a good understanding of how they think, learn and interact with others. Blanket behaviour policies and 'zero tolerance' approaches do not suit autistic children and can be discriminatory.

Policies relating to teaching and learning should take into account the differing needs of autistic children – for example, some may find it difficult to take in large amounts of language at once so may need regular breaks. Professionals can help autistic pupils by taking into account speech, language and occupational therapy advice so that they can tailor lessons, their own practices and approaches to individual pupils.

The learning environment can have an impact on how an autistic child feels, so this will also need to be reflected in policy. Safeguarding policies should reflect the challenges that autistic children can experience in recognizing, communicating and reporting inappropriate behaviour, bullying, exploitation and abuse.

Uniform policies should reflect that autistic children can be over-sensitive to items of clothing, so flexibility is also needed in relation to this. New items of clothing can cause some children extreme discomfort and may even cause pain.

Safety and behaviour

Reframing 'problem' behaviour can really help autistic pupils in schools. Often difficulties arise due to other people's expectations and lack of understanding about how autistic children think, and sometimes behaviour can be misinterpreted. Common difficulties that autistic children experience include:

- other people not being clear
- other people using too much language and the child feeling overloaded
- the child seeing the other person as being unfair or unjust
- the child being misunderstood
- other people's expectations (for example, thinking that a child is being lazy when they find something genuinely difficult)
- a child not being able to read between the lines
- overloading sensory environments (crowds, noise, lights) and hyper-sensitivity
- too many instructions
- miscommunication
- unexpected changes without warning
- anxiety
- phobias (however unusual these might appear to others)
- too many demands
- unreasonable demands
- exhaustion.

When focusing on behaviour, it can be helpful for adults to view the situation, including what led up to it, from a child's perspective, and consider the following:

- What could **I** have communicated differently?

- Did the child understand what was expected of her and was this reasonable?
- What was **my** body language or facial expression showing her?
- Was she confused or did she misunderstand something? Could I have phrased anything differently or made something clearer?
- Was there a reason why she did not want to engage (for example, fear of failure, confused about what to do, sensory issues)?
- What did **my** tone of voice and volume sound like to her?
- What could **I** have done differently?
- Was sufficient structure provided?
- Did the sensory environment play a part in her difficulties?
- Were too many people around the child or involved? How might she have felt?
- How can this be resolved so that trust can be repaired?
- What can be done to ensure that this does not happen in future? What can the child do and what can the adults do? What changes need to be made?

Be safe – what can autistic girls benefit from knowing or exploring, and what should parents and professionals be aware of?

Autistic girls, and others, can explore what is meant by 'personal safety' and what 'private' and 'privacy' mean (in relation to the body, and in relation to information about the child in real-life situations and online). The reasons why autistic children may be at risk of harm or exploitation should be considered:

- They may have difficulty reading the intentions of other people.
- They may take people at face value (believing that what people say is what they mean)
- They can be too trusting of other people.

- They may be at greater risk of danger if overly 'compliant' when following learnt rules (or if they cannot generalize across situations or struggle to apply different rules to different situations or places).
- They may find it difficult to imagine what the consequences of words or actions might be.
- If they become socially isolated, they may not have other people to ask for advice or support.
- They may have different communication needs to their non-autistic peers: they may be literal in their understanding of language; they may not understand slang or current phrases used by peers and so may misunderstand or may accidentally agree to something they do not want without realizing.
- They may overshare, giving out too much information (which may be personal), telling someone something that should be kept private. However, they should understand that sharing in some contexts can be a positive quality that helps people to build connections with others (judging when and with whom will be difficult for some autistic children).
- They may be honest and open (which is a positive quality) and expect other people to be, which is a problem if the other person is not.

Safety and non-verbal communication

Some autistic children find that learning about non-verbal communication (gestures, facial expressions, body language) is useful in helping them to understand other people and their behaviour (by contrast, other autistic children find this unhelpful), so it is worth exploring if a child thinks it may be of benefit to her. Interestingly, I have met many autistic girls who enjoying observing other people, watching how they interact and behave!

In the same way that some non-autistic people can misinterpret the facial expressions and body language of autistic people and their intentions, sometimes autistic children can experience some difficulty in 'reading' others, though many autistic people have no problem interpreting body language, facial expression and gestures. Some autistic people just have different ways of reading and judging others. Autistic children should be aware that what some people **say** does not correspond with what they **do** (their actions). When trying to judge whether a person is trustworthy, it might be suggested that a person's character can be judged by how they speak about, and behave towards, others. The child should also be made aware that it takes time to get to really know a person and trust them – and even then, some level of caution is needed for self-protection.

Oversharing

Autistic girls can benefit from knowing:

- when it may be necessary to share personal information (for example, to access healthcare or in an emergency)
- when personal information would be better kept private, and when **not** to disclose personal information (and how to judge this)
- strategies to avoid sharing personal details (what to say, what not to say, polite refusal, use of humour to diffuse uncomfortable situations)
- why it is important to have 'thinking time' when making decisions or when asked for information (being aware that some people need more time to process information than others)
- that they do not have to respond immediately to requests for information, especially if these are overly personal.

Safety and non-compliance

There may be times when an autistic girl's safety relies on her ability to be impolite and non-compliant. This is something parents and professionals must be aware of. Rather than teaching autistic girls to always be polite and compliant, it is equally important that they should be encouraged to be assertive, give their opinions and say 'No' in different ways. Autistic girls can find confrontation difficult and some will avoid it, so by teaching them to say 'No' politely as well as impolitely, and by respecting their wishes, we are helping them to protect themselves when necessary. Too often, autistic girls are taught to be compliant, to do as they are told and to respect those in authority or their elders, and in some cases this will endanger them. If autistic girls can learn to recognize inappropriate language and behaviour (in their many forms), then they can be kept safe.

In addition to being able to recognize inappropriate behaviour, it is necessary to teach autistic girls how to seek help and to report any concerns as, sadly, not everyone can be trusted, and autistic girls (and adults) can be targeted in real life and online because they are autistic.

Assertiveness

Autistic girls should be taught what being passive, assertive, and aggressive means. Some girls will struggle to be assertive so should learn strategies such as understanding how tone of voice and volume can convey meaning. Autistic girls should be taught to question others, as being compliant could put them at risk.

Exploring the concept of friendship

Autistic girls can benefit from knowing or exploring what friendship means. For example: there are different types of friends, such as a close friend, a best friend, an acquaintance; people may have different numbers of friends; people can be friends whilst enjoying friendships with others.

Children should also understand why some people enjoy solitude and can benefit from being alone: they may enjoy pursuing their own interests; they may need to have quiet time; they may feel exhausted by prolonged social interaction and need a break from it; they may need time to allow the brain to process information; they may need a low-stimulus environment.

Children can consider the following aspects of friendships:

- How people make and maintain friendships.
- The qualities they appreciate in others and the positive qualities (for example, respect, trust, generosity, empathy, honesty) that might make someone a good friend.
- How friendships might make someone feel (good about themselves, accepted).
- Friendships should be welcoming to others and should not exclude or make others feel lonely.
- Loneliness and how it might feel to be excluded.
- The benefits of having friends (mental health benefits, having a sense of belonging, sharing interests, safety aspects).
- Friends can disagree and have differences of opinion but can still be friends.
- The types of conflicts friends might have during the pre-teen and teen years and how these might be managed.
- Friendships can change or end due to circumstances (girls can explore how to cope with feelings in relation to this).
- People enjoy friendships on different terms and that this is perfectly acceptable. For example:
    * Some friends may not see each other as often as others.
    * Friends may have different communication preferences.

- People may prefer to have online friendships rather than meet with each other face to face. Reasons for this might be:
    * They are better able to manage the time they spend interacting.
    * They do not have to make eye contact if this feels uncomfortable.
    * Convenience – they can be in their own space, experience less pressure, and are able to opt out if necessary.
    * They can have friendships with people who live in another country but who share the same interests.
- How to support friends experiencing difficulties and when to seek adult help.
- Friendships can develop through shared interests or shared values.
- Power imbalances in friendships and what is meant by social status.
- Self-esteem and coping with peer pressure:
    * How a child can know when help is needed if a friend is making her feel uncomfortable or unsafe. (She may need to know **who** she can ask for help and about organizations that can help girls and young people who are experiencing problems. She may explore why stereotyping people, based on sex, gender, disability, sexual orientation, race, or religion, can be harmful.)
    * Why some people might go along with others to fit in. (People might adapt themselves consciously or otherwise to do this. Learning about what is meant by masking, camouflage and assimilation can increase self-understanding. Girls can consider why some people suppress aspects of themselves – stimming, for example – to fit in and how this can affect health.)

  * Girls may gain an understanding that when with good friends they can 'be themselves'.
  * How to be assertive with friends.
- Girls should explore honesty and trust and why these are important aspects of friendship; **but** they should also be able to recognize when **not** to keep something a secret.
- Girls may think about their own expectations of friends and vice versa.

Online friendships and safety

Online friendships can be meaningful for autistic girls and can provide positive connections with others.

Autistic girls can benefit from learning about:

- the advantages and disadvantages of having friends online
- how to manage friendships online
- how communication can be misconstrued when online
- the 'rules' or 'guidelines' regarding online friends and how to remain safe online
- how to deal with comments, images, or online content that cause upset or offence, and **how** and **when** to seek advice or help
- how information and data may be used and shared online, therefore they should not share any images, information or other 'material' that they would not want others to view
- how some things may be difficult to remove once they have been put online
- what is meant by an online 'persona' and that people online may be different to who they are in real life.

Girls also need to be aware of other people's intentions and motives, and understand how their own behaviour online might make other people feel (positive or negative). There can be many advantages and disadvantages for young people in disclosing that they are autistic online: on the plus side, they can connect with other autistic people, and other people can be educated about the autistic person's perspective; on the negative side, other people may attempt to take advantage of or exploit the autistic person or mistreat them in some way. Girls should consider what information can be shared online, and for what purpose, and be aware of what is meant by 'grooming'.

Finally, it is important for girls to consider how much time is spent online and whether this has a positive or negative impact on their life (time online may enable them to relax after a busy day, but too much time online might mean other responsibilities or their own health are neglected).

Bullying

Although many autistic girls have successful friendships with others and are valued in their school communities, some experience bullying because they are different, so educating young people is vital. Initiatives such as Siena Castellon's 'Neurodiversity Celebration Week' (www.qlmentoring.com) can help peers to gain a greater understanding of how other children think, learn, and experience the world, but there is still a long way to go. Sue Fletcher-Watson explains how neurodiversity can be discussed in school:

> Another innovative way of increasing support and acceptance of autistic children growing up is to focus on how people around them can change their knowledge, attitudes and actions. A piece of research led by a team at University of Edinburgh has been aiming to do just that. LEANS, or Learning About Neurodiversity in Schools, is a co-design project in which a neurodiverse team of educators and researchers

> have created a resource pack for teachers to deliver to the whole class, in primary school. Through a series of hands-on activities, stories and reflective discussions the goal is that everyone in the class will learn what neurodiversity is and how it affects school life and learning. The team hope that this kind of approach will be part of a shift towards a more progressive form of inclusion, focused less on fitting in or catching up, and more on acceptance and understanding for each individual, as they are. (Personal communication)

When attempting to resolve conflict that arises in school, it is important that the views of the autistic girls are considered, and their way of thinking and communicating is respected. Bullying should not be ignored as it can have devastating consequences for some children. All children need to understand boundaries, know how to conduct themselves online, and recognize and report inappropriate or offensive content or behaviour. Dr Emily Lovegrove writes about bullying and provides practical and helpful advice in her book *Autism, Bullying and Me* (see 'Further Reading').

Autistic children and others may consider or explore what is meant by 'bullying' and know about the different types of bullying:

- Bullying can take the form of verbal, physical or relational aggression.
- Some bullying can be subtle (for example, sarcasm), so it can be difficult for some people to know if they are being bullied.
- People can be bullied face to face or online and should learn how to report it.
- People can benefit from being aware of how bullying can affect someone, about rejection by peers and how being excluded might make a person feel.
- Children should learn about self-worth, self-care, valuing the self and self-acceptance.

- Children should learn how to support others who may be being bullied, whilst keeping themselves safe.
- Children can be given practical tips and advice in relation to bullying, including literature that focuses on bullying and details of support that is available for people who are being bullied.

Body awareness and knowledge

Autistic girls should develop awareness of their own bodies and explore how people might feel about their bodies as they grow up. They must learn that their bodies belong to them. For safety reasons they need to be taught which areas of the body are considered to be private, vocabulary relating to the body (correct terminology as well as slang words and what they mean), and vocabulary relating to different life stages (adolescent, teenager, etc.). They can develop an awareness of what different bodies look like (both from the front and back) and develop an awareness of their own body.

Children should be aware of what stage in life they are at now (pre-teen, teenager) and the various stages that follow. They may become more aware of the physical changes that take place as their bodies develop. They may also experience pressure to look a certain way. They may learn about body image and how this relates to the media and different cultures.

Girls can explore how their bodies (and other people's) change over time (using visuals to show this) and understand that change is a gradual process. Knowing that change and transition can be more difficult for some people, and understanding why (for example, because sameness feels safe and comfortable, whereas change can lead to uncertainty or extra responsibility), can be validating and helpful.

Children should be aware that other people's expectations of them may change or increase whilst they are growing up (for example, a parent expecting a young person to do more things for themselves), and that in the process of growing up, people develop their own thoughts, opinions and beliefs and develop a sense of self. Sometimes this can cause conflict with other people who have different opinions, expectations or beliefs.

Girls should be able to recognize and name internal and external organs of reproduction and understand their function. Girls need to learn about the physical changes that will take place at different stages of their life, including puberty, pregnancy and menopause. Girls can learn that hormones affect emotions and that some people will experience emotions intensely, may feel more tired or may feel pain at certain times during the menstrual cycle (see 'Further Reading' for Robyn Steward's *The Autism-Friendly Guide to Periods* – a great visual resource). Some autistic girls can be extremely emotional and sensitive around the time of their period, so keeping track of when it is likely to start can be helpful. Girls can learn about the different ways menstrual pain can be managed (for example, with yoga, heat, or medication).

Girls may learn about attraction and what people might be attracted to (the physical, a person's spirituality, their personality, humour, nature, intelligence, or how the other person makes them feel). They may learn that some people need to connect with someone on an emotional level before becoming intimate with them.

Girls may also want to explore feelings about their changing body and know what to do if this is causing distress, and why this might be, and learn who they can communicate with in their family or in their community and which organizations can offer support.

Relationships

The Department for Education sets out what children should learn with regards to relationships but autistic children, their parents and professionals, will need to be aware of additional information as their children's needs may differ. The way that autistic girls think, learn and communicate can sometimes be different to non-autistic girls. Relationship education, health education and sex education will need to be taught in a way that is clearly understood and takes account of the different ways that autistic people experience the world. Honesty, sensitivity and directness are required. This is because autistic children can be literal in their understanding of language and can find it difficult to imagine something they have no experience of. In the past, some children I have worked with have found sex education difficult because these topics signal growing up and this involves change. Any type of change can be tricky for some people. Certain children may have phobias or may find it difficult to hear certain words relating to the body or to sex. Others find it difficult to look at images of people's bodies or body parts, internal or external, so it is important to take the embarrassment and pressure away from children.

Autistic children can learn about what is meant by a relationship and that there are many types of relationships – they can consider what the differences are. They can think about the important people in their lives (family, friends, teachers, and other professionals) and their roles.

Children can benefit from knowing how a person should expect to be treated in a relationship and how to treat others, including how to show respect for others and how other people should show respect for them (by their language and actions).

They might explore the benefits of having a positive, healthy relationship and the characteristics of a healthy, intimate relationship (loyalty, trust, consent, sex, friendship, shared interest and values, respect for each other).

Children can explore what it means to be attracted to someone, the qualities people are attracted to and why (personality, physical appearance, etc.). They can consider how to recognize when other people are attracted to them, how to deal with situations if attraction is not mutual, how to tell if they are ready for a relationship and learn about trust.

Girls learn what 'having sex' means and the terminology (including slang words and phrases) relating to sex. (Some children will be more literal than others, so the language used to explain will be important.) They can explore what is meant by pressure and how to recognize when someone is putting pressure on them. They also need to learn how to manage situations when they are being pressurized into having sex, and about not pressurizing others. They can also learn that it is possible to enjoy an intimate relationship without sex and that they can choose to delay having sex.

Sensory needs

Girls might consider how their own sensory needs and sensitivities might affect them and their relationships with others in either a positive or negative way (for example, they may like or dislike touch and smells). They can also consider how other people can be supportive of sensory sensitivities and sensory needs when in a relationship.

Consent, and withdrawal of consent

Knowing what is meant by sexual consent and understanding when consent can be withdrawn in all contexts is vital. This must be made clear because unless children are told outright they will not know and may be at risk. Be clear and explicit and encourage girls to ask any questions, even anonymously, if they need help to understand. They should be aware that people can give or not give consent. They should know that when consent is given, it can be withdrawn later. They should be able to recognize when consent is given or refused by others. They should know that they do not have to allow someone to touch them and that they do not have to touch others or take part in any sexual activity if they do not want to. They must know that they do not have to take part in any form of sexual activity just because someone (including someone older or 'in authority') has told them to, even if that person is familiar to them.

Pregnancy

It is important for girls to know the facts about pregnancy and learn about pregnancy myths, about how lifestyle choices can affect fertility, about different types of contraception, about reproductive health, about miscarriage, about feelings and emotions relating to pregnancy, and about why the uncertainty of getting pregnant and remaining pregnant can cause some autistic people to experience increased stress or anxiety. They should know that there are options in relation to pregnancy (young people should be provided with accurate and impartial information relating to their options once pregnant, including who to speak to and organizations who can support them if they need help). Girls should be aware that autistic people may need greater preparation for what to expect before, during and after pregnancy and know what might be beneficial to them.

For example:

- being provided with information
- being aware of how the body will change (change can be difficult for some autistic people to manage, so knowing what to expect in advance can help)
- having visuals to aid understanding
- health professionals having a greater understanding and awareness of autistic people (the pregnant person and their specific needs)
- being able to ask questions
- knowing what to expect at appointments

- having trusting relationships with healthcare staff
- having consistency of care (seeing the same professionals rather than numerous people, which can cause stress)
- healthcare staff being aware of how to support them
- being able to make their own choices.

Girls should know who they can talk to regarding sexual and reproductive health, including how to access support. They may learn about sexual and reproductive health through reading and other material. They should be aware that the birth experience (pregnancy and childbirth) can be different for an autistic person and understand how and why this might be (sensory sensitivity, experience of and expressing pain, communication differences). Girls should learn about sexually transmitted infections (STIs): how common they are; how to reduce the risk through safer sex; the impact of STIs; how to treat them.

Families

In the UK the Department for Education provide guidance for what young people should be taught in relation to friendships, and relationships, and family life. Children and young people should be aware that there are different types of families: other families may be different to their own and this should be respected. Their own choices about how to live should also respected. There are also different types of stable relationships that show that people are committed. Girls might learn how a stable relationship can be beneficial to children growing up and that families can provide children with stability, love and security when they are growing up.

Girls can learn about what marriage is: it is a formal and legalized commitment between two people; married people have rights; marriage should be entered into freely by a couple. They might learn what commitment means: people who are committed to each other may live together or may live apart. They can learn what caring about someone means and how this may be demonstrated (for example, how people might behave). They should be aware of the role of a parent or parents (for example, to provide love and security for their children) and be able to explore the characteristics of a healthy family life.

They should consider how their own sensory needs and sensitivities might affect them and their relationships with others (for example, they may be overloaded by noise and need solitude at times). They should learn to recognize when aspects of family life may be making them unhappy or unsafe and learn how and where to seek advice.

Disclosure of abuse

When having discussions around the topic of safety with autistic girls, it is possible that some may disclose abuse that may have taken place in the past or may currently be taking place. If this occurs, please ensure that they young person is listened to, without interruption, and that what is disclosed is written down accurately as soon as possible after it has been discussed. It is important that the young person knows that any disclosure of abuse cannot be kept a secret and that it is necessary to let certain people know. Explain why – to protect them and others from harm, and to help them receive support. Disclosures of abuse should only be discussed with those who need to know. Girls should not be asked leading questions as it is important that what they tell you comes from them only, in **their** own words. Please be aware that not all autistic children will use words to disclose abuse. Ensure that girls have a way to communicate that works for them, whether it is by visuals or other means.

Girls should learn about what is meant by 'disclosure', what happens if a disclosure of abuse is made and why that action is taken (to protect a child from harm, to protect others from harm, to ensure they receive support from appropriate services). They should learn what is meant by appropriate and inappropriate physical contact and how to judge this (relating this to different scenarios and different people) and know how to ask for advice from others if they feel unsafe or uncomfortable about being with an adult or young person.

They should learn how to report concerns about other people. (Please be aware that some autistic girls may find it difficult to communicate in words, especially when upset. Some may lose the ability to speak if overloaded or overwhelmed. Ensure that girls learn other methods to communicate such as; writing, drawing or using visual symbols to alert others. Let them know who they can 'communicate' with. Knowing that they have a consistent person (or people) to speak to can also be helpful. Ensure that autistic girls know that if they have not been heard, then they should try to seek help again. This is particularly important because autistic children and adults often report that they have not been listened to.)

Autistic girls can benefit from learning vocabulary relating to relationships and being clear about the meaning of specific words (some people may use visuals to help them understand more complex words). They should learn how to communicate appropriately with adults whom they may not know (in daily living and online). They may develop a greater awareness of what is meant by sexual harassment, sexual violence, abuse, coercive control and rape. They may learn about different types of organizations who they can contact. (Please be aware that some autistic people may have difficulty in speaking on the phone, so other ways of being able to contact organizations might be preferable.)

Key points

- Having supportive friends can help autistic girls to stay safe.
- Being able to communicate with parents and professionals who are considerate and approachable can have a positive influence on the safety of autistic girls.
- Autistic girls need to know that their bodies belong to them.
- Parents and professionals should encourage autistic girls to question and express their opinions, especially when they do not want to do something. Being overly compliant can sometimes put them at risk. Girls need to understand their own boundaries, when these are crossed, and how to assert themselves.
- Autistic girls my find it difficult to read other people's intentions. They can be trusting of others so need to learn how to judge people, not just by what they say but how they treat others.
- Schools should be aware of the issues that autistic girls face in terms of safety and this should inform policy, and practice.
- The sex education curriculum should be adapted to the needs of autistic children and how they think, learn and experience the world differently from the non-autistic majority.

CHAPTER 4

Be Calm

This chapter explores why some autistic girls experience stress and anxiety, and what can be done to prevent or reduce this. Friendship issues, communication differences and how autistic girls understand and express feelings are discussed. The chapter explains why autistic girls can benefit from developing greater self-awareness, describes how other people's knowledge and beliefs about autistic girls, their expectations of them, and the way they communicate with them can either reduce or heighten anxiety and explores how other people can help autistic girls to 'be calm'. It describes how the environment can either elevate or alleviate feelings of worry and provides suggestions for adjusting it to suit the child. It also discusses how sensory needs, sensory sensitivities and sensory experiences can help autistic children to feel calm and happy. Further strategies to help autistic girls to feel calm are provided, relating to speech and language therapy, occupational therapy advice and specialist teaching approaches.

Be calm – context

As autistic girls grow up, they face numerous challenges: as they explore their own identities, they are expected to adjust themselves to meet other people's demands and expectations (academic and social) and must manage their own expectations of themselves; they also have to navigate social situations and the complexities of friendships and relationships, and cope with sensory sensitivities in a variety of environments. All this is happening whilst their brains and bodies are developing.

How autistic girls deal with these and other issues depends on how they feel about themselves, to what extent they understand themselves (their thoughts, feelings, actions, sensory and other needs), whether or not they know they are autistic (and how they feel about it), how able they are to express thoughts and feelings in words (or by other means), and what strategies and skills they have learnt to help them manage stress. How well they cope will also depend on how well they are understood by others, what support they receive and whether their needs are met.

Many girls will experience anxiety, whether this is diagnosed or not. With greater understanding of the causes of anxiety, girls can learn how to reduce it and how to understand their own needs better. Other people, too, can learn how to help girls so that they do not reach the point of overwhelm, overload or crisis.

Stress and anxiety in autistic girls

Many autistic girls enjoy school when they are understood and adaptations are made rather than the child being expected to adapt. However, for others, school can be a cause of stress. In the following poem, a parent asks professionals to recognize the differing needs of their autistic child who is expected to conform to fit in.

My child is not rude, or lazy in any way
My child is exhausted from just being here today
Exhausted from anxiety and overwhelm and so much more
Social demands and expectations, wish-
ing they could just run out the door
Reframe your thoughts about them be curious to why
Put yourself in their shoes, empathy isn't just for when they cry
Empathy works both ways, view life through an autism lens
Don't judge me as a parent or insist we comply with your ways

JODIE SMITTEN (2020)

Whereas some autistic girls experience anxiety some of the time, others are highly anxious on a regular basis. Being in an anxious state, for long periods, is likely to have a detrimental effect on both mental and physical health. According to Van Steensel, Bögels and Perrin (2011), 'autistic children and adolescents with autism spectrum disorders...

are at increased risk of anxiety and anxiety disorders.' Gaigg, Cornell and Bird's (2018) 'model of anxiety in Autism' (adapted from South and Rodgers 2017 and Maisel *et al.* 2016) provides many reasons for why this may be and explain that 'an "Intolerance of Uncertainty" is at the heart of anxiety disorders'. They add that the 'intolerance of uncertainty...causes high levels of anxiety, which autistic individuals may attempt to manage by engaging in repetitive behaviours (to make the world more predictable)'.

It could be presumed that autistic people are predisposed to anxiety just because they are autistic, but how autistic people are understood (or misunderstood) and treated in society can have an impact on their mental health. If someone has limited knowledge of autism, has stereotypical views, or presumes all autistic people are alike, that can have a detrimental effect and cause anxiety or distress to an autistic person. It is also one of the many reasons why some autistic people choose not to disclose – for fear of being misunderstood, misjudged, infantilized, having their capabilities underestimated, or being treated differently.

Some autistic girls hide their feeling and appear to be coping well on the outside. This is concerning because it means they are overlooked and do not gain the support they need. In many cases, girls are storing up feelings and sometimes it is only their family that witnesses the crying, the meltdowns, the exhaustion and, in some cases, the outbursts of physical aggression. This is not 'challenging behaviour' but an outpouring of pent-up anxiety, frustration and distress from being pushed too far and feeling overloaded. As a result, there can be discrepancies between schools and families about how they believe autistic girls are coping. As one parent of an autistic girl comments:

> At school she knows she can use her time-out card, but the feelings and frustration will still build and will overspill at home. We are helping her to deal with her feelings.

Identifying the signs of stress and anxiety

As some girls will mask and camouflage their anxiety, it can be difficult to recognize when a girl is not coping, so it is important for schools and families to work collaboratively. Some aspects of the school day can be mentally and physically draining for some autistic girls, but others will enjoy the routine and predictability that it can provide.

What are the signs that tell us that a girl is feeling increasingly anxious or beginning to feel overwhelmed? What are **her** signs, however subtle? Does her behaviour become more repetitive? Does she 'appear' to be controlling of other people? Does it 'appear' that she is not listening when asked questions? Does she seek something out or avoid something? Does she struggle to sleep, isolate herself or cry? Does she stim? Each girl is unique, so how she shows that she is anxious may be different to how a non-autistic child may show it. Whatever the signs may be, it's important to be able to recognize them so that anxiety can be dealt with and stress reduced

What can cause autistic girls to feel stressed or anxious?

The following are common factors that can lead to an autistic girl's anxiety, discomfort or distress (this list is not exhaustive):

- Having to manage social situations and/or having social anxiety.
- Communication differences (for example, other people not directly saying what they mean).
- Friendship and relationships issues (for example, not knowing how to resolve conflict, not knowing how to remove herself from difficult situations, not being sure if she has upset someone or not).
- Perfectionism (a girl's own expectations of herself and what she can achieve, wanting to do something in a certain way, comparing herself to her non-autistic peers).

- Other people's expectations (for example, expecting her to conform or be more 'non-autistic').
- Others not being flexible.
- Others not understanding her.
- Having a lack of context and not understanding something.
- Finding it hard to judge what someone else might be thinking or feeling.
- Having difficulty predicting what might happen.
- Being with unfamiliar people or in new, unfamiliar places.
- Feeling overloaded (too much information to take in, too many demands, being overstimulated).
- Sensory sensitivities and the environment (for example, too many noises at once, being sensitive to smells in the environment, coping with fluorescent lighting, which may cause pain).
- Being overly tired (sleep is very important).
- Having phobias.
- Being afraid of being judged for making perceived 'mistakes'. (Some girls will not attempt a task if they feel under pressure or are afraid of criticism or failure. Being misjudged and their needs or behaviour being misunderstood or misinterpreted can lead to stress and anxiety, though this is often not mentioned in research.)
- Injustice and being treated unfairly.
- Being excluded, isolated, mocked or bullied.
- Unpredictability and uncertainty in a variety of situations can make a child feel unsafe, so predictability and routine are needed.
- Being in pressurized situations (for example, examinations or being put in the 'limelight') can lead to overwhelm and overload, so these are best avoided if possible. A calm, organized environment is preferable.

- Situations that have not been resolved or do not have a definite ending.
- Having to cope with change and transition (including changes to routine, unexpected change, bodily change, increasing independence, changes in the family, moving home, being expected to stop a task without prior warning).
- Issues relating to identity, feeling different, feeling confused.

Autistic girls and friendships

Friendships can improve well-being, and many autistic girls and women enjoy successful friendships. Many autistic girls are socially motivated, like their non-autistic peers. Cook, Ogden and Winstone (2018) mention that 'girls with autism may have perceptions of friendships that are different to those of their neurotypical peers'. Autistic girls may enjoy friendships but may prefer to socialize with friends on different, more manageable terms – for example, they may wish to see friends less frequently or for shorter periods of time, or they may want to communicate with friends online rather than by phone or face to face (this can be less intense, provides sufficient time to process language and respond, and does not involve having to figure out facial expression and body language, all of which can drain energy). This does not mean their friendships are any less meaningful. In addition, some autistic girls enjoy having one close friend or being part of a smaller group, rather than a larger crowd, as this can be overwhelming. Being in the minority, autistic girls are having to adapt themselves as they attempt to meet other people's expectations to be accepted. Masking their true selves (whether they are aware of doing it or not) can mean that some girls lose their own identity.

All autistic girls are different, so their attitudes towards friendships (including who they want to be friends with, if at all) will vary. This can relate to their identity, how they view themselves and their own preferences. Some autistic girls will want to be with others who are autistic (or neurodivergent); others want to have non-autistic friends; others do not have a preference.

Friendships and camouflaging

As autistic girls grow up and become more self-aware, the differences between them and their non-autistic peers can become more apparent. Friendships become increasingly complex and some autistic girls will find initiating friendships and maintaining them can become more challenging. Some girls find this difficult to cope with, so helping them to recognize their own strengths and personal qualities can help to build their self-esteem. Being autistic, they have different needs (as well as different strengths). If they are not aware of these differences, autistic girls can unfairly compare themselves to their non-autistic peers, and some put pressure on themselves to be like others, adapting themselves, rather than feeling free to be themselves. Although autistic children can benefit from gaining greater self-awareness and self-acceptance, they are more likely to be able to be themselves if they are better understood by peers and differences are accepted.

The 'Camouflaging Autistic Traits Questionnaire' (CAT-Q) developed by Hull *et al* (2018), separates 'camouflaging behaviours' into three categories:

1. **Compensation** – strategies used to compensate for social communication difficulties.
2. **Masking** – strategies used to present non-autistic or less autistic person to others.
3. **Assimilation** – strategies used to fit into uncomfortable situations.

Although this was devised as a self-report measure of camouflaging in adults, it may be helpful to autistic girls, their parents and professionals as it details specific types of camouflaging behaviours that also apply to younger autistic people.

Whether girls are aware that they are autistic or not, many girls will camouflage by moulding themselves to be more like their non-autistic peers. This may be because they want to be treated like others, rather than be rejected or excluded, and not because they are unhappy being themselves or because they are purposely trying to be deceptive. Autistic girls, including those who have social anxiety, can enjoy being with others and many gain benefits from having friends (for example social 'protection' and belonging). However, some will internalize their anxiety, submerging their own feelings, and will use compensatory strategies to blend in. Lawson (2017) explains the hidden difficulties many autistic girls and women experience, stating:

> copy behaviour in social settings that suggests they have an understanding and the true nature of the effort this takes is not seen. Therefore, when they appear not to understand or exhibit 'challenging behaviour', they are thought of as being naughty, difficult or attention seeking.

When autistic girls camouflage to mask social challenges, it can appear to others that they are coping when, inside, they may be struggling. Cook *et al.* (2018) suggest that camouflaging can lead to 'internalization of problems' leading to 'even greater stress and anxiety'.

Moyse and Porter (2015) recognize that 'autistic girls...appear to develop coping mechanisms that mask their problems, such as becoming observers or social chameleons'. In the absence of being explicitly taught to understand themselves, and other people, many autistic girls learn by observing and copying others in real life or by copying fictional characters in books. Mimicking other people is a strategy that some girls will use to make themselves less obvious. Some autistic women report to copying other people's accents, using learnt phrases, or even copying speech patterns. Some build up an image or persona from television or the media; others copy popular peers or characters in books (Bargiela, Steward and Mandy 2016).

Autistic girls can find it difficult to deal with conflict and are 'exposed to more relational bullying...than any other group'. They will then either 'assume they are entirely to blame and do whatever they can to resolve it' or 'will withdraw from the relationship', according to Sedgewick *et al.* (2019).

Cook *et al.* (2018) also highlight that almost half of the autistic girls involved in their research had been subjected to bullying. Some girls who experience difficulties in forming and maintaining friendships deal with social difficulties by avoiding others, a fact recognized by Moyse and Porter (2015): 'A major conflict for Scarlett was that she wanted to be included and yet one of her main coping strategies when she was unhappy or got stressed was to withdraw, thus excluding herself.'

Although being alone can make girls stand out, it can also be a means of self-preservation. Solitude can be beneficial as it provides time to recover from the overwhelm of social interaction and the fast-paced 'chit chat' of peers. It can also relieve some of the overload caused by the sensory environment. Being alone is also less stressful than dealing with conflict.

What impact adapting has on mental health is an important question. Hull *et al.* (2018) state:

> Other studies have demonstrated autistic females' greater use of camouflaging strategies during communication than males, whether through gesture (Rynkiewicz *et al.* 2016), or filling pauses in conversation (Parish-Morris *et al.* 2017), despite overall comparable social skills. These methods measure camouflaging by identifying discrepancies between different measures of social ability or autistic characteristics, such that individuals (especially females) appear less autistic in some settings yet still meet autism diagnostic criteria in others and raise the important question, 'What is the relationship between camouflaging and mental health outcomes?'

Autistic girls should be taught explicitly about friendships (and the differences that autistic and non-autistic people might have in terms of friendships) and should be able to explore their own preferences, boundaries and limitations. Equally non-autistic peers should learn that people who are neurodivergent may enjoy friendships on different terms and that this should be viewed as perfectly acceptable. Greater appreciation that autistic young people may do things differently will help children to maintain strong, successful friendships. An autistic teenage girl explains why some friendships can be difficult,

> I don't have any real-life friends. I never have. I'm extremely picky. Most of my friends just give up on me as I feel I cannot give them what they want in a friendship. I have online friends, and we play games, but I also like debating topics like politics and religion, and also the LGBTQA+ community.

Autistic girls can learn about the qualities of good friends and how true friends help you to feel good about yourself, how friends should treat each other, the different types of friends and, importantly, how to manage differences of opinion and conflict. Autistic girls should not have to adapt to appear more non-autistic but should feel that they can be themselves in the company of others. An autistic teenage girl shares some of the difficulties she encounters with friends when she feels she has to adapt,

> I struggle with everything at least once. Some [things] more than others. I really struggle with making friends. I can often misread what they are saying or what they want from me and I am often left confused by what is expected of me. I get anxious as I don't know what they are going to want to talk with me about. Eye contact is very difficult for me so I prefer online friends as I have an easy way out of a conversation or situation I don't feel comfortable with.

Being with people with whom they have a trusting relationship enables autistic girls to be themselves, without having to mask. Opportunities that enable them to develop friendships (for example, through clubs that relate to their specific interests, where they can take part alongside others, without pressure) can help girls to gain the benefits of being with others in a way that works for them. Since research by Hirvikoski *et al.* (2019) shows that some autistic women are at increased risk of suicide, and Pelton and Cassidy (2017) recognize a sense of belonging as being a protective factor against suicide, being part of a group, and a valued member of the school community, may be important for autistic girls who feel socially isolated. Connecting with other people can enhance well-being.

Those devising groups can help autistic girls to develop friendships in a way that suits girls and takes account of their differing needs (for example, language needs, sensory needs, social and emotional needs). Cook *et al.* (2018) suggest:

> As they move into adolescence, opportunities should be provided for them to share company through joint activities where they have similar interests. This might in turn enable them to feel more comfortable in social situations, and reduce the need for them to mask their autism in an effort to fit in.

The challenges that some autistic girls face in terms of friendships could be reframed as being due to the difficulties that non-autistic people display rather than due to 'deficits' and 'impairments' of autistic people. Crompton *et al.* (2020b) state:

> Non-autistic individuals have communicative difficulties when interacting with autistic individuals. Non-autistic people struggle to identify autistic mental states (Edey *et al.* 2016), identify autistic facial expressions (Sheppard *et al.* 2016), overestimate autistic egocentricity

> (Heasman and Gillespie 2018), and are less willing to socially interact with autistic people (Sasson *et al.* 2017).

Crompton *et al.* (2020b) call this a 'bi-directional disconnect in communication and understanding between autistic and non-autistic people' that is known as the 'double empathy problem' (Milton 2012; Milton, Heasman and Sheppard 2018) . Crompton *et al.* (2020a) explain that 'recent research has found that autistic people prefer interacting with other autistic people, and experience close social affiliation with them (see also Morrison *et al.* 2019). Taking this into consideration, autistic girls can benefit from being with others who are like them. Cook, Ogden and Winstone (2018) reiterate this:

> Where successful friendships had been formed, they were often with other girls with special needs, or who were different in some way. While this is expected for those students in special school settings, this tendency was also found in girls in mainstream settings who tended to gravitate towards other girls with autism without realizing it.

An autistic woman provides the following advice for autistic girls:

> Whoever autistic girls choose to be friends with, a mutual appreciation and understanding between autistic and non-autistic children would result in less need for autistic children to mask and camouflage. If you are looking to make new friends, it's crucial to find the right ones. When you meet new people, see how they treat others and ask yourself: 'Is this person nice and kind to other people?' I know it can be tempting to try and become friends with people who seem popular, but if they don't treat others well, it's probably not a good idea to become friends with that person. Also, when looking for friends, it's important to find ones who share similar interests! I love playing 'The Sims' (a computer

> game) with my closest friends. For my friendships that have lasted a long-time, I have always had a lot in common with them.

Autistic girls enjoy successful friendships when with people who understand and accept them as they are. Many are loyal and honest and will often be willing to stand up for friends against injustice even when they find confrontation difficult. Many autistic girls are extremely kind and considerate and are willing to support others, such as younger members of the school community. I have worked with many autistic girls who have been a joy to be around and have brightened the classroom with their smiling faces and sunny outlook on life.

Promoting well-being

Fewer difficulties will occur if we focus on how we speak, what we do and what we can change in the environment or provide, as opposed to making the child conform and adapt, which leads to poor mental health. Being aware of what causes an autistic girl to feel upset, stressed or anxious (and discussing what her signs might be) will help some girls to recognize these herself, independently, and can help her to become more aware of what to do when stressed. If she can learn to understand her own needs, she will be more likely to be able to address problems and avoid feeling overwhelmed. It can be useful for parents and professionals to identify the causes of stress, anxiety and outbursts, too, and their role in helping girls to cope. As we have seen, writing these down can be beneficial in preventing problems.

Providing routine and predictability

Autistic girls can feel safe when life is more predictable. Too much uncertainty can lead to anxiety and stress. The level of routine that each girl needs will vary greatly from person to person. Some will need high levels of routine and structure throughout the day whereas others will feel more comfortable having a routine but will be able to be able to cope with some change.

Many girls can benefit from using visual and/or written schedules or itineraries as these make life more predictable and provide routine and structure. Visual and written schedules can be used to show the order of activities during a day or week and can be used to sequence an activity. Some children benefit from a two-step sequence – 'now' and 'next' – as too much information can be overwhelming. Others need a greater amount of information and detail and need to be informed of all events throughout the day.

Using visuals can also increase independence and self-esteem and can be helpful to many autistic people regardless of age or ability (stage not age), but this depends on the individual. The type of visuals used will depend on each girl's needs and preferences. Some girls will need photographs of specific items whereas others can use more generic images or symbols. Visuals can be differentiated and can be used discreetly so that they are not obvious to peers (some girls won't want to be seen as different to their peers). Girls who do not want to use visual schedules might prefer written or colour-coded timetables that show what is going to happen during the week. Calendars (or their own diaries) can help girls keep track of what is going to happen, when and for how long. This helps some girls to feel informed and provides routine during less structured times such as the school holidays.

For those girls who do not require a visual schedule or timetable at school, structure can still be provided by making instructions clear and concise during lessons and by showing examples of exactly what is expected of her. Instructions (written and/or visual) can be provided for everyone so that the autistic girl in the class does not feel singled out. If girls are expected to work with others, then provide the 'rules' and give them time to prepare their contribution in advance. Girls who prefer to work alone can be given structured guidelines to be independent. Many autistic girls enjoy self-study as being independent gives them control whilst building confidence in their own abilities.

Life is unpredictable, so although it is not possible to bring order to every area of life or control what other people say and do, it is appreciated if other people can respect an autistic girl's need for structure and routine.

> My daughter cannot cope with changes to her strict routine. If her grandma arrives at the house one evening in the week, she becomes very stressed to the point of meltdown. Someone arriving at the house ad hoc always causes her stress.

Asking others to arrange times to visit in advance can minimize stress caused by unpredictability. Preparing the child by letting them know what time the visit will take place and for how long will provide the structure they need. If a child is anxious about communicating socially with visitors, including family members –because conversation can be unpredictable – and this adds to their anxiety, then teaching them a few conversation starters or chatting about topics of conversation in advance can relieve some stress. In addition, teaching the child phrases to politely excuse herself, will allow her to opt out of social situations when necessary. Some autistic girls will need time to 'recover' after social interaction as being with others drains energy. Providing time out or time to relax, recuperate and recharge will ease anxiety and improve well-being. It is not that some autistic girls do not enjoy socializing – it can just be difficult and exhausting!

Avoiding overload

Sometimes, if too many plans have been made during a day (or week), this can gradually lead to overload. Busier days can be offset by quieter days, with fewer demands being made. Sometimes, rescheduling plans can help a girl to cope.

The school day can involve having to process vast amounts of language and instructions, coping with social times, meeting expectations of professionals and managing sensory sensitivities. All this can leave an autistic girl feeling exhausted. Sometimes being too busy or having to take in too much information can lead to the brain feeling overstimulated (as if the brain is still running when we want it to switch off) and this can cause sleep difficulties. It is important to allow time for the brain to process the day and for the body to recharge. What extra-curricular activities and events an autistic girl will be able to manage needs careful consideration, so building in 'down time' into your schedule can help.

Many autistic girls see school time and home time as very separate entities. Some will struggle when asked to complete homework tasks because they need their own time to recuperate, enabling them to cope with what the next day will bring. Some will push themselves past their limits because they want to be able to do the same as their peers but also because they are keen to please others. Each girl will have different limitations. Ensuring that girls have time to re-energize will help them to pace themselves. Autistic girls can be overloaded by people asking too many questions at once without enough time to think and process what has been said, so providing enough time to answer will really help. Too many people asking questions or talking at the same time can also be stressful as it can be difficult to focus on two people at once. This is also true of someone speaking when there is background noise to contend with. It feels as though there is too much to cope with at once.

Avoiding exhaustion

Things that might seem simple or straightforward to others can be exhausting for autistic girls. Using the example of being invited to a social event that will be draining (lots of social interaction, unfamiliar people, unpredictable conversations, the sensory environment, different noises at once), there are choices and the pros and cons must be weighed up: there's the choice of not going (conserving energy, but possibly causing offence to the host); the choice of going but leaving early (using up some energy and hoping the host won't mind); the choice of going (knowing it will use up immense energy and that afterwards solitude will be needed to recover).

Adults can sometimes make decisions based on experience and knowing themselves. However, many younger autistic girls are still learning to understand what their limitations are, so knowing how to achieve balance and how to pace themselves will be a valuable skill enabling them to achieve their goals without compromising their health in the process. It will be equally important in later life when greater resilience may be needed for coping with the additional responsibilities of being an adult. Autistic people use up energy very quickly (processing situations and language, for example) and need to gain that back.

Using the Energy Accounting Activity (developed by autistic author and speaker Maja Toudal and clinical psychologist Dr Tony Atwood; see McKay 2020), or other similar strategies, can help autistic children achieve balance and prevent overload or meltdown. Energy accounting involves writing down in two separate columns what drains energy and what restores it, under two headings:

'Withdrawals': Things that drain energy (for example, being in crowds, unexpected change, noise, assemblies, break times, certain lessons, sensory sensitivities).

'Deposits': Things that restore energy (for example, being alone, reading, being with a pet or listening to music).

Each of the items on the list are scored out of 100, based on how draining or restoring it is for the individual. For example, 10 is slightly draining or slightly restoring, 80 is highly draining or highly restoring. (Some girls might like to draw each item too.) Each child will have her own individual list. Some girls will need more help than others to think of what might be included on their list. For girls who might struggle to think of ideas and who may find imagining something difficult, visuals could be provided to choose from, and more items can be added as a child experiences them. When one or more withdrawals has been made and energy used up, this should be replenished by the deposits. Being able to offset experiences that are challenging with those that are pleasurable can lead to improved well-being. Energy accounting is a helpful way to avoid distress and exhaustion.

Developing self-awareness and being able to judge beforehand what type of situations might cause overload or drain energy will be a useful skill for autistic girls in later life. Knowing how to pace themselves and take care of themselves will enable them to manage the demands of study and/or working life, though this is not always easy.

Providing time for intense interests

For some girls, being able to pursue an interest in extreme depth or for long periods of time, referred to in this book as an 'intense interest', can replenish energy. (Some people may use the term 'special interest' or 'hobby'.) Intense interests can sometimes seem unusual to other people, but having differences is what makes each girl an individual. Many autistic girls are also interested in similar things to their peers, but will pursue their interests in greater detail and are happy to devote vast amounts of time to a topic or subject of choice. Wood (2019) explores how intense interests can be viewed as obsessions or, in more positive terms, as an advantageous thinking style. Being able to pursue their own interests could provide autistic pupils with satisfying learning experiences as well as opportunities for them to interact successfully with others

Having a specific interest feels safe and predictable (unlike life in general) but the extent to which girls will be able to step out of their comfort zones to develop new interests will vary as change can cause stress. Repetition feels comfortable. Although focusing on one specific subject of interest can be viewed as repetitive behaviour, often one interest can develop into another and can broaden experiences. Intense interests can become strengths or in-depth knowledge or skills that can build confidence and self-esteem. Some autistic girls will also take great pleasure in talking to others about their interests.

> My child enjoys walking in the woods or on the beach. She loves going to big cities and people-watching in places with fashionable or quirky people. She loves going to restaurants and having something from the adult menu. She likes being in her room on her own and she enjoys playing computer games with her friends and flitting through social media. She loves make-up and fashion. She adores watching Japanese animations on Netflix. At the moment this is her passion and she loves to tell me the full plot of each animation!

Interests can also be a form of escapism, a distraction, even self-preservation, allowing girls to shut off from an overstimulating world. Autistic girls and women enjoy reading for many reasons.

> Reading brings me a creative and expressive escapism [from] the stresses of everyday life and the world around me. It gave me the voice I struggled to have at a young age, and the more books I read the amount of vocabulary grew until I became one of the top readers in my class.

Some highly creative girls enjoy writing their own stories or poetry and some have a strong interest in drawing and can lose themselves in it for hours. Whatever their passion, autistic girls should be given opportunities to indulge in whatever field they are interested in, without being stereotyped or judged.

A further benefit gained from having intense interests is provided by Kourti and MacLeod (2019), who recognize that 'autistic individuals have been described as being monotropic in their pursuance of personal interests, which, in turn, can become a very important part of their identity', referring to the work of Murray, Lesser and Lawson (2005) and Lawson (2010). Whether at home or at school, being expected to 'change channels' too quickly can cause distress, so children need to be made aware in advance when they are going to have time to enjoy their hobbies and for how long. They will also need preparation when an activity is coming to an end. Some girls may be engrossed in what they are doing and may not hear you or will be unaware of what is happening around them. They are not purposely ignoring anyone – they are just hyper-focused on what they are doing.

Pursuing intense interests allows autistic girls to be themselves, something denied to them too often as they camouflage themselves (and inhibit their 'natural ways of being') to fit into a non-autistic world. If nurtured, interests can lead to meaningful opportunities or even careers in later life. Dr Sarah Bargiela, a clinical psychologist and design researcher who specialized in the study of autism in women for her doctoral research, says: 'Some of the autistic women I interviewed are incredibly successful in their professional life because of their dedication to a special interest they've pursued, be it in academia, the arts or athletics' (cited in Hill 2019). Whether or not autistic girls decide to develop their intense interests into a career, their intense interests are still of immense value in relation to achieving better mental health.

Helping with organizational skills

Autistic girls can feel increased pressure due to uncertainty, so advance planning can alleviate some anxiety.

> A lot of my daughter's issues are caused by school. When it is the holidays, we have a great decrease in meltdowns and stress. It's bliss! On a school night my daughter struggles to sleep because she is anxious about what the next day will bring. Is the work completed? Is the bag packed? What will others say if she wears her hair down? Where will she go at lunch time?

Because of the way they think, some girls will find organizing themselves difficult, so helping them to forward plan will provide some order, enabling them to feel more in control. Starting tasks, sequencing, ordering, carrying out tasks and problem solving may be challenging (especially for children who also experience difficulties with memory), so providing support in this area can ease pressure. In contrast, some autistic girls are highly organized and have a love of order as it gives them safety and stability. Those who find it difficult to organize themselves can continue to struggle throughout their lives (and sometimes other people find it difficult to comprehend why, especially if they have been reminded several times) but it's not that the child isn't listening, it's just that her brain thinks in a particular way that's perfectly natural to her. So understanding this and developing support strategies such as using visual task lists or tick lists can enable some girls to manage. Sometimes, autistic girls and women can be very able in certain areas but can find simple things extremely difficult.

Reducing pressure

Some autistic girls can feel pressure when communicating (one to one, in pairs or in groups) and do not want to feel they are the centre of attention. This may be one of the reasons why some girls find it difficult to access therapies or services. Taking the focus away from the can help to minimize anxiety and help girls to engage.

In schools, allowing girls to work alone can be a good option, whilst providing the choice to join a small group when ready. In Chapter 2, Be Unique, Dr.Craig Goodall provides advice about supporting autistic girls in schools. Some girls like to make their own decisions about whether they want to be involved in an activity (and at what point) as it can take time for them to become accustomed to other people and the environment they are in. Some girls prefer to be observers first before choosing to involve themselves. Some girls find it difficult to work in groups due to the increased pressure of social interaction, especially when tasks are not specific or when open-ended questions are asked. Being specific and concise with language, providing structure, rules and guidelines can be helpful. Providing a visual and written schedule of what work/activities are going to happen will help girls to feel calm when working alone or with others.

When working one to one with an autistic girl, communicating in a way that suits her (not necessarily with words but perhaps by using visuals or by doing something physical) can reduce pressure. Providing girls with a resource to focus on (something to look at or read) or a task to do also means that she is not expected to give eye contact. Sitting side by side rather than opposite each other (which can feel intimidating) works well as no one is forced to provide eye contact. Walking (or moving around) whilst talking can minimize anxiety. Letting a girl know that she has the option to take time out when needed – and agreeing a cue if necessary, such as a visual card she can show you when she needs a break – can also reduce stress as communication breaks are sometimes necessary.

Structure is important to autistic girls as it provides safety. Without sufficient structure (and during times of change) autistic girls will often attempt to create order for themselves. This can be interpreted as a girl being domineering, rigid or overly controlling, but this occurs because life feels unpredictable and out of control. It can also happen when a girl is feeling pressurized, unable to cope with demands or is feeling overloaded by people or the environment. 'Repetitive behaviours' (doing something familiar, many times, such as singing, moving, watching the same thing) when under stress can provide predictability, helping girls to feel in control and safe, and having a calming effect.

When under pressure, some autistic girls can be perfectionists, wanting to make sure that something is done properly to an impossibly high standard. They may take considerably longer than they would normally, or than their peers, to complete an activity or task. To help to take the pressure off, provide time out or remove time constraints. Larger tasks that feel overwhelming and unachievable can be broken down into more manageable chunks. Perfectionism can be positive and means that a child will do something to the best of her ability, but it can also be frustrating for the child, especially if she puts pressure on herself. Health and well-being are more important than making something 'perfect', so it's important for an autistic girls to know that balance is needed in life. By encouraging and complimenting her on what she has achieved, you will help her to grow in confidence and learn to be kinder to herself. Sometimes it can take until adulthood to understand this fully.

If autistic girls are to voice their thoughts and opinions honestly, they need to feel comfortable and secure with other people and know that they will not be judged negatively. Some autistic girls can be sensitive to perceived criticism and this can erode their self-confidence. Wording questions, and our responses, with care and consideration can help to build trust. Some girls will be reluctant to say what they think for fear of making 'mistakes', but they can be encouraged to participate in discussions (or activities) if they know there are 'no wrong answers' and that whatever response they provide is their own valid opinion and this is respected.

Making the unfamiliar more familiar

Autistic children can be apprehensive about going into an unfamiliar environment, so making the unfamiliar more familiar by looking at pictures first can make them feel at ease. Different environments can have an impact on the senses (due to lighting, smells and acoustics, for example). Some autistic girls will need time to familiarize themselves with the environment (for example, walking around the perimeter and touching the boundaries can help them to become more accustomed to the space) and need time to feel comfortable somewhere new.

The same applies to meeting new and unfamiliar people. Looking at photographs in advance can make them seem more familiar, which reduces anxiety. Knowing how long a visit or meeting will last can help an autistic girl to cope. Providing choices can help her to feel in control, although giving too many options can have the opposite effect and increase stress. If routine is going to be disrupted, it can be helpful to provide as much preparation for change as possible so that a child has time to familiarize herself with the new plans. Where this is not possible, calmly explaining why the changes have occurred can sometimes help.

Understanding feelings

Expressing feelings and emotions in different ways

Not all autistic girls are able to talk about feelings (or have the strategies to express negative or uncomfortable feelings), although it could easily be presumed that they do, especially if they are capable in other areas. How autistic girls express themselves is also discussed in the chapters, 'Be Expressive' and 'Be Healthy'.

Although we can teach autistic girls to understand how non-autistic people express their feelings, it is equally as important that non-autistic people also understand that autistic people may express feelings in a different way to them, and that this is no less valid. For example, some girls may show little facial expression but this does not have feelings.

If others (professionals included) are unaware of such differences, this may mean that some autistic girls and women may be unable to access support or services when needed. They may appear to be calm, but their outward appearance does not reflect their internal state. Levels of stress can sometimes be wrongly interpreted by others: 'I felt like I was having a breakdown inside but I didn't know how to make the inside feelings show to other people' (Camm-Crosbie *et al.* 2019).

Social situations can already be difficult for some girls to manage (for example, because of communication differences between autistic and non-autistic people, having to process language or social anxiety) and some girls may experience further issues in expressing their emotions. 'Females on the spectrum often experience Alexithymia. This means describing how they feel in social situations is hard,' explains Lawson (2017). Alexithymia (see Sifneos 1973) is a difficulty describing emotions in the self and others and is thought to affect approximately 50 percent of autistic people (Bethoz and Hill 2005). Gaigg, Crawford and Cottell (2018) also explain:

> Alexithymia has been linked to difficulties in accurately sensing the internal signals of arousal that often accompany emotional experiences, such as changes in heart rate or a rush of adrenalin (Gaigg, Cornell & Bird 2018; Garfinkel *et al.*, 2015). This can make internal sensations confusing and unpredictable, leading to anxiety in a similar way to how sensory processing difficulties do.

In contrast, some autistic girls are highly emotional, have extreme highs and lows, experience the world intensely, and show this outwardly. Sometimes there are outpourings of emotion in public, which other people might find inappropriate but which the girls find difficult to hold in. Some highly sensitive girls will seek out music, literature or drama full of emotion (hospital-based dramas, romances, disaster films), and I have known girls to write their own moving stories, emotive poetry or compose beautiful pieces of music. These girls are gifted **because** they are autistic, not in-spite of it.

Autistic girls should know that it is perfectly normal for people to experience a range of emotions, even over a short period of time, and that how we feel can depend on whether we are alone, with other people (whether they understand us and our needs and whether we understand them) and the situation we are in. The environment can affect feelings, especially for those who have sensory sensitivities. As all autistic girls are unique, there will be great variability in how they express feelings and how emotionally literate they are. Sometimes it can be difficult to communicate feelings in words, so finding other outlets can be useful.

Some girls talk about going through the motions of displaying emotion (for example, 'smiling because that's what you are supposed to do when you are happy/because that's what is expected'), whilst others can talk about their feelings at length using complex emotional vocabulary. If we can gauge what understanding an autistic girl has of her own feelings and to what extent she is able to interpret how other people think and feel – by asking her and observing how she manages different situations – then it will be possible to support her with what she finds challenging. When teaching autistic girls about feelings, some approaches will be successful, whereas others will be less effective. Whatever language or imagery is used, it must be that which suits the individual.

Dr Alex Sturrock, a highly specialist speech and language therapist, says:

> Many autistic girls feel they don't have the vocabulary to explain their emotions. Clearly this is a problem if they need to seek help from others. One strategy which some girls have reported is having the opportunity to write down their stories. They need quiet time and space to do this and maybe the opportunity to discuss what they have written with a trusted adult afterwards. When these things are in place it appears that autistic girls can be very good at reporting their difficulties. This is important to note, as it means we can

> include autistic girls in discussions about setting their own targets. (Personal communication)

Autistic girls will express their emotions in their own way. Some girls might show happiness in an unconventional way, so 'happy' might look different for each individual. Some girls show happiness by being still and quiet whereas others are more vocal. Knowing and understanding the individual is key. Helping autistic girls to develop vocabulary around emotions can help them to communicate, but visual resources can help too. Each girl can develop her own system of expressing how she feels (for example, by using images she has selected herself).

Learning about feelings can help girls understand themselves, and other people, which can make life less confusing. It can help them to understand their own feelings, thoughts, behaviours and actions, and to express themselves in safe ways. However, autistic girls also need other people to understand them too.

Understanding feelings

Gauge each girl's level of understanding of her own feelings and to what extent she can understand other people might feel. You can help her understand feelings by doing the following:

- Build understanding through real-life situations.
- Increase vocabulary relating to feelings through speech and language work.
- Explore how to show intensity of feeling (using visuals or numbers, levels, scales and charts but also by developing vocabulary: 'I am in agony/extreme pain' as opposed to 'it hurts') in a 'language' that works for her (not necessarily in words).
- Use visuals to aid understanding of people and situations (her own thoughts and other people's, what was said, actions).

- Teach strategies that help to calm and soothe the mind and body and encourage girls to be open about which strategies work best for them as well as those that don't.
- Use visual supports to remind girls to use different strategies (for example, a visual reminding her to take time out, listen to music, ask for help).
- When knowledge has advanced, help the child to link the following together:
    * Problem/causes of stress (What is causing anxiety/stress?)
    * Thoughts (What am I thinking?)
    * Feelings (How do I feel?)
    * The body (How do those feelings affect my body? For example, tense muscles, faster heart rate.)
    * Actions (What do I say and do when feeling like that? For example, fight, flight, freeze mode.)
    * Solutions (What can I do to help myself, and when? What strategies can I use? Do I need any help from others and if so, what can they do?)
- Help the child to understand what she can and cannot control. She cannot control what other people might say or do but she can have some control over how she feels and how she reacts.
- Help an autistic girl to understand her own sensory needs and sensitivities and what strategies she might use to manage them. You can help her to recognize how different environments can affect how she feels and how her physical state can heighten sensory sensitivities (for example, being tired can make someone more sensitive to noise). Help her to understand that other people may need to make adjustments for her due to her sensory needs. you might model how to ask for these to request help when needed. Further advice about the type of adjustments that might be needed may be provided by an occupational therapist.

- Identify the girl's strengths and encourage her to pursue interests and passions that will help her to experience positive feelings about herself and her abilities.

Practical resources for understanding feelings

When asked how they are feeling, some girls might only be able to express themselves by saying 'I'm okay' or 'I'm not okay'. Others will not feel comfortable being questioned but will prefer to show you by using visual symbols (for example, thumbs up/thumbs down, or happy/sad faces, or the words written down) without pressure to speak. Some like to choose colours to represent feelings, using their own colour code for example, red = angry, blue = calm), keeping them on a keyring or in a pencil case. Others like to use more subtle ways of showing how they feel, such as reversible wristbands that show 'I'm okay' on one side and 'I'm not okay' on the other. When experiencing uncomfortable emotions, it can be more difficult to speak, so communicating in ways other than words can often work better. Each girl should be able to choose what the best option is for her.

Some girls say that some feelings are difficult to understand but they can grasp the idea of being 'comfortable' and 'uncomfortable'. Whatever language or imagery is used to describe feelings, it must be that which suits the autistic individual.

> I refuse to accept that feeling 'low' isn't an emotion. If it's the best word I can find to explain how I am feeling at a particular time, I will use it.

Feelings board

For girls with a greater understanding of feelings, but whose vocabulary is limited, a feelings board can be useful (see Figure 4.1). Symbols showing basic feelings are placed into categories by the child; 'comfortable' and 'uncomfortable' and those that are 'neither' or 'both' can go in the centre. At various intervals during the day, a girl can select an appropriate symbol from the board to show you how she is feeling at that moment, and she may also explain why in word (or use drawings, symbols or writing/typing). If she chooses an 'uncomfortable feeling', for example, you discuss why this is to help her to find a solution. Equally, if she feels over-excited, she might need to talk about this and what strategies she can use to help her to calm down. Using symbols and talking about feelings can be the difference between a young person having a good day or a bad day as minor difficulties can be rectified so that they do not escalate into bigger problems. More complex feelings can be added to the board as they are learnt (for example, over-excited, jealous, frustrated) and this will help to expand emotional vocabulary.

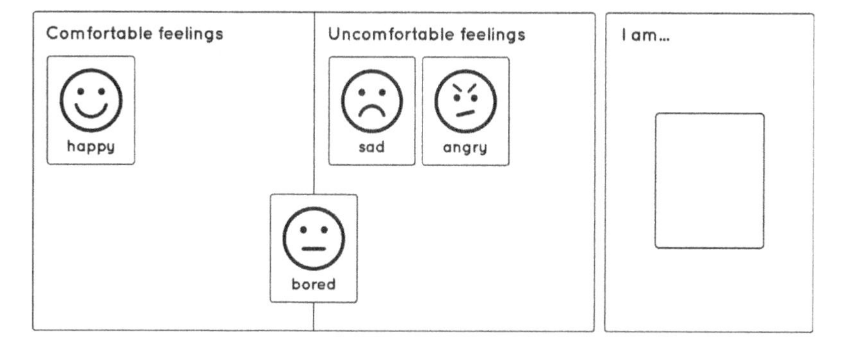

Figure 4.1: Feelings Board

Feelings scale

A visual scale or chart can be used for a variety of purposes. It can show the level of emotion someone is experiencing (for example, if talking about anxiety, a scale of 1–5 could be used, with 1 being a little anxious, 5 being highly anxious). It can also be used to show different feelings as they escalate from being in a relaxed/lethargic/under-stimulated state to 'okay/calm' through to being very 'unhappy/angry/overloaded' (see Figure 4.2). Some examples of strategies can also be provided. A visual scale or chart can help autistic girls to recognize how they feel and consider what action they can take (what tools and strategies to use and at what stage) to change thoughts and feelings so that they can calm themselves before becoming overloaded. As a scale can go up or down, it can show when feelings are escalating as well as de-escalating. A scale can also allow the child to alert other people to when she is becoming increasingly overloaded or anxious so that they can provide support if needed.

	How I feel	Strategies
5	 Overwhelmed	• Go to my safe space • Get soft blanket
4	 Agitated/ annoyed	• Speak to an adult • Use Comic Strip Conversations™
3	 Unhappy	• Take deep breaths
2	 Okay	• Use sensory toys to stay calm
1	 Lethargic, tired, understimulated	• Drink water • Go for a 5-minute walk

Figure 4.2: Feelings Scale
Adapted from Dunn Buron and Curtis (2012)

Dealing with worries

As some autistic girls can internalize anxiety, the following activity can help girls to release pent-up worries, getting stress 'out of the system' and onto paper instead. It is a good way of providing resolutions to difficulties. Parents/carers should choose a suitable time to do with this the child – perhaps during the day rather than too near to bedtime, as thinking about problems might affect sleep.

1. Divide a piece of paper (or wipe board) into two sections by drawing a line down the centre. On the left-hand side, write 'Problems/Worries'. On the right-hand side, write 'Possible Solutions'.

2. Next, draw circles of different sizes (small, medium and large) on the left-hand side and ask the girl to write in the circles (or write it for her as she speaks) any things that are troubling her and causing her to feel anxious, using up as many or as few as she needs. She should decide whether worries are 'small', 'medium' or 'large' and write each worry in a circle of the corresponding size. For example, in the large circles she can write down what the 'bigger worries' are, such as things that are causing extreme worry or issues that need dealing with immediately. In the medium sized circles, she can write down things that are worrying her but which are not as troubling or as immediate. In the small circles she can write down 'small worries', such as things that are only causing a little anxiety and don't need immediate attention. (Some girls might want to represent worries visually and then discuss them rather than writing them down. An adult can annotate the pictures to clarify what each problem is, to ensure that it is a correct representation of what the young person has said.) Some girls might only have one worry to discuss, others might have many more.

3. Tackling the big worries first (and dealing with problems only one at a time so as not to overload the child), write down the first worry and give it the number '1'. Then, discuss it and write down possible solutions. Number the rest of the worries '2', '3', '4', etc) and discuss these in turn.

Here is an example:

Problems / Worries Things that worry me in order of importance	Possible Solutions Please tick the right solutions or write in your own
	.... ☐
	.... ☐
	.... ☐
	.... ☐
	.... ☐
	.... ☐
	.... ☐
	.... ☐
	.... ☐

Figure 4.3: Problems and Solutions Chart (blank)

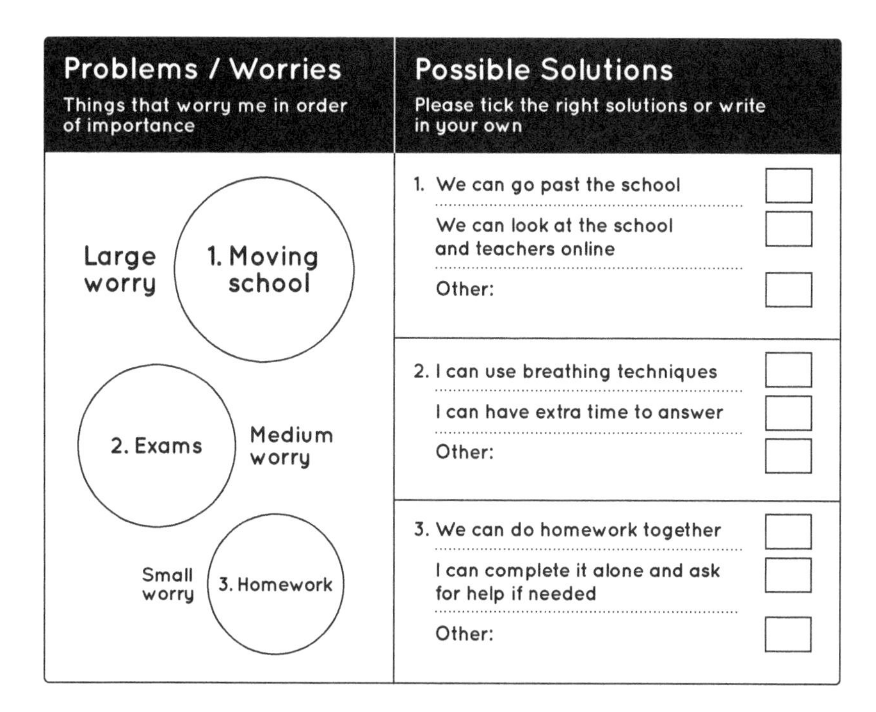

Figure 4.4: Problems and Solutions Chart (completed)

Completing this together encourages a girl to problem solve for herself – she has control over decisions, whilst being supported. If a girl finds it difficult to think of possible solutions, the adult can provide them, but the girl can take ownership by choosing those solutions she feels are manageable. She can make choices by using a tick list that the adult provides on the right-hand side. Solutions should be practical, 'do-able' and specific, stating what can be said or done, and when, so that the child can feel calm knowing that worries have been, or can be, resolved. Some worries can be resolved easily and immediately; others will take time to fully resolve. Although there may be some situations that are beyond the control of an autistic girl and the adult supporting or working with her (for example, worries relating to parents who are going through divorce, illness or bereavement), it is possible to focus on proactive steps that can be taken to help the child feel less anxious and more in control (i.e. compiling a list of 'solutions' that relate to how she can manage change, self-regulate and communicate her thoughts and emotions). It's important to be open with autistic girls about what you **can't do** (things you cannot control) as well as what you **can do** (things you can control) so that trust is built up. Autistic girls can learn that although they can't control other people and situations, they do have control over themselves.

Working through this activity together, one worry at a time, can help an autistic girl feel supported, knowing she has a trusted adult to rely on, if necessary. Once a worry has been resolved, the girl can cross out each circle and each corresponding statement so that there is a definite end to the problem. She should then plan to address any other worries with a list of achievable solutions. For girls who would be overwhelmed by tackling all their anxieties at once, other less immediate worries can be dealt with at a specific time on another day, but they can be physically put away for now. This activity could be followed by a calming activity such as listening to music or reading, depending on the individual girl's preference.

Other similar activities involve writing down worries on separate pieces of paper, working through them together to resolve them, then crumpling them up and physically throwing them away. This is both visual and physical so it can help autistic girls feel they are offloading worry. Another option that works for some autistic girls (particularly younger girls) is for them to write down anxieties and place them inside a worry box to be dealt with at a specific time.

Feelings wheel

Some girls can become more self-aware by considering where specific difficulties stem from (not all children will know this) and how 'problems' affect thoughts and feelings. They can then understand how these feelings affect the body physically and directly affect actions (i.e. what they might do or say, such as run away from a situation or shout out). Girls can then connect these thoughts to solutions, considering how the situation can be put right in a safe and appropriate way. Girls can use this tool (see Figure 4.5) to help them to reflect. This will enable some autistic girls to help themselves manage difficult situations in the future by linking thoughts to feelings to actions.

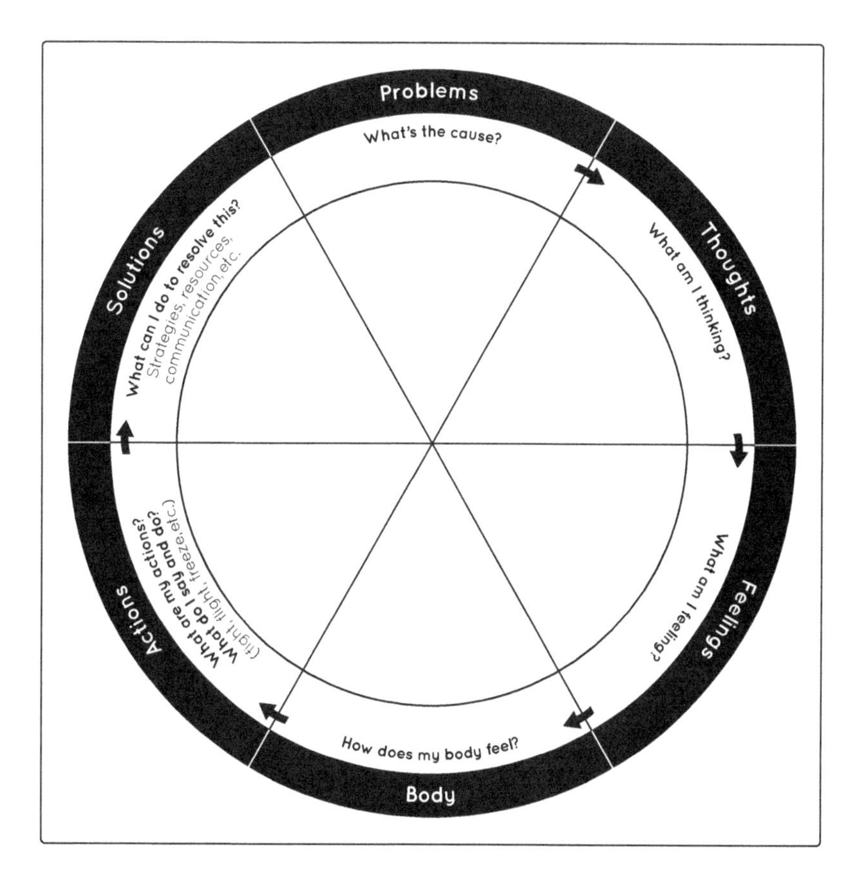

Figure 4.5: Problems and Solutions Wheel

Sensory needs, sensory sensitivities, and sensory joys

Sensory needs, sensory sensitivities and sensory joys can affect an autistic girl's quality of life. Interestingly, in his study 'Autistic disturbances of affective contact', Kanner (1943) refers to three autistic girls he observed, including 'Elaine C.':

> [She was] 'frightened' by noises and anything that moved toward her. She was so afraid of the vacuum cleaner that she would not even go near the closet where it was kept, and when it was used, ran out into the garage, covering her ears with her hands... Any noise disturbed her.

Kanner described another girl, 'Barbara', as very timid girl who was frightened of several things including the wind. He observed Barbara, whose father was a 'prominent psychiatrist' and whose mother was 'a well-educated kindly woman'. It was Barbara's mother who recognized that 'appendages fascinate her, like a smoke stake or a pendulum'. Interestingly, Kanner also remarked on Barbara's 'phenomenal ability to spell' and 'read'. He said that she '[is] a good writer' but 'still has difficulty with verbal expression. Written language has helped the verbal.' Kanner also mentions the 'neat and tidy girl' of 11 years old, known as 'Virginia', with an IQ of 94, who is 'self-sufficient and independent' and 'hums to herself'. Each of the girls that Kanner observed display what could be considered to be sensory sensitivities (being over-sensitive) and sensory-seeking behaviours.

Many autistic children have sensory processing differences and can have hyper- or hypo-sensitivity. As autistic girls and women are generally diagnosed later in life compared to boys (Begeer *et al.* 2013; Giarelli *et al.* 2010; Shattuck *et al.* 2009), it is possible that many of them have little understanding of their own sensory needs, and their sensory sensitivities and sensory-seeking behaviours may have been misunderstood by others, possibly being seen as 'behavioural issues' such as avoidance or intolerance. (This may also explain absenteeism when environments have not been adjusted.) They may have spent a considerable number of years without the understanding and support that might have reduced any difficulties they may have experienced.

However, having a diagnosis does not automatically mean that sensory needs will be met. For young girls of school age, this depends on the knowledge and skills (and consideration) of other people. In schools it can also depend on whether staff and resources are available. Moreover, not having a diagnosis does not mean that sensory needs will not be understood and met. There are many parents and professionals making the necessary adjustments and accommodations for autistic girls who don't yet have a diagnosis.

Though teachers are not generally trained to deliver occupational therapy programmes, some teachers who specialize in working with children who have special educational needs and disabilities, and/or autism, have sufficient knowledge to implement and monitor simple strategies to help autistic girls to regulate themselves (i.e. to be more alert or to help them feel calm).

Autistic girls can be involved in discussions about their own sensory experiences and, if able, can share what experiences cause them either discomfort or enjoyment. They may also be able to offer opinions about strategies that might help them. Parents and carers should be involved in discussions about the sensory needs of their child so that there is consistency across settings.

Sensory processing

Sensory processing is the process of taking in information from our environment, making sense of that information and using it to act or respond in an appropriate manner. For autistic girls who have sensory processing difficulties, these can inhibit the ability to correctly organize and interpret stimuli so the girls' responses are likely to be 'inappropriate' and may interfere with learning.

When the brain takes in too much information (is over-responsive) or too little sensory information (is under-responsive) it is more difficult for a person to react in a meaningful way:

Over-responsive: The central nervous system of the over-responsive child registers sensations too intensely. An autistic girl may feel overwhelmed and overstimulated by sensations; this may result in the child being distractible and losing focus; it may also result in the child actively avoiding sensory input. She may have difficulty blocking out incoming information and being distractible or be 'sensory avoiding,' actively engaged in reducing the frequency and intensity of sensory stimulation received. She may be resistant to change and may develop rigid rituals.

Under-responsive: The central nervous system of the under-responsive child registers sensations less intensely; the child does not receive enough sensory input from everyday events; this results in the child needing increased amounts of stimulation to achieve typical alertness levels.

Information about our own body and the world around us is gathered from seven senses: touch (tactile), movement (vestibular), body position (proprioception), sight (vision), sound (auditory), smell (olfactory), taste (gustatory). Everyone can have some sensory processing difficulties as no one is well regulated all of the time. For some autistic people, sensory processing can have a significant impact on their everyday life. For example, some people can be overly responsive to touch, sight or sounds; some may be under-responsive to movement, sight or touch; others may experience difficulties in organizing and carrying out everyday activities. The diagnostic criteria for autism include being over- or under-sensitive to, or having an unusual fascination for, sensory aspects of the environment. (This might include being averse to smells or textures, finding lights painful, being frightened by noises, or seeking them out). The exact diagnostic criteria for autism can be found in the Diagnostic and statistical manual of mental disorders (5th edition) and is known as the DSM-5.

For an autistic girl who may have sensory sensitivities and who may be over-sensitive (hyper-sensitive) or under-sensitive (hypo-sensitive) to different stimuli (and where those issues are having a significant impact on her life), an occupational therapist may provide a sensory assessment (a process that includes observing and gathering information relating to each of the senses to gain an understanding of how each individual experiences the world) before planning how to support the child with any difficulties.

A sensory profile

Although some autistic children will receive an individual assessment from an occupational therapist, others will not. This depends on how significantly sensory needs affect a child's life, and in some cases may depend on the budgets and resources of education or healthcare providers. Private assessments can also be carried out. Sometimes, occupational therapists may invite parents, as a group, to attend sensory workshops to equip them with the skills and knowledge to reduce the effects that sensory processing difficulties can have on their children's daily lives.

A sensory profile or checklist would include questions relating to each sense. (Yes or no answers and further information would be required to establish what impact sensory processing difficulties have on an individual's everyday life). A girl's medical and developmental history, whether she has an autism diagnosis, and any other co-occurring conditions would be considered.

A sensory profile may include questions relating to:

Tactile (touch) sense: Whether the child is sensitive to touch or whether they seek it out. Some autistic children will dislike getting messy or may dislike bathing and grooming because they may dislike the feel of a hairbrush, cloth, or towel. They may show some sensitivity to items of clothing such as labels or may only want to wear clothes that they have had for years, not wanting to wear new items. Children may not like standing too close to others or queuing.

Auditory (sound) sense: This can relate to whether the child seeks out noise, becomes easily distracted or responds negatively to sound. Some children will make noises for no apparent reason, whereas others will seek out and enjoy noise. Questions may relate to how this sense is affecting the child's everyday life.

Visual (sight) sense: This can relate to the autistic child's experiences of taste/texture/smell senses. Some autistic children can be overly sensitive to lights and this can cause pain. Some will seek out darker environments. Some children can be distracted by visual stimuli, noticing lots of detail in the environment, or may seek out items that light up or spin.

Taste/texture/smell senses: Questions will relate to whether a child seeks out or avoids tastes, smells or textures. Some children may dislike certain foods, smells or textures and even certain utensils. Some may gag easily, may be unaware of food on their faces or may enjoy chewing or licking non-food items.

Vestibular (movement) sense: This relates to how children experience movement. Some autistic children can find it difficult to sit still; others may spin around or rock themselves.

Proprioception (body awareness): Some children may seek out tight hugs from others or enjoy being wrapped in tight blankets. Some may bump into others, jump around or crash into furniture, appearing to others as being clumsy. This relates to their awareness of their body in space. Some children will place their hand against a wall as they walk along or may pace around the perimeter of a space to become familiar with the environment. Others will balance on their toes when walking.

Sensory needs and sensory suggestions

Problems with information processing can cause sensitivity in one or more of the following areas: tactile, oral, visual, auditory, olfactory, vestibular. This section describes the types of behaviours that may be observed, relating to each of the senses, depending on whether a child is hyper- or hypo-sensitive, or both. Practical strategies are suggested that can be explored with autistic children to help them manage any sensory sensitivities they may have and enable them to feel balanced and calm (or more alert when necessary). Other people can help autistic girls by considering what adjustments can be made to the environment and the approaches taken (including communication) when supporting them, depending on the sensory needs and preferences of each child. Autistic children will generally know which sensory experiences they need, which ones to avoid and which ones they may benefit from, depending on whether they are under- or over-responsive, or a combination of both.

Please note that the following examples and suggestions are not intended as a substitute for the services of a qualified occupational therapist. All autistic children are individuals, and the way they experience the world is unique.

Auditory (hearing)

Some autistic children can have problems with hearing and a general practitioner will be best placed to advise parents and carers. Others may have what is known as 'hyperacusis'. This is when noises sound louder to a person than they should and can have an impact on daily living in numerous ways and affect well-being.

Children who are over-sensitive to sounds can experience stress at what they consider to be loud or unexpected noises. Some autistic children have a dislike for a certain word or sound, and this can also cause feelings of discomfort or stress. Some autistic children who are over-responsive to noise will put their hands over their ears when reacting. Unexpected noises can be quite frightening, and it can take time to recover. Common noises that can cause stress include a door-bell ringing, a hand dryer or vacuum cleaner being switched on, thunder, a school bell ringing or a dog barking.

Some autistic children in schools find it difficult to filter out noises, especially if they hear background noise whilst the teacher is talking. This can affect learning because listening to two competing sounds can make it difficult to concentrate and cause overload. Some autistic children will be able to hear sounds that other people don't notice: the buzzing of lights in the room, the sound of technical equipment, a dripping tap at the back of a room. For some, this can feel overloading.

Wood (2019) highlights how noise in the environment can affect autistic children's learning in schools, stating: 'It is...clear that the physical school environment, if it is not carefully managed, can be inherently exclusionary for autistic children, with noise arguably being the biggest culprit.' She encourages us to consider the impact of the environment on the learning experience of autistic children – how noise in the environment can affect their communication abilities – and rightly forces us to question our own perceptions of children's abilities:

> The children in my study who were seated with a TA [teaching assistant] in a corridor, for example, or to one side of the classroom while the rest of the children were noisily engaged in another activity, were having to deal with more noise and disruption than their peers. Therefore, while the children demonstrated difficulties with speech, these problems could be compounded by the challenging circumstances within which they were expected to communicate. (Wood 2019, p.150)

Would these children who demonstrated 'difficulties with speech' be more able to communicate in a calm, quiet environment?

For some autistic children, crowds and crowded places (for example, assemblies, school corridors, theatres, cinemas and shopping centres) can be overwhelming because of the noise. Some noises seem to be amplified in certain environments (for example, swimming pools or school dining rooms). Some autistic children may dislike going to social events if they are noise-sensitive, though this depends on the child. One way to help noise-sensitive children manage social events and gatherings is to be the first ones to arrive. This helps the child to get accustomed to the environment and manage noise gradually as other people arrive. This can help her to feel more in control. I do this myself and find it reduces anxiety.

Too much noise can be overstimulating, and some children find it difficult to calm down. A strategy that some autistic children use to drown out noises is to make their own noise (for example, shouting, screaming, singing or humming).

There are many things that can help noise-sensitive autistic children. Some like to wear ear defenders at certain times, though parents should be aware that the environment might appear louder to some children when taken off as they have been accustomed to silence. Some autistic children prefer to wear more discreet earphones, and others enjoy listening to music as this can block environmental noise. Some brands of earphones allow some noise to filter through, which some children prefer. Some autistic children like wearing a hooded item of clothing, or two, as this helps them feel more protected from noise. For a noise-sensitive child, being able to wear a hood up, wear a hat, wear earphones or wear ear defenders should be viewed as 'reasonable adjustments'. Other alternatives to managing noise sensitivity might include relaxation techniques such as breathing exercises. Listening to quiet music or nature sounds can also be calming.

Having a quiet place to go to in school such as a library, a sensory room, a quiet room or outdoor space (for example, an area of a playground or sensory garden) can help a noise-sensitive child to avoid overload or overwhelm and manage the school day. A quiet place in the home, where this is possible, can also be beneficial, even if it is a small area. Some children to have dens or small tents to retreat into, though it must be a safe space.

Allowing an autistic child to control the noise within the home can be helpful, such as giving them the remote control for the television. Some children will want no noise at all if trying to concentrate, whereas others can manage with background noise being turned down low. Where children are given autonomy in relation to sounds, they are able to control how much noise they can manage.

Other people can help by preparing children in advance for noise. For those working in schools it can be worthwhile to walk around the school building and grounds at different times of day to view the school from the perspective of the child. Listen to all the different noises in different classrooms and areas before considering what adjustments and changes can be made to accommodate the autistic children you know. I once worked with an autistic girl who was struggling to concentrate and was overwhelmed at the end of each day. She was sat at the back of the class, farthest away from the teacher, next to an open window, with a busy road outside. Lots of verbal information was being shared without visuals or demonstrations. Closing the window a little and allowing her to sit where she felt comfortable nearer to the teacher helped her to feel less overloaded. Being autistic, she was burnt out because she was already having to work harder than her peers to process the volume of spoken language (from a distance) whilst having to cope with sensory issues. This was a very inclusive school that had already put in place many things to support her and they wanted to do everything they could.

Some autistic children seek out noise or make their own (for example, they may hum or sing constantly, or bang or tap things). Introducing children to musical instruments can bring lots of enjoyment.

Children who are under-responsive to noise may not respond to their name being called in class or at home. They are not trying to ignore anyone, but just miss cues. Others hear loud noises but do not seem to react. Playing listening games can be helpful. For some children, being under-responsive to noise can mean speech is delayed or their pitch and tone are affected.

Visual (sight)

Some autistic children can be over-sensitive to light and may try to block it out by shutting the curtains, or closing or covering their eyes. Some like to wear dark glasses or hats/caps to block out lights that can feel painful.

In addition to light sensitivity, some environments can be visually distracting. For example, schools can be full of what Wood (2019) describes as 'visual clutter'. She suggests that 'this phenomenon is generally considered to have a potentially overloading impact on autistic children who are already very sensitive sensorially'. Viewing the environments from an autistic perspective can help to make environments more accessible.

How to reduce visual distractions within schools

- Displays could be kept within borders within a certain area of a room. Visuals can be placed away from the board area or where a teacher is standing. Resources or work that hangs from the ceiling can cause additional distraction, so might be removed.
- Muted/pastel colours are less distracting. Keeping the classroom clear and clutter-free can help provide order.
- Screen overlays can be used, or screen settings adapted to reduce glare.

These suggestions can help a young person to concentrate. Other visual distractions can be other people's clothing! When communicating with others, a child might take in all the visual details of the person, including what they are wearing (especially if a person is wearing patterned, striped or bright clothing); alternatively, she may focus on the background, which might distract from what the person is saying.

The following are some suggestions when developing resources for autistic children who may be visually overstimulated:

- Think about how the information is set out (often autistic children like order and symmetry).
- Consider the colours you use, including the colour of the background (some colours cause contrast and can be difficult to read), depending on the needs and preferences of the child.
- Think about the amount of information you put on each page.
- Use visuals to back up information.
- Some children like written information to be contained within borders as this breaks it up on the page and helps them to feel less overloaded.

Children who are under-responsive can miss visual cues. They are not purposely ignoring people. Some may have difficulty in reading or scanning for information in lessons.

Some autistic children like to seek out visual stimulation. They may enjoy watching lights flashing or gain enjoyment from stimming (for example, flapping their hands or other items in front of their eyes), or they may focus on the visual aspects of some things. Creating a sensory area or visiting a sensory room (with bubble tubes, lights, etc.) can be beneficial for some children. Others I have worked with enjoy painting pictures with UV paint or neon markers as this really shows up well in the darkness. Some children enjoy stimming or swirling brightly coloured fabrics (nets, silks, etc) and others enjoy wearing brightly coloured clothing in the sensory room.

Tactile (touch)

Some children who are over-responsive to touch find certain aspects of personal grooming painful and may, for example, dislike having their hair washed and brushed, teeth brushed, or nails being cut. Having hair brushed can feel painful, but soft bristle brushes and detangling shampoos and conditioners can help some children. Cutting nails after a warm bath can make things feel moderately better though this depends on the child. Clothing and footwear can feel uncomfortable, so allowing children to wear what they find comfortable in can help. Children may have favourite items of clothing, enjoy the feel of certain textures and dislike others. Schools can help autistic children by being flexible about school uniform. New items of clothing can feel harsh and often have a distinctive 'new' smell that some children either love or hate. Washing new clothes several times before the child wears them can help. Labels may need to be removed from clothing as these can cause irritation.

Autistic children who are over-responsive to touch may dislike being too near to other people so may avoid queuing and lining up; they may dislike being touched and avoid being hugged or kissed as this feels uncomfortable. They may dislike getting messy so might like to get washed straightaway. Autistic children should not be forced to do activities that they find uncomfortable due to being sensitive to touch but can be encouraged to explore textures if they feel comfortable doing so.

Some autistic children find messy, sensory activities calming. Some children who are sensory-seeking may attempt to touch or hug others. I used to work with an autistic girl who was sensory-seeking and who tried to hug **everyone** very tightly, including me! Knowing what is appropriate and inappropriate, with whom, and in what situations can keep autistic children safe. There are often alternative ways for autistic children to gain the same input and feelings that they are seeking. If a child is unintentionally behaving 'inappropriately', as well as helping them to understand personal boundaries and different types of relationships between different people, showing them what they can do instead and allowing them to choose what works best for them, can help. Hugging a friend, hugging a teddy, hugging a pillow, self-hugging (wrapping their arms around their own body) or wearing a weighted jacket/vest might provide the feeling they are seeking. Some children enjoy being wrapped up in blankets or sleeping bags at home, though it is important that they are safe, supervised and can easily get themselves out. At bedtime, some children enjoy the feeling of being tucked up tightly in bed as this feels safe and comforting. In school, sensory-seeking children who love the feeling of certain textures can find certain items calming (for example, soft pencil cases, journals, tactile keyrings and small soft toys). Depending on the child, sensory experiences can be built into the school day. One of the teaching assistants I worked with noticed that one child was spending a lot of time at the sink and loved playing with bubbles in our art lessons, so we made sure to provide sufficient time in lessons for him to enjoy this sensory experience in addition to others. School should be a fun place to be in, and a happy child will always learn more. All subjects can provide sensory experiences and it is worthwhile spending time focusing on the curriculum and how more sensory experiences could be included.

As well as thinking about textures, you might also like to think about sensory experiences involving temperature. Some children like to wear clothes that give a feeling of warmth; or they may like the warmth (and weight) of a hot-water bottle on their lap as this can feel calming and soothing. Other products that provide warmth include microwaveable handwarmers and soft toys, some of which are scented, though please check these are suitable for children.

Children who are under-responsive to touch may not feel pain. They can appear to be clumsy and can bump into things by accident. They may also have poor fine motor skills. Some children may bite or scratch themselves if under-responsive to touch. This is considered self-injurious behaviour. Children can gain sensory input from tactile games and experiences such as art and craft activities, which can be a fun way to introduce a child to different textures. Some children like to carry around fidget toys. These can be made freely available in a box in every classroom. Some autistic children love immersing themselves in nature, so doing messy activities outdoors can be fun. Some like the feel of different textures on the skin and may enjoy being barefoot.

Gustatory (taste)

Some autistic children prefer to eat bland foods and may have a limited diet as they refuse to eat other foods. Some are averse to certain tastes or textures. Children who are involved in preparing, cooking and baking their own foods (without pressure to eat it) may choose to try different foods. Some children feel comfortable just touching or smelling a 'new' food before deciding if they want to lick or taste it. Some children do not like different kinds of food to touch each other (for example, wet food must not touch dry food).

Children can explore the world through taste and textures. Some will put things in their mouths and will chew or eat things that are not supposed to be eaten. Children who are under-responsive may enjoy foods and drinks that have strong flavours. Sometimes they can appear to be messy eaters. Some things that children might enjoy include ice lollies, trying different flavours, cooking and baking foods with different textures, and drinking thick milkshakes through straws

Olfactory (smell)

Smell is an important sense that we rely on for our own safety. Some children who are over-sensitive to smell are alert to danger and can therefore sometimes prevent a dangerous situation from occurring (for example, a gas leak, fire, etc.). Others who are under-responsive to smell can be unaware of danger and can find it difficult to distinguish between different smells.

I have known many autistic children who are sensitive to smells in the environment. Some autistic girls will find that when tired their sense of smell is heightened. Everywhere a child goes will have associated smells, depending on location, time of day and different products being used. Children may have favourite places to go because of how they smell, or they may refuse to go into certain environments. They should be given opportunities to communicate their likes and dislikes.

Autistic children often link smells to their experiences and there is no doubt we 'store' smells in our memory. The impact of smells should not be underestimated, and the fear of smells is very real. In contrast, smells can evoke feelings of happiness, of being with certain people, of past experiences or of a time or place when we felt happy. Although a simple idea, it is useful to work with children to identify their favourite smells and use this to their advantage. An autistic girl I once worked with explained how wearing her favourite perfume helped her to feel calm enough to sit an exam that she was going to opt out of.

If a child has a strong sense of smell, wearing unscented products around her might be considered. Wherever children go, there are smells in the environment; in schools, hospitals, shops, parks, and in our homes. The products and resources that we use should be given careful consideration as should the environments children spend time in. Some children dislike certain smells whereas others may seek smells out. Some children dislike these smells while others may seek them out. Some children dislike scented bodywash, air fresheners, scented candles and cleaning products (they may prefer natural products as artificial ones smell too strong). Others, by contrast, like strong-smelling products and enjoy using strongly scented toiletries. Incidentally, having poor personal hygiene can be the result of being under-responsive to smell. Even clothing has a particular smell and can be pleasant or unpleasant. Some children will smell clothing before putting it on and may also like to smell food before eating them as it helps them to feel more comfortable.

Some autistic children find certain smells so unpleasant or uncomfortable that they feel nauseous. They may find it difficult to sit in the school canteen because they dislike the smell of food cooking or the smell of the meals their peers are eating. This can be interpreted as being fussy or intolerant, but it is not – it is genuinely difficult for these children. For some, having to sit next to a person eating a certain food they dislike the smell of can be unbearable. Therefore, some adjustments and flexibility may be needed at mealtimes (for example, children may be able to eat in other areas or rooms, supervised, away from unpleasant and overpowering smells).

In a school environment smells can affect learning. Things that can help children who are over-sensitive to smells include: allowing them to sit where they choose to avoid smells being flexible about your own expectations and adapting lessons, allowing children to use alternative products (in art lessons for example), enabling children to observe experiments from a distance (in science lessons), using (or not using) strong smelling products, being aware of other smells in the environment, incorporating pleasant smells into lessons (for example, in art lessons, using natural products, fruits and vegetables to paint with or create sculptures with) and taking children on trips that allow them to experience pleasant smells!

Some children enjoy school trips that involve going to places where they can experience strong smells (for example, fairgrounds, bakeries, restaurants, zoos). Learning experiences can incorporate multi-sensory activities and games that involve smells. Some children enjoy using scented stationery such as markers, pens and erasers. There are even scented products (balls, for example) that can be used in P.E. lessons. In other areas of the curriculum, strong smells can be incorporated into lessons such as life skills or cookery, where herbs and spices might be used. Schools might consider creating their own sensory garden or space.

Vestibular (movement)

Some autistic children enjoy moving around a lot and enjoy rolling and spinning. They may find it hard to sit still in one place. Places like fairgrounds or activity centres can provide them with experiences and sensations that are enjoyable. Other children, in contrast, feel worried about moving around or being off the ground (for example, escalators and elevators might cause stress), so movement that they can control is preferable. Some enjoy the slow, rocking feeling of being in a hammock or a rocking chair, but no child should be forced to take part in movement activities that they find uncomfortable. Fast movements can be over-stimulating, whereas slow movements can help a child to feel calm.

Under-responsive children may sometimes be found slouching at their desk in the classroom. Regular movement breaks can help children to feel more alert. They can be asked to collect equipment, run an errand or take a short walk; alternatively, the whole class can take part in a short, fun movement activity. Under-responsive children sometimes struggle for various reasons in P.E. lessons as they may become tired quite quickly and can have poor balance.

Proprioception (muscles and joints)

Some children will move around and fidget a lot. They might chew things, tap their feet, bounce, rock themselves and seek out rough play with peers. I have often seen children running their hands along the wall in the corridors as this helps them to understand where their bodies are in relation to the environment. Some children also walk around the perimeter of a space to become accustomed to the area. Children may touch themselves or try to touch other people. Under-responsive children may hug people too hard, not realizing how 'heavy-handed' they are being. Sometimes they appear to be clumsy and bump into things (and people) accidentally, which can be a source of conflict between peers due to lack of understanding and awareness. Children who are under-responsive may not realize how much noise they are making moving around. They may have poor posture and may drop or spill things by accident. They also might not be aware of how rough they are being with pets and animals. I have worked with children who travel across a classroom and fail to recognize that there are people or items in the way.

Some children feel embarrassed at appearing clumsy, which can affect their self-esteem, so providing reassurance is important. Accepting the child for who they are is important. Things that can help children who are under-responsive include doing chores, gardening, laundry, and activities that involve pushing and pulling, lifting and carrying. Children can use products such as a weighted lap pad or do wall push ups. Some children love the feeling of weighted jackets or weighted 'snakes' or shoulder cushions and may find it helpful to use fidget toys, chewy sweets or gum. For those who struggle with fine motor skills, using pens and pencils with pencil grips can be helpful, but the child is the best person to ask as they will be able to communicate their own preferences and what works for them.

Advice about the proprioceptive system, from an occupational therapist, Helen Murphy

The proprioceptive system has an important regulatory role in sensory processing as proprioceptive input helps to control responses to sensory stimuli. Proprioceptive input can be calming for children who are easily overwhelmed by sensory stimulation and can be alerting for children who need increased sensory stimulation to facilitate attention and learning.

The proprioceptive system is input received through the joints and muscles through movement and heavy work. It is activated any time we push or pull on objects, as well as at any time the joints are compressed together or stretched apart (for example, jumping up and down or hanging on apparatus). In sensory terms, proprioception is often referred to as the 'magic sense' as it is the 'go to' activity to use.

Consider activities which work the muscles and joints:

- Weight bearing activities such as push ups and cardiovascular activities (for example, running, jumping)
- Resistance activities (for example, pushing/pulling)
- Heavy work activities (for example, rearranging furniture, carrying classroom supplies)
- Oral activities (for example, chewing and blowing).

If proprioceptive input is being used to calm an anxious girl, try to identify her trigger points and introduce the activity before she becomes anxious (for example, prior to going into the assembly hall or lunch room). Activities can be incorporated into a child's timetable to help her remain calm during these times.

Proprioceptive activities can also be used to calm a girl who becomes unexpectedly distressed by sensory input. It is beneficial for such activities to be familiar to her so that they can be performed easily.

Some children will be able to recognize when they are becoming stressed or anxious and may be able to request a sensory break; others may not have the ability to recognize this themselves and are therefore reliant on an adult to direct them towards appropriate activities.

If proprioceptive input is being used to alert a child, try to identify times when they lose focus and become disengaged, and incorporate activities just prior to this. This will often be before or after more sedentary tasks such as independent, quiet work.

Activities that provide proprioceptive input can be used with children individually as needed or as a whole class activity. Activities do not need to be lengthy; little and often is just as beneficial.

Points to remember in relation to proprioceptive input:

- Input to the muscles and joints is regulating, therefore it can be calming or alerting.
- Activities in which the girl is actively engaged are more effective than passive input provided by an adult.
- Participation in activities that provide increased proprioceptive input are required at regular intervals throughout the child's day.
- It is beneficial to allocate a child daily responsibilities which involve proprioceptive input depending on her ability (for example, carrying heavy supplies to another classroom or stacking chairs, putting away equipment, wiping tables).

Interoception and sensory processing issues

Autistic girls with sensory processing issues may have difficulty organizing information from sight, smell, hearing, taste, touch, proprioception and vestibular senses. Some may also have difficulties relating to the eighth sense, known as interoception.

Just as there are receptors in the muscles and joints that help us to understand where our body is in space (proprioception), similarly, there are receptors inside our organs, including our skin, that send information about the inside of our body to our brain. Interoception helps us to understand what is happening on the inside of our bodies. It can help us know if we feel too hot or too cold, recognize when our bladder is full, feel our digestive system working, notice when we feel nauseous, alert us to danger (the physical sensations we experience such as tense muscles, nervousness in the stomach or a rise in body temperature when stressed), feel sensations relating to the menstrual cycle and understand what is happening in the body at a particular time of the month, and feel pain.

An autistic girl who has sensory processing difficulties may find it difficult to interpret what is happening in her body and as a result may have trouble 'feeling' her emotions and bodily sensations. If girls struggle to understand their emotions or find it hard to interpret what is happening in their body, this can lead to meltdowns or bedwetting. A girl may find it hard to understand how she feels and may have difficulty explaining this.

Some autistic girls seek out interoceptive input. They may move around quickly or breathe quickly as this feels comfortable to them. They may not eat as much as others because the feeling of being hungry or thirsty may also feel comfortable.

For other girls, interoceptive input can be annoying. Some may eat more than other children because they want to avoid hunger pangs; others may not eat or drink as often as others because they don't feel hungry or thirsty. Some children may go to the toilet more often because they do not like how their bladder feels. Some girls may respond 'inappropriately' to interoceptive input. For example, if they are under-responsive, they may not respond to sensations when they should, and they may take longer to learn to use the toilet or have toileting 'accidents'.

It is possible that mindfulness activities and meditation may help those with sensory processing difficulties relating to interoception because this helps them to be more aware of their bodies. Activities involving heavy work can also be helpful in regulation.

Calming ideas

As many autistic girls internalize feelings, mask their true selves and adapt themselves to fit in, having strategies to use can help them to feel calm and balanced. This is needed to offset stress and mental exhaustion. Helping autistic girls to understand themselves and what helps them to feel calm can improve mental and physical well-being. Each girl is unique and will have her own preferences for what she likes to do and where she likes to go.

Animals: Animals are easy to be with and make good company. Spending time with animals can be very calming for some autistic girls who may love their soothing sensory qualities. Some schools have school dogs as they recognize how children can benefit from being able to spend time out of class with animals (for example, it can lead to greater focus). Some girls are very in tune with animals and enjoy the responsibility of looking after a pet. For autistic girls who love being with animals, this interest can sometimes develop into a career opportunity, but even if it does not, it is good for well-being.

Clothing: Some girls prefer certain clothing because of sensory issues. Others like to be able to hide themselves away in clothes such as hoodies or wear tighter clothing (such as weighted vests and t-shirts) as being tucked away feels safe and provides proprioceptive input.

Nature: Being outdoors can be calming for many autistic girls. Being in a natural environment is low-arousal and can be restorative. The outdoors allows some degree of solitude, which is calming for the mind, allowing girls time to recharge. Gardening, too, allows the mind to focus and provides escapism, whilst the exercise involved (mowing, raking, lifting, carrying) can be calming for the body and helpful for autistic girls who have difficulties sleeping. It is also creative and rewarding and provides satisfaction for autistic girls who like a sense of order. Some find environmental sounds are calming. Forest 'bathing', which encourages slow and mindful enjoyment of nature through all of the senses, is also highly recommended.

Water: Some girls find bathing or swimming is calming and helps them to regulate their emotions. Being in water helps to relax the body. Some autistic girls like the feeling of being underwater.

Music: Music can be a calming influence and can also reflect how girls might be feeling – it can be helpful for girls who struggle to describe feelings in words. Music allows the mind to relax and can help to block out other unpleasant noises that can be distracting, distressing, or overloading. Listening to music can be uplifting, helping to change a person's mood and make them feel more positive. Some girls enjoy spending time playing instruments and making music as this is something that requires focus and attention.

Rocking, swinging, jumping: The back-and-forth motion of a swing or rocking chair can feel calming. Girls can read, or listen to a story or music, whilst moving on a swing. Trampolining can also have a calming effect and may help to improve focus. Bouncing and jumping are very regulating because linear movements are calming in contrast with rotary movements, which are alerting.

Weighted blankets: Weighted blankets can help to relieve anxiety and stress by helping a child to feel safe and secure. For some children, they can aid sleep. Shoulder wraps, lap pads, and jackets that are weighted can be used to aid relaxation, but this depends on the young person's preference. Some will enjoy being tucked inside a sleeping bag and others will like the tight hug of being wrapped up in a blanket. (For reasons of safety, a child using any of these products must be able to remove them themselves and the correct weight of product must be used. Please seek the advice of an occupational therapist where necessary before using this type of product.)

> When I feel stressed or anxious and I am able, I lie under my weighted blanket. It doesn't make things completely better, but it makes me feel a bit better as being tucked away feels safe and provides proprioceptive input.

Stimming: Although autistic girls stim for different reasons, some girls say that stimming can help them to relax.

> I stim a lot. This helps me so much. I have many stimming ways that help me to calm down, but I also stim when I am happy and excited. Music is great for stimming, too. Art is a big help and hours can go by while I am drawing. I love having a cup of coffee or any warm drink, and spending time with my family makes me feel safe and secure and I can be myself in front of them. Stroking my dog and cat really helps too. I also have a weighted blanket that really helps with sleep as I can find falling asleep hard.

Hugs: Some girls like to have a soft toy or cushion to hug. Self-hugs (where a girl can wrap her arms around herself pressing her hands tightly into her arms) can also be a discreet way to gain proprioceptive input, helping her to feel calm. Some girls seek out people to hug. (Just teach her what is appropriate behaviour, what is not, when and with whom.)

Sensory toys: Sensory toys have properties that distract and calm and appeal to different senses. Oil and water toys and spinners work well for those who like visual input. Some girls prefer sensory toys to squash and squeeze as they are more tactile. Some like to play with dough and others like the feel of different swatches of materials (silky, fluffy, furry) kept on a keyring, as stroking different textures can be very soothing. With any sensory toys or equipment, it is important to demonstrate how they can be used.

Sensory rooms: Some girls benefit from time to themselves in a sensory room as this allows them to recuperate. Some like light, airy, plain, calm and uncluttered rooms, whereas others prefer a dark background with bright lights and visual stimulus.

Smells: Some girls find certain smells calming. Smells can evoke good memories and happy thoughts.

Visuals: Visuals, such as lava lamps, oil and water toys and even fish tanks, can provide some children with relaxation.

Sorting and organizing activities: Some autistic girls enjoy sorting activities because they provide a sense of order which helps them to feel calm. Sorting small items into separate compartments can be completed alone and helps to focus the mind. Some girls like to organize their own belongings (or their own rooms) as having order feels comfortable. Some girls enjoy craft activities that have a sequence, as it allows them to get into the flow.

Breathing exercises: Breathing exercises are a way to help autistic girls to calm themselves when stressed. They can help girls to slow themselves down, allowing them to think situations through so that they can avoid meltdown. This can be beneficial for girls who are impulsive and quick to react.

Drawing and colouring: Some girls enjoy colouring patterns (for example, mandalas) as this requires focus and is a distraction from the outside world. Some girls gain enjoyment from repeatedly drawing safe and familiar images (for example, favourite cartoon characters), whereas others gain a considerable amount from creating their own work.

Reading: Reading provides escapism whilst building up knowledge and vocabulary, and can help girls to grow in confidence. Reading can also help girls to relax and can aid sleep. Many autistic girls and women are highly creative so as well as being avid readers can also enjoy writing their own stories.

Solitude: Sometimes being able to spend time alone, without having to communicate, can allow an autistic girl to zone out and recharge her batteries. Some autistic girls are so drained from school that they need time to relax before discussing their day. This is especially important for autistic girls, according to Hull *et al.* (2017), who state that females may report high levels of subjective stress, anxiety and exhaustion, and a need to withdraw from social interaction to 're-set'.

Affirmations: Affirmations can help to build confidence and self-esteem through positive statements, `I am confident', `I am strong', `I am amazing', `I can do this'. Girls can use visual representations of these if they like and personalise them to remind themselves to use positive self-talk.

Gratitude journal: Autistic girls can enjoy focusing on the positive aspects of life by recording what they have enjoyed or appreciated during the day, however small. This encourages a positive mindset. Gratitude journals can enable children to reflect on happy memories.

Yoga practice: There are numerous benefits to yoga practice for autistic girls and yoga should be differentiated so that everyone can be included whatever their needs.

Advice from a yoga teacher, Julie McKnight

A good yoga practice should be accessible and suitable for the individual, offering challenges but not unrealistic expectations. It is also important to remember that yoga should not be competitive, and success should not be measured just by physical and visible achievements.

Practising yoga alongside others can enable girls to feel connected without the pressure of having to communicate, although they will often chat naturally when they feel comfortable and when they are not feeling under pressure. Yoga can be enjoyed alone if preferred.

Yoga practice has many physical, emotional and mental benefits, which can really make a difference for autistic girls. Simply "checking in" with the body, the breath and the mind can often offer surprising improvements to well-being.

Benefits to be gained from physical practice and simple breathing, relaxation and meditation techniques include:

- **Relaxation:** Learning how to relax the body and mind is a skill that takes practice and is often easier when guided by another person.
- **Focus and concentration:** Learning to maintain focus by using physical sensations or the movement of the breath as an anchor.

- **Emotional regulation:** Being able to recognize emotional states, including anxiety, and having the tools available to change them.
- **Self-awareness, self-discipline, and persistence:** The repetitive, simple routines send out a message that practice makes progress rather than practice makes perfect, and work towards self-acceptance and self-love.
- **Improved vagal tone:** The vagus nerve helps the body and brain to communicate. The brain picks up messages from the body – in particular the lungs – so altering the way we breathe can change the messages received and help us to return from an agitated state to a calmer place.
- **Flexibility:** Yoga postures (asanas) maintain ease of movement in the spine and joints.
- **Strength:** Yoga builds and maintains muscle strength and bone density.
- **Body awareness (proprioception):** Yoga helps to gain an understanding of how the body moves and where it is in a space. (How does your body feel when you move in a certain way?)
- **Balance:** Feeling the ground beneath the feet and improving physical body control.
- **Safety:** Yoga can also provide autistic girls with valuable lessons about safety, their bodies and their boundaries, as well as other people's. Whilst on the mat, girls have their own physical space which can help them to learn about personal space. Yoga also provides mental space as girls can learn to release negative thoughts, allowing them to focus on being calm in the present moment, thereby improving well-being.

Be calm – what can autistic girls benefit from knowing or exploring, and what should parents and professionals be aware of?

Feelings

Autistic girls can benefit from knowing that emotions affect all aspects of life, including sleep, diet, choices and habits. They should be aware that not everyone expresses themselves in the same way. What is important is for the child to understand herself and express herself in a safe way that works for her, and for other people to understand this. Feelings can fluctuate and people can experience a wide range of emotions even in a short period of time.

Autistic girls, and others, should know that some people find it difficult to talk about and describe feelings. There are many reasons for this, such as alexithymia or feeling under pressure. Children and other people can benefit from knowing that people can feel and express emotions in different ways. Some people, for example, experience feelings intensely and are emotionally affected by how other people feel, which has advantages and disadvantages. The advantages are that some will be very considerate to others, which is a positive quality in terms of friendships and relationships. This quality is a particular requirement for certain jobs, such as caring roles. In contrast, a possible disadvantage might be that being highly emotional could result in a person being exploited or taken advantage of by others. This is not the fault of the person themselves.

Autistic girls can benefit from being more aware of the physical sensations that some people experience when feeling a certain emotion (for example, body temperature might increase or the heart beat faster). They can also benefit from knowing more about interoception, as some people find it difficult to read the signs that their body is sending them. Children may also understand that people can have different perspectives of the same situation and experience different feelings.

Autistic girls can explore how they might express emotions verbally or non-verbally. They might express feelings in a variety of ways: by clapping, stimming, becoming withdrawn or louder or more talkative, talking faster, making a particular noise, being more physical, behaving in a more repetitive way or seeking out favourite things for comfort. It depends on the person. This may be different to how some non-autistic people may express emotions but is perfectly acceptable.

Autistic girls may benefit from exploring the reasons why children might express themselves in unsafe ways and this will help many girls to develop greater self-awareness. Exploring safe ways to express difficult feelings can be helpful though it's important that the young person has ownership and can make their own suggestions about what works for them. Adults can support children where necessary by suggesting alternative and safe ways to release negative emotions if the child finds this helpful.

Autistic girls and those who support them should be aware of what triggers stress and anxiety and should explore how these can be prevented, avoided, or better managed. Autistic girls should develop their own strategies, or those they have devised with others, either independently or with support or prompting. If a child finds it difficult or impossible to communicate verbally, she can use resources to alert others that she is feeling upset, angry, jealous, confused, frustrated, etc. For example, she may use a visual scale, a symbol or a gesture that has been agreed with a trusted adult – if my reversible bracelet is orange, I'm okay; if I turn it inside out and it's green, I'm not okay) – diaries, charts, graphs or other methods.

Children, and others, should also be aware that some people will seek out intense emotions in the media and on television (for example, dramatic films and hospital dramas).

Children, and others, can benefit from knowing what a meltdown is, what can be done to avoid meltdown and how they can be supportive before, during and after a meltdown so that further stress can be avoided. They may also be aware of what 'burnout' means, what causes it and how to avoid it. Children may learn why some people suppress feelings and should be aware that this can affect mental and physical health. 'Camouflaging' and 'masking', which many children do unintentionally and intentionally to protect themselves and to help themselves fit in, are other relevant topics that should be explored. Children and others can benefit from knowing what is meant by 'shutdown' and what causes it. Please find explanations of these terms in Chapter 3 (shutdown) and Chapter 4 (camouflaging). Autistic children are often expected to adapt themselves to fit in to systems not designed for them, so they should be given opportunities to consider why it is important for them to be able to 'be themselves'. They may think about what this means to them personally: how, when, and in what situations, and with whom they can be themselves without having to adapt.

If we can help autistic girls to develop a greater awareness of the things that cause them to be stressed, anxious or uncomfortable, and other people are also more aware of these things, they can be better managed so that situations don't feel overwhelming. Girls, and those who support them, can benefit from knowing the main causes of stress which are changes to routine, what other people say or do, sensory issues, crowds, social occasions, social anxiety, being unprepared, not having sufficient information ad being confused. Autistic girls may learn that they cannot control what other people say or do, but they **can** control their own reactions. They may consider what difficulties they can resolve alone and be able to recognize when to seek help from others. They should be aware that transition from one activity to another or from one place to another, as well as other changes, can cause some people to feel increased levels of stress; for some people, transition is very stressful if they are not given sufficient warning of change, especially if they are involved in an activity of great interest to them. In addition, the environment can be calming or a stressor. Autistic girls may consider the types of environment they personally find calming (for example, nature, being in water) and what aspects of different environments can cause increased stress (for example, crowds, shopping centres, noisy events or, alternatively, places that are too quiet).

Sensory needs and sensitivities

It is important, where possible, for children and other people to be aware of their sensory needs, understand what being hyper- and hypo-sensitive (or both) means, know about the different senses (including vestibular and proprioception) and sensory overload, and learn that sensory sensitivities can cause overload. Some girls will benefit from knowing that their sensory needs may change (for example, they may become more sensitive to noise if tired). They may consider their own needs and how to request or be able to make adjustments for themselves when necessary.

Phobias

Some autistic children have phobias, which can sometimes relate to sensory perceptions. Phobias can have an impact not only on how the child feels but also on her learning and everyday life. Professional advice may be required to support the child to manage any difficulties, though this will depend on their severity. Sometimes it is possible to work with the child to find solutions to make life more manageable. Trust is important so that the child knows that what has been agreed will be followed through.

Being calm

Autistic children and others should be aware of what factors can cause some people to experience stress and anxiety, including:

- being misunderstood and misjudged by others
- lack of understanding of the autistic person
- needs not being met
- uncertainty, unfairness and injustice
- being undervalued or underestimated
- other people's expectations not being fair or realistic
- misunderstanding and miscommunication
- difficulty interpreting other people's feelings
- difficulty expressing themselves
- friendship difficulties
- phobias
- sensory sensitivities
- the environment
- tiredness, exhaustion and not having time or opportunities to recuperate
- too much information or too many requests without sufficient processing time
- lack of routine and predictability
- other people changing their minds
- other people not being clear
- being confused, lacking context or information
- not knowing how to manage difficult situations
- insufficient preparation for change and transition.

Children may be able to use this knowledge in a variety of situations, developing a greater awareness of what can cause them to experience stress/anxiety so that they can judge **when** they feel stressed/worried/anxious, know **why,** and know **what** to do to reduce these feelings.

They may explore calming strategies, activities and resources they **personally** find most useful, including:

- using sensory strategies (for example, sensory toys, weighted products, favourite smells, textures, tastes, or chewing or crunching foods)

- visual resources such as a booklet or keyring that the child has created, showing favourite people, places, etc.
- technology
- personal belongings or other items that are meaningful or comforting to the child
- special interests
- taking time out
- solitude
- quiet space or den
- sensory room
- calming music
- writing down thoughts or recording them in other ways
- drawing, painting, colouring, writing
- physical exercise
- activity involving repetitive movement (for example, swing, rocking chair, trampoline)
- yoga and other movement activities that involve repetitive sequences
- breathing and relaxation techniques
- being outdoors
- getting rid of feelings visually and/or physically (writing them on a piece of paper and then throwing it in the bin)
- changing thought processes (slowing thoughts down in order to think things through rather than react too quickly)
- any other strategies the child suggests.

Girls may reflect on difficult situations with others who are non-judgemental at an appropriate time after the event. They can learn to link experiences to thought, thoughts to feelings, feelings to the body, the body to actions, and use this cycle to be more conscious of actions to improve their own well-being By exploring a range of scenarios and learning **why** certain situations can evoke difficult feelings, children can learn how to manage them better in the future, either independently or with support from others.

Change and transition

Change and transition from one activity to another or from one place to another can cause some people to feel increased levels of stress, especially if they are given insufficient warning or involved in an activity of great interest. Children may explore what can help them manage change (prior warning, visuals, schedules, itineraries, information, explanations) and what other people can do to help them to manage change and transition.

The environment

Children and others should be aware that some environments can be calming but others can be stressful. Some girls need time to familiarize themselves with an environment before feeling comfortable in it (this might mean they walk around the perimeter of a space to 'feel' it or they may need time to sit quietly in order to adapt to new surroundings). Children should have opportunities to consider the types of environment they personally find calming (some people like quiet environments whereas others prefer some noise and feel uncomfortable with silence). Other people can be considerate and supportive by being aware of the impact of the environment on an autistic child. They can ask the child what might help them and suggest adjustments or accommodations, depending on the child's needs.

Key points

- Anxiety and stress can be an issue for many autistic girls.
- Helping autistic girls to recognize what causes them anxiety and stress can help them to understand themselves and reduce those feelings.
- Sensory aspects of the environment can be either enjoyable or cause overload, so understanding an autistic girl's sensory profile can aid well-being.
- Parents and professionals can help autistic girls feel less anxious by adapting how they communicate with them, changing their expectations of them, understanding the specific needs of the child, and providing routine and predictability.
- Friendships are important to many girls, so helping them manage conflict when it occurs can be really helpful.
- Intense interests make autistic girls feel happy and can provide some rest and relaxation. Intense interests can be a form of self-preservation as they allow time to recharge.
- Autistic girls can benefit from being taught strategies to calm themselves when anxious or stressed. They should be encouraged to offer their own strategies where possible. Strategies might include breathing techniques, time out or physical activity.
- Some autistic girls find it difficult to understand or express feelings or may express themselves in their own valid way.

CHAPTER 5

Be Healthy

This chapter focuses on mental and physical health and well-being, and explores self-care, food and nutrition (including sensory issues with food), exercise, hygiene, rest, relaxation and sleep. It seeks to raise awareness of a range of health conditions that are more common to autistic girls and women. Through focusing on the experiences of autistic girls and women, it discusses what can be done to address the barriers they experience in accessing health services and how health-care professionals can make positive changes. Also discussed is how the environment can impact on health.

Be healthy – context

Autistic girls and women should be able to live long, happy and healthy lives, and their mental and physical health should be a priority. This is because autistic girls and women experience many health inequalities, as well as challenges, but there is much that can be done to address these issues. Autistic girls are diagnosed later in life than autistic boys, and many autistic women have only been diagnosed as adults. Many others remain undiagnosed. Lockwood Estrin *et al.* (2020) state:

> A clear delay in diagnosis for cognitively able girls compared to boys... evident, despite there being no difference in the number of appointments with healthcare professionals during the diagnostic process (Siklos and Kerns 2007), the age at which parents express concern (Begeer *et al.* 2013), or the duration of assessment (Wilson *et al.* 2016). It has also been shown that even with comparable levels of symptom severity, females are less likely than males to receive a diagnosis (Geelhand *et al.* 2019; Russell, Steer and Golding 2011).

As many girls are not being recognized as autistic by schools or by health services, this will have an impact on education and health, which are often inter-related.

Accessing health services

For some autistic girls and women, diagnosed or not, being able to access an appointment with a health professional (general practitioner or other) can present problems. Some find it difficult to speak on the telephone; therefore, the possibility of being able to make appointments in other ways can enable greater access to services for girls and women who might otherwise go without treatment. Making and remembering appointment dates and times can be problematic for some, due to difficulties with planning. Some women find it difficult to think ahead or organize themselves; others can become engrossed in a task and may not remember. This could easily be avoided if reminders could be sent out to those patients who need them. In some cases, when appointments are missed, services are withdrawn, meaning that autistic women who require healthcare do not receive it. Greater understanding and consideration for the needs of autistic girls and women would help them to receive the care they need. Even minor adjustments to the system can make a big difference.

Consistency in care can be beneficial for autistic girls and women. Being able to see the same healthcare professional during appointments can reduce stress – autistic people need sameness, routine and predictability, and having to see an unfamiliar person can heighten stress levels. Preparing for and attending a one-to-one appointment with a health professional can be exhausting for some autistic girls and women, but often this goes unseen. Energy may be used up even before an appointment, due to stress. Waiting rooms can be crowded places, uncomfortable for those who need their own space. Lighting (especially fluorescent lighting), noise (telephones constantly ringing) and smells, for example, can be off-putting for those who have sensory needs or sensitivities. If appointment times are delayed, some autistic people can find this difficult and the pressure can build.

Having to speak to someone in a short, allotted time can increase pressure and many autistic people will feel uncomfortable because they do not like to be put 'on the spot'. In a one-to-one situation there is increased pressure to give and maintain eye contact (to not appear rude) and this can make some girls and women feel uncomfortable. Social contact, for some, can be extremely draining. In addition to this, there is the uncertainty of not knowing what questions might be asked, which some people may find stressful. For those autistic girls and women who find appointments difficult or who may have social anxiety, 'recovery' time may be needed afterwards. Either sitting quietly or having time to enjoy their own interests can help them to wind down. Older girls and women who are self-aware know that situations such as these will cause exhaustion, and are sometimes able to plan the day around an appointment, giving themselves time to recoup energy; younger girls, however, may not have this self-knowledge. Teaching autistic girls about self-care is essential.

Relationships with healthcare professionals are important and there are many working compassionately with autistic girls and women. However, some autistic girls and women worry that when they report concerns about their health, they may not be taken seriously or believed. Some will avoid seeking support or health services as a result. Some say that when they have sought help, they have been dismissed and ignored; that their voices have not been heard. With greater training opportunities for those working in healthcare in relation to autism, there will be increased understanding of the needs of autistic girls and women. With this knowledge, health professionals will become aware of what can stand in the way of accessing the right support and misunderstandings can be avoided. Some examples of scenarios include:

- An autistic girl who appears expressionless may be wrongly interpreted as having no feeling, so is not provided with appropriate support or treatment.
- An autistic girl who is not given time to process language may not be given sufficient opportunity to talk about her own health.

- An autistic girl who cannot communicate in words when in pain is not offered an alternative way to communicate such as a visual pain scale.

People working in health and education can have a positive impact on the mental and physical health of autistic girls. Throughout their lives, autistic girls and women will require services that are adapted to their needs and different perspectives.

Mortality, self-harm, suicide ideation and suicide

Autistic people experience health inequalities not just in childhood but across the lifespan. Those working in health services can help to bring about change by not only adapting how autistic people can access services, but by being aware of the inequalities that exist and adapting their own practice to be more inclusive. There is, according to Hirvikoski *et al.* (2016), 'accumulating evidence indicating that ASD accounts for substantial health loss across the lifespan' and that 'the risk of premature mortality has been reported to be elevated among individuals with ASD, compared with the general population'. It is suggested that this could be because autistic people may have 'difficulties in social interaction and communication [which might] seriously reduce the ability to seek and receive help and treatment'. However, it must be recognized that services and interventions are often not adapted to the needs of autistic people. 'Gender is another possible moderator of excess mortality in ASD', state Hirvikoski *et al.* (2016), who recognize a 'markedly increased premature mortality in ASD owing to a multitude of medical conditions. The risk was particularly high for females with low-functioning ASD.' These women were described as an 'especially vulnerable group in which the mortality risk was nine times higher than in the general population control group'.

Karim and Baines (2016) draw attention to anecdotal higher rates of self-harm, suicidal ideation and suicide attempts in autistic children compared with non-autistic children:

> Nationally and globally there has been considerable concern regarding the apparent increase in the number of young people under the age of 18 who self-harm. This is in comparison to rates of suicide in the UK which have which have remained fairly stable. For autistic children and young people, there are concerns from parents, carers and professionals that self-harm is an even greater problem, but the extent is unclear due to limited research. Significantly however there are reports that suicidal ideation and suicide attempts are 28 times more common in autistic children than in non-autistic children.

What is equally worrying is that autistic women without comorbid learning disability have been found to be most at risk of death by suicide. It is possible that autistic women may not have the same protective factors that many non-autistic women have, such as a wide social circle, and they may have greater difficulty in accessing professional support. Hirvikoski *et al.* (2016) explain:

> For most diagnostic categories, the pattern of mortality risk was comparable in females and males with ASD. Nevertheless, males with ASD had a higher relative risk than females of mortality owing to diseases of the nervous and circulatory systems. On the other hand, females with ASD had higher relative mortality risk than males in diseases owing to endocrine diseases, congenital malformations and suicide.

Fortunately there is increased awareness of the health inequalities that autistic people experience. In the UK, *The Oliver McGowan Mandatory Training in Learning Disability and Autism* seeks to 'ensure staff working in health and social care receive learning disability and autism training, at the right level for their role. They will have a better understanding of people's needs, resulting in better services and improved health and wellbeing outcomes.' Health inequalities are also featured in 'The national strategy for autistic children, young people and adults: 2021 to 2026.'

Mental health and how schools can help

Professionals working in schools can make a positive difference to the mental (and physical health) of autistic girls by valuing, supporting and accepting them as they are. Putting certain measures in place in schools can also help to improve their mental health. Where adults are given adequate training and resources and meet need, autistic girls are less likely to experience mental health issues.

Schools can help autistic girls in the following ways:

- They can provide a structured environment (clutter-free, well-organized and low-arousal) allowing girls to be independent.
- They can provide routine during lessons (including a schedule of what is going to happen during the lesson and in what order).
- They can adapt their practice to take account of sensory needs and sensitivities.
- They can adapt how they communicate (and how much language they use, to avoid overload).
- They can provide opportunities for structured activities at break.
- They can enable girls to attend interest groups or allow them to spend time alone.
- They can support girls with friendships.
- They should take reports of bullying seriously.
- They can help girls to build social understanding.
- They can teach girls to understand and express emotions and help them to understand how other people might think and feel.

- They can be understanding of autistic girls (see the world from their perspective).
- They can help girls to cope with change.

Girls should be listened to and valued. They will benefit from opportunities to spend time doing what they are good at, achieving goals at the right pace. They should be taught to understand themselves, calm themselves down and relax. They will also benefit greatly from being taught to problem solve and make decisions (they should be encouraged to think things through rather than act impulsively).

Professionals can be supportive of autistic girls by understanding why they camouflage and mask, and how girls are often forced to adapt themselves (see Chapter 4). When girls understand their own strengths and needs, they can become more positive and accepting of themselves. Mental health issues can arise for a combination of reasons – for example, the strain of having to adapt on a regular basis, tolerate unbearable environments, and cope with being misunderstood and misjudged by others can leave girls feeling overwhelmed..

Flexible approaches can allow schools to take into consideration the specific needs of each child, which helps each one to feel they are valued and accepted as they are. Children need boundaries, but what one child needs is different to that of another. Flexibility is preferable to having rigid rules or systems and policies that must be adhered to at all costs (for example, strict uniform, behaviour and homework policies). Accepting autistic girls for who they are means they are less likely to compare themselves to their non-autistic peers and view themselves as 'broken', ' wrong', or 'an outsider' who doesn't fit the mould, all of which can also lead to mental health issues.

Food and nutrition

Autistic girls can benefit from learning about healthy eating as being more aware of the different nutrients in food can help them understand why a balanced diet is necessary. For girls who are more literal in their understanding, the choice of language will matter. For example, girls should be made aware that no food is a 'bad' food but that all foods can be consumed in moderation.

Some autistic girls have issues with certain foods because of sensory sensitivities. They may detest the smell of certain foods, which can cause problems when eating out or at home, but this can be avoided if they are seated away from strong smells. Some autistic girls will seek out certain foods and will enjoy strong flavours (spicy or 'hot'), which is not a problem unless too much is consumed; others prefer bland foods. The textures of certain foods can be enjoyable or intolerable, depending on preference. Sensory aspects of the environment can also affect an autistic child – having either a positive or negative impact – so a regular routine in a calm, non-pressurized environment can make mealtimes more enjoyable.

Because of the need for routine and predictability, eating the same foods on a regular basis (for example, the same school lunch everyday) can feel safe and predictable. Some children know immediately if a certain food product has been substituted with another brand. While some will have no problem with this, others will refuse the substitute outright or become upset by the change. Sarah provides the following advice to autistic girls who may struggle with trying new foods:

> Food has never been easy for me. I only ate a few foods as a child because I am extremely sensitive to taste, but in my teen years I managed to start expanding my diet. My advice is if you want to be able to eat more food, I would do it slowly and gradually, so your senses get used to new tastes and textures. Also, do not try new food under pressure – it is important to feel relaxed and comfortable when you are trying new food. At first, I started trying food that was similar to what I could eat. I would smell it first (sometimes a few times) before I would

> try a bite. I would only eat a tiny amount the first time, and if I found the food okay, I would eat some more. After a few times of thinking a particular food was okay, I would generally be happy to eat it.

Some autistic girls may like to eat foods in a certain order, or in a certain way; others may have an issue with the temperature of foods and drinks, having a preference for either hot or cold. Sometimes, even having certain foods together on the plate, or touching, can cause upset. This can be because one food may make another food wet, and the person may prefer to keep certain foods dry. Some autistic children have a preference for the type of cups, plates and cutlery they use; others need particular items of crockery and cutlery to aid independence on account of their motor skills.

Not all autistic girls are able to read the body signals that tell them that are hungry or full, so they may need to be reminded when to eat or when to stop. As well as considering the sensory aspects of eating, it is important to consider the social aspects of mealtimes and eating out, as this can be problematic for some girls, especially if they have social anxiety. Some girls might prefer to eat alone or may prefer to eat with their family rather than in the presence of others, whereas others will find eating out enjoyable. Eating out to celebrate special occasions can, for some girls, be difficult to manage, but advance preparation can help. Being able to select foods from the menu and being able to choose where to sit in advance can reduce stress.

Change and transition can sometimes cause stress levels to increase, which may affect eating and weight gain or weight loss. Some autistic girls who lack the structure and routine they need may attempt to control what they eat as a way of providing themselves with order. Recognizing this, and providing greater structure in the girl's life, can help her feel in control. Another reason why some autistic girls may not eat is because they become so engrossed in an activity or interest that they simply forget, so an alarm or other reminder can be useful.

It can be difficult for some autistic girls and women to achieve balance in life – managing demands and expectations, as well as finding time to care for themselves, taking time out when needed, and remembering to eat. Those who also have a family to care for may find this especially difficult, though having a routine can help. Self-care is vital to well-being, especially for autistic girls and women.

Some autistic girls give much consideration to what they eat, taking a keen interest in food and nutrition. For some, food can become an 'intense interest', as Mandy and Tchanturia (2015) highlight: 'It is interesting to note that she has some interests, such as fashion and veganism, which are not inherently unusual, but which she pursues with an unusual, and possibly autistic, intensity.' Some autistic girls like to learn about food, nutrition, and particular diets such as vegetarianism and veganism because they care about the planet or about animal welfare, or because they have food allergies or to certain foods. Having an intense interest in food and nutrition can be a positive thing, and some autistic girls will go on to be nutritionists. It is important, however, that an intense interest does not develop into something that negatively affects health. Some autistic girls can become overly detail-focused, counting calories and logging food intake.

There is growing awareness that many girls and women who have an eating disorder may be autistic. A 'PEACE Pathway' blog (PEACE stands for Pathway for Eating disorders and Autism developed from Clinical Experience) states that women with anorexia nervosa have 'been found to possess greater number of autistic traits than typical women.' We also know that eating disorders are more prevalent in females than males. According to Mandy and Tchanturia (2015), 'males are at greater risk of ASD than females, whereas EDs [Eating Disorders] shows the converse gender ratio, affecting 10 females for every male (Mandy *et al.* 2012; Smink *et al.* 2014).' Mandy and Tchanturia (2015) recognize that 'more work is needed to test the hypothesis that ASD is a causal risk factor for ED', but it is thought that possible explanations might be due to the need for repetition and sameness, inflexibility of thought (though autistic people can be very considerate and adaptable to the thoughts of others), being obsessive (though I prefer the term 'intense'), and social and communication differences. It is suggested that some autistic girls may restrict their food intake as a way of fitting in with peers.

It is thought some autistic girls and women who have an eating disorder may be less concerned with weight or body shape, but may have sensory-related food issues or alexithymia. Vuillier *et al.* (2020) state: 'Our findings showed that alexithymia, most particularly difficulties identifying emotions, may partially explain the prevalence of eating disorder symptomatology in females with high autistic traits.' Some women experienced social difficulties prior to the onset of an eating disorder. Mandy and Tchanturia (2015) state:

> Reports from the women with autism spectrum classifications suggested that their difficulties were longstanding, and predated the onset of their ED. Neither appears to have ever had a close or sustained friendship, and their eating difficulties were preceded by painful experiences of social isolation and bullying at school.

ARFID (Avoidant/restrictive food intake disorder) Awareness UK say:

> Eating disorders such as Anorexia Nervosa (AN) or Bulimia Nervosa (BN) can appear in adolescence or early adulthood... For some autistic girls and women, controlling eating is a way to manage overwhelming feelings of anxiety. This can be particularly true during adolescence where physical changes such as puberty and social and academic pressures can cause anxiety to spiral out of control. As a result, it is very important that such anxiety and associated eating problems are recognized early and given the right support. (ARFID nd)

With increasing interest and research in this field, sharing expertise means that treatments can be adapted to take into account the differing needs of autistic women: their communication differences, social and emotional needs, sensory sensitivities and requirements. Environments could be adapted to be more calming rather than overstimulating.

ARFID Awareness UK say it is known that 'autistic people are much more likely to develop ARFID...as are those with ADHD and intellectual disabilities [and some children will have a] pattern of eating that avoids certain foods entirely/or is restricted in quantity (eating small amounts)' (ARFID nd). They state that some people have 'sensory sensitivity, fear of negative consequences or a lack of interest in eating'. Moreover, they can be 'sensitive to the taste, texture or appearance of certain types of food, or have had a distressing experience with food [which may] cause the person to develop fear and anxiety around food'.

Advice and insights on eating disorders

Hope Virgo, author and founder of #DumpTheScales

> Eleven years ago, I was standing in a hospital doorway, my hair thinning, my skin a yellowish colour. I was wearing a short denim skirt and a pink jumper that drowned me. Tears were welling in my eyes as my mum signed me in. I begged her to let me come home, begged her for one more chance. I promised her I would begin to eat. But mum said no. She couldn't take it anymore: the lies and the deceit. I hated her then, and everyone around me. I couldn't understand why they were interfering in my life. There wasn't anything wrong with me. I had lost a bit of weight, yes, but I wasn't that skinny. I was nowhere near thin enough to die. (Virgo 2019)

Current stats show that eating disorders affect over one million people in the UK, and that anorexia holds the highest mortality rate out of any psychiatric disorder. In the majority of cases, eating disorder is still an illness that is misunderstood and the fixation is purely on how it presents itself physically. There are many different types of eating disorders, and each person who develops one will have their own unique story around it. Specific eating disorders include anorexia nervosa, bulimia nervosa, binge eating disorder, diabulimia and pica. It is important to remember that whilst these conditions are about eating behaviours, there is so much more to them than food.

I was diagnosed with anorexia when I was 17 years old but had lived with the illness for the previous four years. When I was 13 years old, my family life got harder and I was sexually abused. These things took those painful feelings to a whole other level: a level of uncertainty and distress, a level where I just knew I didn't want to feel things anymore. Instead of trying to talk about things, I needed to find other coping mechanisms. Like so many others who have eating disorders, the eating disorder behaviours for me were a symptom of something else, whether trauma-related or other. It is vital in recovery that the underlying issue is properly dealt with, or the person is likely to go back to those unhealthy coping mechanisms.

The other issue that often comes up with individuals is that they are unable to accept something is the matter; and when they do, the guilt they feel around it can be huge. When I think back to my diagnosis, this is exactly what happened. It was at my second appointment that they diagnosed me with anorexia. At this point I was in complete and utter denial about it. I didn't think there was anything the matter with me – definitely not anorexia! I just had this best friend in my head and I loved it. I convinced myself that everyone wanted to make me fat, that they were just jealous of what I had and wanted it, but I wasn't going to let them. Instead I was going to up my game. What followed after that appointment was six months as an outpatient where I convinced myself (well, Anorexia convinced me) that I was super-happy. But actually I wasn't. There were times when I hated that voice in my head. Times when I didn't have the energy to even stand up in the shower, sitting there with the water pouring over me, my brain battling it out.

Eating disorders present in so many different ways. They are illnesses that are secretive and devious, but the fact remains that recovery is 100 percent possible. Recovery will look different to all of you, and it might change over time and that is okay (it certainly has for me – going from a place of functioning, to living a bit more, dipping my toe in and then really starting to commit to this fully!).

If you are starting your road to recovery, I would suggest reaching out to your GP. More often than not they will turn you away if your Body Mass Index (BMI) is not quite what they are looking for (see my #DumpTheScales campaign) – but be bold and go back, keep asking for that support. When you go to your doctor, ask them what they are doing to offer you support. Look at other support that is out there, from charities to other professionals. If you feel able to go with someone else to the appointment, it might help you to write down the facts beforehand. You might think about how you feel, whether you are able to express it, and you might think about how long you have been feeling like this. If they are not able to refer you, please do ask for some additional interim support. What also helped me was journaling my thoughts afterwards!

The eating disorder will make the individual feel really

guilty for reaching out, but it is so important to make that initial step.

Right now, there is no denying it, eating disorder services are massively overstretched, so if you are struggling with an eating disorder and unable to seek support, there are a few things you can do:

- Keep going back to your GP. Be persistent. (I know this might make you feel uncomfortable but you do deserve support.)
- I wrote meal plans to help me get back on track.
- Each day I reminded myself why I wanted to get well.
- My mum and sister would text me to check I had eaten.
- My boyfriend monitored my exercise.
- I booked lots of fun things to do.
- I talked a lot. I told people I was struggling, that I wanted to give up but at the same time didn't want to. I was so vocal that I didn't have to express myself with food.

An autistic woman

Growing up undiagnosed, I knew there was something 'wrong' with me but I didn't know what it was. I struggled to make friends and made social mistakes that resulted in scolding from adults and exclusion from peers. At the same time, I had extreme food selectivity issues, which were rooted in cognitive rigidity and sensory sensitivities. The kinds of food I would eat caused me to gain quite a bit of weight, which worsened the bullying and consternation from adults. I came to understand that I was a bad person – I must be, based on the things people said and the way they were around me. I think a good deal of the bullying was actually more related to my weirdness and social difficulties than my weight, but weight is something a lot easier for a child's mind to grasp. At some point, my badness became inseparably centred around my weight, which illuminated a pathway to a happier life. If only I could lose weight, if only I could get thin, the bullying would stop, people would like me, and I would be a good person.

Throughout my teenage years, I was on one crash diet after another – absolutely desperate, because being me was so intolerable, I was such a worthless person. Puberty added an extra layer of awful into the mix – I struggled with personal hygiene, so became even more alienated and bullied. In my head, my weight was cemented as the 'thing that was wrong with me' – perhaps it was the easiest thing for me to grasp, with my concrete, black-and-white thinking. I did not descend into a restrictive eating disorder until I reached my 20s, when I finally learnt how to eat salads and vegetables. As soon as I could do this, I ate nothing else, and I finally had the means to lose weight.

I was a bloody good dieter. Here is where all the autistic features come in handy. I can eat exactly the same thing every day and be quite happy. I have these convictions around my weight being this thing I have to fix in order to be good and likeable, and like other autistic people, my thinking is very fixed and obsessive. I don't have days off. I don't have what my friend calls a 'f*** it' button – I don't have those moments which other people have where they just say, 'Oh sod it, I'll break my diet today.' I dieted like a fiend, utterly fixed on one numerical target after another. I started dieting from a high weight, and because Western society is highly fat-phobic, I received intense praise and social reinforcement for my weight loss. I had friends, a boyfriend, and felt likeable for the first time in my life, so why would I want to stop?

That single-minded obsession came in here – I just had to

focus on getting to a number, then I just kept going, because of that black-and-white thinking – there was no point where it wouldn't be good to go further, because the less I weighed, the better I would be. I didn't think further than the numbers in terms of what it meant and where it would stop. I had these rules, and if I followed them, I was good and I felt okay. If I broke them, I was bad, and I had this feeling that 'bad things would happen'. These were around gaining weight again, because in my head, there was really no state in between where I was right then and me at my heavier, bullied state. The lower my weight, the further away I was from that, the safer I was.

Anorexia also made my world small, predictable and controllable. Social relationships were still exhausting and highly stressful, and I found it impossible to manage conflict. At one point, I had a crystal moment of clarity, realizing that I didn't NEED to feel – 'Let's go running, right now!' Not a sensible thing to do in the middle of the night as a young woman, but... It was like a revelation. I got my music and off I went, and then I wasn't crying any more. I didn't need to worry about my relationship, my job and career – I could go running, I could diet. My world narrowed to that point where all I needed to worry about was how to lose weight. The more I lost, the lighter I was, the better I would be.

Having gone into science, I now understand how my experience appears to align with the literature around vulnerability for eating disorders in autism (for example, Brede *et al.* 2020; Kerr-Gaffney *et al.* 2020). Factors which have been suggested to make autistic people vulnerable include: difficulties with social interaction (which cause distress and low self-esteem); alexithymia and difficulties with emotion regulation (for instance, where an individual discovers that eating disordered behaviours help them 'feel better', even if they don't understand what they're feeling); and cognitive rigidity and black-and-white thinking (perhaps around food rules and rituals). The intense focus of autistic people could lend itself to dieting if an autistic person so chooses. Some autistic people struggle with interoception, which means that they have difficulty identifying signals like hunger and thirst – this, again, is a 'useful' trait for dieting. Autistic people are also very likely to struggle with food selectivity (Kinnaird *et al.* 2019; Reinoso *et al.* 2018) – having a very restricted diet, which can cause them social difficulties and, like me, problems with their weight and nutrition. Perhaps relatedly, they are more likely to have higher BMIs and larger bodies (Matheson and Douglas 2017). This is a difficult intersection, if it occurs. If eating disordered behaviours result in weight loss and subsequent praise, then this makes them powerfully reinforcing for a person with low self-worth. Eating disorders are often identified later in those who previously were at higher weights, such that behaviours are more likely to be entrenched. Psychologically and physiologically, individuals who present with higher weights but greater proportionate weight loss can actually be more compromised than those who are thinner when diagnosed with an eating disorder (Matthews *et al.* 2021; Meierer *et al.* 2019).

Anecdotally, I believe early diagnosis is crucial in the hopes of avoiding other labels that might be attached to the individual (for example, 'bad'). A diagnosis may also be helpful in that it may allow parents to recognize how the autistic profile could fuel an eating disorder if turned that way; they may be more alert to ideas their autistic child expresses around food, weight, shape and self-esteem.

Exercise

For autistic girls, physical exercise can improve health, being beneficial for the mind and body, though the type of exercise each girl will enjoy, or be able to take part in, will depend on the individual and her specific needs. For autistic girls who like routine and predictability, trying out new activities can be challenging so it's important to find suitable activities to do, as an autistic woman in her twenties explains:

> One thing I have learnt about myself is the importance of finding exercise that is sensory-friendly for you. I don't like most forms of exercise, but I have found the ones I enjoy, and that makes me feel good afterwards. For me, I love the feeling of bouncing on a trampoline or swimming in water. It may take some time to find the right exercise for you, but it's worth trying something at least once if you feel comfortable taking part.

Autistic girls are more likely to try out new experiences if they are prepared in advance, if there is no pressure to take part and if new environments can be made more familiar. Allowing them to first observe, rather than participate, can help them to feel more comfortable. Going past the venue a few times and looking at photographs of the venue and the staff can make the experience feel less uncertain.

Health needs, mobility and motor skills also need to be considered as autistic girls can sometimes have co-occurring conditions that affect the type of exercise they can do, as well as how often. These include ADHD, dyspraxia and hypermobility, with hypermobility being more common in women (Casanova *et al.* 2018; Green nd; Hakim and Graham 2003).

Some girls have difficulties physical exercise, motor skills and co-ordination. They can appear to be clumsy when taking part in sports, though this can relate to not having an awareness of their body in space (proprioception), meaning that they may accidently bump into other people or things. In P.E. lessons at school they may find verbal instructions or rules difficult to follow (this can relate to language ability and sometimes memory). Often they cannot imagine something they have no experience of (therefore, demonstrations can be helpful). Sequencing can be difficult, too, especially if there are too many steps to follow.

Some children may have sensory sensitivities that interfere with exercise (for example, the acoustics of a large sports hall can interfere with listening, it can be difficult to listen whilst concentrating on movement during a game, lighting is often an issue, clothing can be a problem). Some girls find it difficult to switch from one activity to another too quickly (or from one rule to another rule). They may be afraid of making 'mistakes' in front of peers. They may find that winning and losing is an issue or they may not like being competitive. Autistic girls can benefit from concise instructions and being shown what to do. This can be reinforced through visuals if necessary. Sensory sensitivities can be taken into consideration when planning activities. Providing sufficient time to finish an activity before preparing for the next can also be helpful. *Social Stories*™ (Gray 2015) and other visuals can aid understanding in relation to winning, losing and being competitive.

In contrast, some autistic girls have incredible balance or become highly accomplished due to having an intense interest in a particular sport. Whichever type of activity autistic girls engage in, there are numerous benefits for the body. Exercise can also provide many mental health benefits, especially for autistic girls who ruminate or who over-analyse social situations, which can lead to stress. Some girls prefer to exercise alone, whereas others will enjoy the connection gained from being part of a group.

Exercise as an outlet for stress and can help girls to deal with difficult emotions in a safe way. For girls who find it difficult to express emotions in words, or for those who are not given the opportunity to express feelings, or for those who feel they are not heard, this is especially important. Teaching autistic girls to link the causes of stress directly to strategies that help, including exercise or physical activity, can improve their physical and mental health. Physical exercise can help girls to feel calm, as can finding time to engage in intense interests or other activities. Florence Neville (co-founder of Autism Health and Wellbeing) explains how finding time for self-care can help autistic people to feel less overwhelmed with life, allowing them to recharge.

> It is really important for autistic people to find or create the time and space just 'to be'. It helps us to avoid getting too overwhelmed, reduces the chance of a meltdown, and gives us the energy we need to manage the challenges we face every day. Sitting quietly under a tree, walking a dog, planting seeds, paddling in the sea, finding somewhere cosy to read, knit, sketch or dream, playing an instrument, coding, dancing... Finding your own way to just 'be you' will help you to feel calmer, stronger and happier. (Personal communication)

What non-autistic people might find straightforward or routine, can be stressful for some autistic children. Florence says:

> Building in recovery time after what might seem like routine day-to-day activities is vital. If you plan something like going to a supermarket, changing a bedroom layout, going on a school trip, starting a new routine, going back to school after a holiday, having a friend visit, or getting a haircut, you may also need to plan for a lot of rest time afterwards. A nap, re-watching old episodes of a favourite show, some planned stim-time or playing a computer game may be helpful. Planning for a few hours' recovery after stressful events allows us to adapt and revive quicker than when we are expected to carry on without a break. (Personal communication)

Change, transition, and health

Many autistic girls and women experience significantly increased anxiety and stress during times of change and transition in their lives and this can have an impact on their health. Changes that may seem insignificant to some people can cause worry or anxiety for others. For a school-aged autistic child, changes in staffing, room changes, unexpected activities, being asked to do something at short notice, changing year groups, moving schools could all potentially cause upset. Other changes across the lifespan might include changes in friendships or relationships, getting a new job, changing jobs, having a child, separation, divorce or bereavement.

All autistic people will react to change differently. Some will become being quiet or withdrawn; others will react loudly. Stress due to change can have an impact on the body resulting in stomach aches, constipation or diarrhoea. Muskens, Velder and Staal (2017) note: 'The study of Valicenti-McDermott *et al.* found that children with ASD had a significantly higher rate of gastro-intestinal (GI) symptoms than children with either typical development or other developmental disabilities'.

Change can affect a person's sleep, ability to relax, eating habits, weight, thoughts, choices and actions. Change can make life feel less certain, so helping girls to plan for change in advance can make life seem safe and familiar. Autistic girls need to be aware of how change can affect their health so that they are better equipped to manage different life events, especially those that are unexpected. Autistic girls can be prepared for changes such as puberty by informing them about what to expect (physically and emotionally) before they reach that stage. As well as learning about body awareness, girls need to learn about privacy. As they mature and their bodies develop, some will become more self-aware and self-conscious, whereas others will not pay attention to their changing body. Some girls will not be aware of how other people see them or of other people's intentions, so it is important to explore various topics around the subject of safety.

Self-image, body image and the media should be discussed, as autistic girls will learn from watching others and this may not be a true representation of real life.

Autistic girls also need to build up social understanding – learning about what's considered appropriate and inappropriate, with whom and when, as these are not the type of skills that they can pick up in the same way as their non-autistic peers might. Helping girls to develop communication skills will enable them to build good relationships with others and others should adapt the way they communicate, respecting the autistic girl's communication differences. Autistic girls need to understand what is meant by a healthy and unhealthy relationship, how people should speak to each other and respect each other, and about responsibility and choices in relationships. They should learn about security and stability.

Pregnancy

When teaching autistic girls about pregnancy, it is necessary to explain this from an autistic perspective as autistic women will experience different issues and needs. Firstly, girls need clear, concise, direct information and need to know the facts about contraception, sexually transmitted infections (STIs), how people become pregnant, the stages of pregnancy and what to expect after the birth of a child. Pregnancy will raise many issues for autistic people, especially as the body changes so dramatically. Many will have sensory issues (for example with foods, smells and clothing). They will also be expected to attend appointments with unfamiliar people, in unfamiliar environments, and be expected to communicate preferences, which may be difficult if in pain.

Karen Henry, who created the 'Pregnancy Passport' (East Suffolk and North Essex NHS Foundation, Leeds and York Partnership NHS Foundation Trust nd) that allows autistic people who are pregnant to share their thoughts, needs and preferences with healthcare staff explains:

> For many women with autism, pregnancy can provoke fear and anxiety due to a changing body and changing routines. Women are expected to understand information to enable decisions for care. This can be difficult for women who find that listening and retaining information in new surroundings can be difficult due to sensory difficulties. For such women, differing methods of communication may be required.

The health of autistic girls and women is paramount, especially as research suggests that autistic women are at greater risk of having a 'medically indicated preterm birth' and that there may be 'a need for individual prenatal care for women with autism with a better understanding of the difficulties related to autism, especially regarding the communication with healthcare professionals' (Sundelin *et al.* 2018). For autistic girls and women to experience better health, professionals need to be fully trained in understanding the needs of autistic people and should make adjustments to accommodate them.

Sleep

Getting sufficient sleep can improve well-being as it allows the body and mind to relax, provides us with enough energy for the day ahead and helps us to be more resilient. Insufficient sleep can affect the physical body and our emotions and how our brains function. Unfortunately, I have met many autistic children who have sleep problems, and the reasons why they struggle to get to sleep, find it difficult to stay asleep, or cannot get enough sleep, vary.

Some autistic children need the advice or guidance of a health professional in relation to sleep difficulties, but there are various strategies that children, their parents and professionals should consider first.

Sometimes at school (or when home learning), some children find it difficult to take in and process vast amounts of information. If a child spends six or more hours learning, listening to people talking, reading and socializing, her brain has a considerable amount to process. She cannot just switch off, and may need time to relax before going to bed. Environments can also overstimulate (for example bright lights, smells, colours, disorder), so this is an additional factor that can lead to autistic children feeling overwhelmed. Schools can help by being clutter-free and well ordered. Professionals working in schools (and parents teaching children at home) can help children by breaking lessons down into manageable chunks and by providing breaks or time to pursue interests in-between formal learning. Another way to help autistic children to feel less overloaded is to base their school work on their own interests.

In the home, keeping the bedroom orderly can help the child to feel more comfortable (some will find patterned wallpaper, bedding and curtains overstimulating, but ask the child). The temperature of the room and bedding will be important. Some girls like soft, fluffy bedding whereas others may prefer cool, cotton sheets and layers they can pull off if they get too hot. This depends on the child and their sensory needs and sensitivities.

Some children benefit from a routine (for example, having a shower or bath, doing a calming activity such as reading or looking at something of interest) before going to bed.

Some children find it difficult to sleep if they start to dwell on worries about what has happened during the day or worry about the day ahead. Chapter 4 discusses strategies for managing worries and Dr Craig Goodall (Chapter 2) offers advice about getting organized for the next day.

Sensory toys, soft lighting and listening to music can help some children to feel calm at night time. As always, it is important to work with the child to figure out what will help – often they know best and are happy to make suggestions. Pavlopoulou (2020) states:

> It is thus important for the sleep practitioners and healthcare providers to move beyond providing standardized sleep hygiene interventions. A Lifeworld-led care model that pays attention to personal experiences, promotes sense of agency, evaluates both autism-specific strengths and struggles could and should complement biomedical approaches.

Pavlopoulou (2020) recognizes:

> It is important to further examine both the daytime and evening factors that may affect bedtime and the quality and quantity of sleep, as well as the role of intense focused interests and physical activities that cultivate positive feelings and help autistic people to relax before bedtime.

Be healthy – what can autistic girls benefit from knowing, exploring or learning, and what should others be aware of?

Parents, carers and professionals should know that autistic children will learn, experience and perceive the world in different ways and that this can have an impact on mental and physical health and general well-being.

They should be aware of the following:

- People have different personalities.
- People have different coping mechanisms and can be more/less resilient than others.
- People's perspectives are different (some people focus on positives rather than on negatives).
- People think differently to each other.
- People have different bodies.
- People have different needs.
- Some people have sensory needs or sensitivities.

- People have different beliefs that can affect their health and choices.

People should be treated fairly and equally and with respect, whatever their needs are. Children should learn why it is important to care about their own mental and physical health, and develop vocabulary that relates to their health and well-being (reinforced by visuals where this is helpful).

Mental health

Autistic girls should learn what is meant by 'mental health', how physical health can affect mental health and vice versa, and that how a person feels can affect their mental and physical health. They should explore the factors affecting mental health (a sense of belonging, being excluded, self-perception, how people are treated by others, experiences) and be able to recognize **when** support is needed in relation to mental health, **who** to ask for support and **how** to develop an awareness of what affects their mental health either positively or negatively (this might be when they are with a particular person or people, when taking part in certain activities, when involved in activities alone or as part of a group, when engaging in hobbies or interests, or when working towards a goal). They may learn what is meant by mental illness, and what anxiety is (including the difference between 'worry' and 'anxiety'). They may learn about depression and be aware of the reasons why autistic people may be at greater risk of anxiety and depression (for example, being misunderstood in society by others and being expected to adapt). Children should know about people who can help if a person has anxiety or depression (for example, GP, mental health services), understand what can be done to alleviate (or reduce) stress and anxiety (what they can do for themselves and what other people can do to help, and how the environment and sensory needs have an impact on anxiety). It is important that other people, as well as the child, explore the barriers that autistic people might have in relation to accessing mental health support and are aware of organizations that support people in terms of mental health.

Physical health

Children should learn about self-care and how to look after their own body (sleep, rest, relaxation, a balanced diet, exercise and the consequences of being inactive). They can learn why and how others may be needed to look after their physical health, and they may be able to identify who these people might be (parents, health professionals) and their role. They should develop an understanding that those who support them health-wise should behave respectfully towards them and treat them with dignity (in terms of language used, touch, withholding support, threatening behaviour). They should know who to communicate with (and explore alternatives to speaking if this may be difficult) if there are any concerns. Children will need different levels of support at different ages and stages, depending on their specific needs. Children should be aware that they may have expectations of themselves, and that other people will have expectations of them, in relation to self-care. A girl might consider:

- What do parents/teachers/health professionals expect me to be able to do for myself, and is this reasonable given my needs?
- Are there some things that are difficult for me to do that other people might be unaware of?
- Do I find it difficult to start looking after myself?
- Do I find it difficult to manage change as I am growing up?
- What help might I need?

Girls can consider difficulties in terms of remembering and attending appointments (reminders, schedules, reading materials). They can be taught to recognize different types of physical illness (for example, if they have lost weight or notice changes in their body). They should know that some people may find it difficult to recognize when they are unwell or in pain, whereas others will be hyper-sensitive; some people may find it difficult to explain in words how their body feels or the severity of their pain so may need to use non-verbal methods of alerting others to health issues.

Sleep, rest and relaxation

Autistic girls should consider the importance of sleep: how it helps us to feel refreshed and allows us time to process the events of the day. They may learn about the difficulties some autistic people experience in relation to sleeping. For example, they may:

- have difficulty getting to sleep
- have rigid routines about going to sleep (thinking they must go to bed at a certain time although they may not be tired)
- go to sleep but wake up many times throughout the night
- go to sleep, wake up and be unable to get back to sleep
- need to seek help from health professionals and may need medication to help them sleep.

Autistic girls should explore the factors that can cause difficulty sleeping for some people:

- Their brain has been overstimulated due to too much information.
- They have not had enough opportunities to take time out or to feel calm throughout the day.
- They have a medical condition.

- Social contact can drain energy leaving a person feeling exhausted (this can mean being overtired and unable to sleep, or sleeping too much).

Lack of sleep can affect the mind and body, so it is important for children to find out about methods and strategies that aid sleep for some people and consider what might work for them. They also need to know when and how to seek help for sleep difficulties. Some people experience sensory issues in relation to sleep and the environment: some prefer to sleep with some light whereas others do not want any light at all; some may need 'white noise' to help them sleep, whereas others may prefer quiet; some may dislike textures, or feel too hot or too cold; some may dislike a cluttered, busy room and find coloured, patterned wallpaper/bedding overstimulate them, etc.

Children can learn that autistic people may enjoy repetitive activities and that these can provide them with rest, relaxation and well-being. Girls can explore what helps them to feel relaxed and know that this might be different for other people. They should understand that autistic people may need solitude to recharge and relax. Autistic people may have intense interests that they find calming (at the same time they can develop strengths due to the time devoted to these interests). Children can learn to understand that, for some autistic people, social situations can cause anxiety and that some people need information and advance planning and information before events to help make them less stressful.

Hygiene

Depending on their needs and level of independence, autistic children should learn what is considered appropriate or inappropriate in relation to keeping their bodies clean. They should also learn about keeping themselves private in different places and environments and what is appropriate or inappropriate behaviour on the part of others. Autistic children should learn, explore and consider how to keep their body clean and how often, how to keep their teeth clean and how often, how to keep their hair clean and how often to wash/brush it, and how to look after their own nails (or ask for help if necessary).

They may also learn about:

- personal choices in relation to hygiene (i.e. products that help to keep the body, hair and teeth clean, including those that are natural or chemical-based)
- keeping hair healthy – brushing it, sensory issues (the child may dislike having her hair brushed), having it cut (including being prepared for and managing hairdresser appointments), choices in relation to hair removal
- privacy when undressing and washing
- the consequences of not keeping the body/teeth clean
- hygiene in relation to clothing and keeping clothes clean (including when and how to wash, iron, fold, and store clothing)
- types of clothing and what is meant by formal and informal clothing – they may think about personal choice when choosing clothing and expressing the self through clothing
- keeping themselves private when getting changed inside and outside of the home (for example, close the door if in a cubicle when getting changed at swimming)
- what help might be needed from others to keep themselves and their clothes clean
- sensory perceptions and how these affect hygiene (they may be under-responsive to their own body odour, they may like the smell of their own body, they may be over-responsive and dislike the smell of certain products, they may dislike the texture of sanitary products)
- sensory perceptions and clothing (for example, some children

may like the feel of certain clothing, some may dislike tags in clothing, others may want to wear the same clothes repeatedly and may struggle with new clothes).

Dental hygiene

Autistic children should know how to keep their teeth clean and the consequences of not doing so. They should be informed about how often to brush their teeth and the variety of products that can be used to keep teeth clean, including when and where to buy them and how often to replace them. They should understand about sensory issues (for example a dislike of the flavour of toothpaste, or the feel of dental floss) that might affect keeping teeth clean and how these can be resolved. They may become aware of how food and drink (and other life choices) can affect their teeth.

They should understand why visiting a dentist for check-ups and treatment is necessary and know how to make a dental appointment and what to say if they are able. They should learn that some people find it difficult to express pain such as toothache, but might be able to communicate it in ways other than words (visuals, for example). For people who struggle with organization, an appointment reminder might be necessary (perhaps a calendar for them to check the week ahead). Children may need to be prepared in advance for an appointment and should be aware of what visiting a dentist might be like (the room, the sounds, the smells, how the dentist might be dressed) to minimize anxiety. It may be worthwhile visiting the dental practice in advance of the appointment so that the child becomes more accustomed to it. Some children will experience other difficulties and challenges, so it's important to consider how these could be addressed (i.e. sensory needs, bright lights, smells, uncertainty, noise).

Food and nutrition

It is important for children to learn about what is meant by a balanced diet and a healthy lifestyle. They may learn about balance and moderation and consider what healthy eating is. They should be taught that foods contain different nutrients and know why these are needed by the body. Some people like to eat the same foods repeatedly and prefer predictability and sameness in relation to **what** they eat, **how** they eat and **where** they eat.

Some people may be averse to, or seek out, different foods because of sensory sensitivities or needs. They may not like the smell, texture or colour of certain foods, have difficulty trying new foods, prefer bland foods or, alternatively, strong flavours. The environment where food is eaten often has a positive or negative effect on a person (for example, they may find it difficult to be in a room, café or restaurant due to sensitivities to smell). Some have food-related phobias (this can relate to smells, noises such as the crinkle of a crisp bag, colours, etc) and can explore how these can be managed. Some people are highly attuned to differences in the tastes of certain foods, so may only like specific flavours or brands.

Autistic girls, parents and professionals should be aware that some people can be detail focussed or goal oriented and this might affect their food intake. Some people might become overly interested in calorie counting, be determined to reach a certain weight, may be dedicated to achieving a specific aim in relation to how they might want their body to look (whether this is achievable or not, or healthy) and may be intensely driven. They should also be aware that when hyper-focussed on other things, some people may accidentally forget to eat because they are engrossed in an activity. They may (or may not) appreciate reminders or other strategies to remind them to stop and eat.

Some people may be interested in calorie counting or achieving a certain weight. Children should learn about eating disorders as they can affect autistic people, especially girls and women, and how to receive support.

Physical exercise

Autistic girls may understand why being active can be beneficial for health (it reduces the risk of illness, can help us to live longer and improve mental health) and learn about different types of physical activity, personal preferences and needs. Some people prefer physical activity that is done alone, while others prefer to be part of a group or alongside other people. The benefits of different types of activity should be explored (for example, some may like the sense of belonging without the pressure to communicate, some may prefer a quiet, solitary activity as they need to wind down following social contact). Some people prefer to do exercise in certain environments or may need adjustments (for example, gyms may be too bright, too noisy or too smelly for people with sensitivities). The benefits of exercise can include being outdoors in the fresh air and connecting with others (even if momentarily), so that they feel less isolated, refreshed, revitalized and calm.

Drugs and alcohol

Autistic girls need to know about the effect of alcohol and drugs on the brain and body, and the wider consequences of alcohol and drug misuse for their health, their family, employment, finances, decision making and behaviour. Children should learn what legal and illegal drugs are, explore the reasons why people take them, understand the law relating to drugs, and the risks associated with using them. Autistic children should explore healthy ways to relax, socialize and manage sensory sensitivities and social anxiety. (Strategies for relaxation and sleep are discussed in Chapter 4.) Autistic girls should be aware of the dangers of using alcohol to feel less socially at ease and the risks this might entail for health and safety. Autistic girls should be aware that it is beneficial to be with people who understand and accept them and their boundaries.

For those with an interest in this topic, please see further reading.

Health and communication

Autistic girls should explore what being healthy means and have some awareness of the signs of illness. They should learn what to do if they feel unwell, understand when and how illness can be managed alone, and when, where and how to access support. Knowing what to do if they or others need help in an emergency, and what to say, is vital. Children may learn basic first aid skills and learn how to keep themselves fit and well.

Autistic children can benefit from knowing know which professionals can support them in relation to physical health and it is useful for them to identify who these people are and their roles. Autistic people may, however, find it difficult to communicate their health concerns for a variety of reasons. They may dislike speaking on the phone or avoid appointments because they find it daunting to be in a doctor's surgery or in a waiting room with other people. Some people may not feel pain; others may find it difficult to express levels of pain in words, or distress and pain may affect their ability to communicate. In such cases, non-verbal methods of communication should be explored (for example, visuals, alert cards, etc.). In addition, facial expressions may be misinterpreted by others, and healthcare professionals who lack understanding of autism may dismiss health concerns. Children and others can benefit from knowing the reasons why some autistic people have greater difficulty accessing healthcare and services than non-autistic people and how this can be addressed (for example, they may need support from others when attending appointments as well as adjustments relating to sensory needs, mobility and communication in certain healthcare environments.).

Children should understand that when they need to attend health appointments, they should be treated with respect and dignity by professionals, and vice versa. They should also know how to find out information about health and, where possible, understand their rights in relation to healthcare.

Organizational skills and how this can affect access to health services

As people think differently, some experience differences in their ability to organise, remember, and manage information and tasks. This may have an impact on them being able to access health services: they may accidentally miss appointments and in some cases this can mean they are discharged from services. Some people might need help from others to organize themselves and strategies should be explored that can help an individual (calendars, reminders, alerts, support from other people). Some people might need to be prepared in advance for appointments and will need to know:

- where they are going, what the date, the day and the time
- who they are going to visit, their role, what they look like
- what the room looks like
- what will happen and in which order
- how long the appointment will take (if time is a difficult concept, relate this to something familiar such as 'one TV show'/'one game', etc.).

Others may need to plan necessary adjustments where possible, consider sensory sensitivities and how anxiety might be managed (for example, listening to music whilst waiting). The child may need time to relax after the appointment to recoup energy.

Pregnancy

Girls may learn about different types of contraception and choice. They may learn about sexually transmitted infections, how people become pregnant and the facts about pregnancy, including the sensory aspects of being pregnant and what happens during labour and birth. (Communication preferences and potential communication barriers should be addressed in advance.)

Girls should be aware that some autistic women experience worry/anxiety due to uncertainty (for example, not knowing if they will get pregnant, not knowing if they will remain pregnant, and not knowing exactly when the baby will be born). They may also worry about the health of their baby and how they will adjust to motherhood. Pregnancy involves change, which for some autistic people may be difficult. Having to attend appointments might cause some women anxiety due to meeting new people, visiting new places, sensory issues, coping with sickness, feeling tired and managing emotions.

Knowing what happens at each stage of pregnancy can help, whereas not knowing what to expect can be extremely stressful. Communication issues in pregnancy and during birth, especially in relation to pain, should be explored. Adapting to a different life with a newborn may increase stress, so it can also be helpful to consider the emotional impact of having a baby.

Key points

- Autistic girls and women can experience many health inequalities across the lifespan. There are many positive steps that can be taken to address these.
- Self-care, rest, relaxation and pursuing intense interests are all important for autistic girls, who may experience exhaustion and 'burnout'.

- Providing alternative ways for autistic people to access services will lead to improvements in care.
- Being listened to and understood can have a positive impact on the health of autistic girls and women.
- Consistency of care is important (change can cause stress), and being familiar with people and the environment can help. Sensory aspects of the environment can affect how a person feels.
- Greater understanding of the differing communication needs of autistic girls and women helps to reduce inequalities. Professionals may consider how they can adapt the way they communicate.
- Autistic girls may not express feelings or pain in the same way as some non-autistic people and this should be taken into consideration. Other strategies can be put in place (for example, visual pain scales, visual representations of pain, communication passports), with input from the child about what works for them.
- Health and education are interlinked. Where schools can adapt to the child, and adapt the learning environment as well as the curriculum, there will be less need for autistic girls to access health services.
- Change and transition (bodily changes and life changes) can have an impact on the health of autistic girls and women.
- Masking and camouflaging can affect the health of autistic girls, but being with others who they feel comfortable with or spending some time alone can help. A positive sense of self, good friendships and relationships, and understanding their own needs can lead to improved health. Autistic girls need other people to understand them too.

CHAPTER 6

Be Expressive

This chapter explores the importance of communicating and expressing feelings and how this can improve well-being in contrast to internalizing thoughts and feelings. It focuses on the different ways autistic children may prefer to express themselves and explains why it is important that autistic children are listened to, understood and have a 'voice'. It also describes people's expectations of autistic girls and seeks to explain how they experience the world differently to their non-autistic peers. It also explores how autistic people can be influenced and affected by other people in a variety of situations and how the environment might affect their ability to express themselves.

Be expressive – context

People communicate their thoughts, feelings and needs in a variety of ways, communicating basic needs from birth and using different methods of communication throughout life: the noises they make; the sounds they create; through languages; using pictures, symbols, or drawings (single images and sequences); through behaviour; through gestures, facial expression and body language; through signing; through movement, through using their eyes; through touch.

Autistic girls, being unique, have different abilities and needs, and communicate in different ways. Many communicate using methods other than words; some communicate with support from others; some are minimally speaking (i.e. they may use some words); others may be able to speak but prefer not to with unfamiliar people or in certain situations or environments. In addition, many autistic girls have good expressive language ability and a precise command of language. Communication can be affected when under stress or pressure, meaning that some people lose the ability to speak. How long this lasts will depend on the individual. It can be caused, for example, by feeling overloaded by too many demands, too much language being used, being overwhelmed by the sensory environment, or not feeling that they can cope in a certain situation (which ideally should have been avoided in the first place). Whether or not an autistic person communicates using speech, all autistic people have the right to have their 'voice' heard and have opportunities to contribute their opinions.

However an autistic girl communicates, it is vital to her health and well-being that she is able to express herself. Not all autistic girls are outspoken or extroverts, nor do they want to be. These girls still have opinions, thoughts and ideas, but are sometimes overlooked.

Gill Loomes (creator of VoiceSpaces, nd) says:

> I'm well aware that individuals and groups in society both want and need to speak in different ways, at different times – and I know that those individuals and groups can be silenced by social oppression. I care about how, and when we can speak up – and the circumstances and reasons why we may be silenced. I'm curious about the myriad ways in which we can express ourselves, and make our mark; and I'm interested in the social politics of interaction – and what this means for those of us who do not, or cannot, access normative approaches to communication.

Valuing what autistic children have to say (not just using words) is just one of the many ways we can help to improve mental health. Greater consideration of the different ways autistic children communicate at different times (for example, writing down thoughts or opinions, or drawing) will help them to achieve their potential, feel more connected and grow in confidence.

Why is self-expression so important to the wellbeing of autistic girls?

In a society that places an expectation on girls to be sociable, autistic girls are under pressure to conform. Therefore they often mask, camouflage and adapt their communication to appear more like their non-autistic peers and fit in. This involves having to suppress aspects of themselves, including how they express themselves. Processing language and responding to other people can take considerable effort. Autistic girls often need longer to think about what has been said before replying, and have the additional worries both of making sure that what they say is relevant and that they are going to cause offence or upset others by saying the 'wrong' thing. These are not easy things to judge and use up a lot of mental and emotional energy. It can also impact negatively on mental health.

If autistic girls find it difficult to express feelings through speech, it is important that they are given the opportunity to express themselves in other ways. They need to have an outlet for their feelings so that they are less likely to engage in harmful or unsafe behaviours. There are numerous ways this can be done but each girl will have her own preferences. Some autistic girls will express themselves by being creative.

> I express myself through my art and I suppose through debating subjects that I enjoy... I need somewhere quiet to go if I am overloaded. Somewhere I can stim would be great.

Autistic girls should not be discouraged from stimming (so long as they are not harming themselves) as it helps girls to express their feelings and allows them to regulate themselves. Understanding and acceptance is of greater use than stopping a child from doing what they need to do to help themselves. Many autistic girls can express themselves through the use of line, texture and colour by drawing, painting and making. Poquérusse *et al.* (2018) state:

> Art allows individuals with alexithymia to express themselves and potentially access the verbal expression system which they need to process and vent their emotions (Meijer-Degen and Lansen 2006);

> interestingly, individuals with ASD have high rates of synesthesia and often use colors to express their emotions (Neckar and Bob 2017).

Other girls express themselves through writing or poetry – whether or not it is shared with others or remains private depends on the individual.

Some autistic girls can express themselves non-verbally through dance or other forms of rhythmic movement in a sequence or flow as this allows the brain to focus. Yoga and other forms of repetitive exercise can help autistic girls to release stress.

Creating music, singing (either alone or as part of a group) and listening to music can also enable girls to feel emotion, not only through the melody but through the vibrations.

Poquérusse *et al.* (2018) recognize the value of music and movement:

> Dance, or rhythmic movement therapy, is another effective outlet for symptoms of alexithymia (Malkina-Pykh, 2013) and may be intricately linked to emotional competence (Bojner Horwitz *et al.* 2015). [...] music is another alternate vehicle for understanding, processing, and communicating emotions (Allen and Heaton 2010; Zangwill 2013).

Poquérusse *et al.* (2018) further note that some autistic people have 'superior musical pitch processing and are able to properly identify the positive or negative emotional valence of music stimuli'.

As well as knowing how to feel and express emotions, autistic girls can consider how they might express their personalities. This can be through their appearance (clothing, hair, etc.), their interests and hobbies, and also how they choose to live their lives (which may be seen as unconventional by others).

The well-being of autistic girls can improve when they:

- can be themselves and express themselves in their own way

- feel good about themselves by doing the things they enjoy or do well
- have a voice and are listened to rather than ignored or silenced
- have ways to release pent-up stress (and know how to get rid of negative thoughts from the mind and feelings from their body) through music, art, writing, drama, movement or exercise.

Communication differences and challenges for autistic girls

Helping autistic girls to explore the communication challenges they face can provide them with greater self-awareness and self-understanding and help them to be more accepting of themselves. Autistic girls should not feel that the way they communicate is inferior to that of their non-autistic peers, and need to be aware that people communicate differently.

Speech and language therapist Dr Alex Sturrock explains that many of the communication challenges autistic girls face can affect learning, relationships with others and self-esteem:

> The profile of autistic girls seems to be distinct from that of autistic boys or even neurotypical girls. Findings from research suggests that their basic vocabulary and sentence grammar in speech will be in-line with other cognitive abilities meaning if they are quite smart generally, they will tend to have very good vocabulary and sentence structure. But other aspects of language and communication are likely to be affected. Narrative is one area where autistic girls had equal amounts of difficulty to autistic boys, and this seems to be driven by poorer sequencing (this happened *and then* this happened) and causality (this happened *because* this happened). They also showed less overall story coherence meaning that it was hard follow for the listener. Difficulties with narrative are reported by the children themselves and their parents as well as being identified in analysis of story-telling samples.

> The importance of narrative is that it allows you to explain events that happened to you and ideas that you have. Without this skill it can be really hard to self-advocate and engage with your peer group. Many girls have reported problems explaining events and ideas, often leading to the girls feeling negative about the whole experience and on occasions withdrawing from the situation. This difficulty is likely to get even more pronounced if they are trying to explain an event which includes important emotional information. (Personal communication)

Sometimes in classroom situations, autistic girls are overloaded by too much language. Social rules, such as having to give eye contact, can make it hard or impossible for an autistic girl to take in verbal information whilst looking at a person's face. In a visually stimulating or noisy environment this can be even more difficult. Dr Alex Sturrock explains:

> Both autistic girls and women report real difficulties with listening to detail in speech. Why and how this can be a problem varies between individuals. However, many individuals report problems listening in crowded environments or in group conversations. Others report difficulties when they are in a visually stimulating environment, meaning they cannot focus on speech because they are too busy looking around. Some report difficulties listening when they can't physically move and others find it hard to listen when they are forced to look at a person's eyes. Many report increased levels of anxiety when trying to listen for detail, which can make focusing even harder. It is not clear if problems with listening for detail are due to underlying difficulties with auditory or language processing, attention, or even verbal memory. (Personal communication)

It is possible that autistic girls experience less pressure and stress when they are able to move around and are not expected to give eye contact both of which would enable them to feel more comfortable (see 'Reducing pressure' in Chapter 4).

Dr Sturrock shares some useful suggestions about how to support autistic girls in the learning environment, either at home, at school or in other settings:

> One strategy which can help is providing important information in a written (or picture) form. Parents sometimes suggest that breaking instructions into chunks (one step at a time) can also help and giving important information should be done in a quiet, calm setting ahead of time, in order to allow time for best responses.

Preparing autistic girls in advance of lessons can help to reduce anxiety – some girls will enjoy reading about topics of study and will feel better prepared when there is less uncertainty about what will be covered. Providing key vocabulary with explanations and visuals can also aid understanding. Since speaking aloud can be stressful for some autistic girls, they may gain confidence and be more likely to contribute to lessons if they can share their knowledge in other ways.

Parents, carers and schools should work with autistic girls to ensure that help with communication is tailored to the individual. Dr Sturrock recognizes the strengths that autistic girls may have, as well as the specific challenges they may face, and suggests how they can be supported through specialist interventions:

> Autistic girls do appear to have some strengths compared to autistic boys, and this is often to do with language used in a social context (pragmatics). They appear to be better than autistic boys at interpreting the meaning behind non-literal language, for example, 'It's very loud out there' might mean 'Please keep quiet'. They also appear to be better at using appropriate social behaviours during conversation, including turn-taking, development of conversational topics,

nodding, smiling, and using gestures. It must be remembered that autistic girls still have difficulties when compared to Neurotypical [NT] females, who appear to be extremely skilled in pragmatic behaviours. This means that autistic girls might not be as nuanced in social communication as their NT girl peers and this appears to become more of a problem in secondary school and teenage years. Specialist interventions can be really helpful for these types of issues, focusing on the individual's set of strengths and weaknesses. Findings on the communicative strengths and weakness of autistic girls are only just beginning to be researched. We also need to bear in mind that group findings are just that: an average of group performance and do not explain every girl's profile. This means some may present much more like a classic autistic boy and, in fact, some boys may present more like the profile outlined for girls. However, these early findings can tell us something about the questions we need to be asking in research and may help us work towards assessments and interventions that work for autistic girls.

Be expressive – what can autistic girls benefit from knowing or exploring, and what should parents and professionals be aware of?

Autistic children can benefit from knowing that their feelings and thoughts are valid and valuable, that people express themselves in different ways, verbally and non-verbally, and that people can express themselves and their feelings in ways other than speech: through creative writing, creative tasks, drama, drawing, painting, poetry, clothing, their interests, dance and movement. How people express themselves can vary depending on the person whom they are communicating with, and they may have their own preferred methods of communication which may differ in different situations. Children should be taught that although some people have greater difficulty than others at expressing themselves for various reasons, their 'voice' is no less important.

Children and others can explore what is meant by 'situational mutism' (when a person finds it difficult to communicate in certain situations) and become aware that the environment can affect communication abilities. For autistic girls, being able to express themselves outwardly, in some way, even if it isn't through speech, will have a positive impact on them both in terms of improved mental and physical health. They should explore the mental and physical impact of keeping feelings internalized and consider the impact of not being listened to (how this might affect self-esteem and confidence). Their opinions should be sought about matters involving them.

Key points

- Autistic girls need to be able to express themselves rather than suppress themselves.
- Some autistic girls internalize feelings, which can affect health, so they should be encouraged to express their feelings outwardly. Some girls need to be shown strategies (written, visual or physical), whereas others will have their own.
- Some autistic girls have difficulty expressing their feelings or may express these differently from their peers.
- The spoken word should be of no greater value than other modes of communication.
- Autistic girls may want to express themselves in a variety of ways (through creative activity, writing, drawing, creating, music, movement).
- When autistic girls feel heard, they feel valued.
- How an autistic girl feels with another person, the situation she is in and the environment affect how able she is to express herself.
- Schools can provide various opportunities for autistic girls to express themselves.
- Professionals can help autistic girls to communicate by providing them with alternative ways to communicate other than through speech.

CHAPTER 7

Be Independent

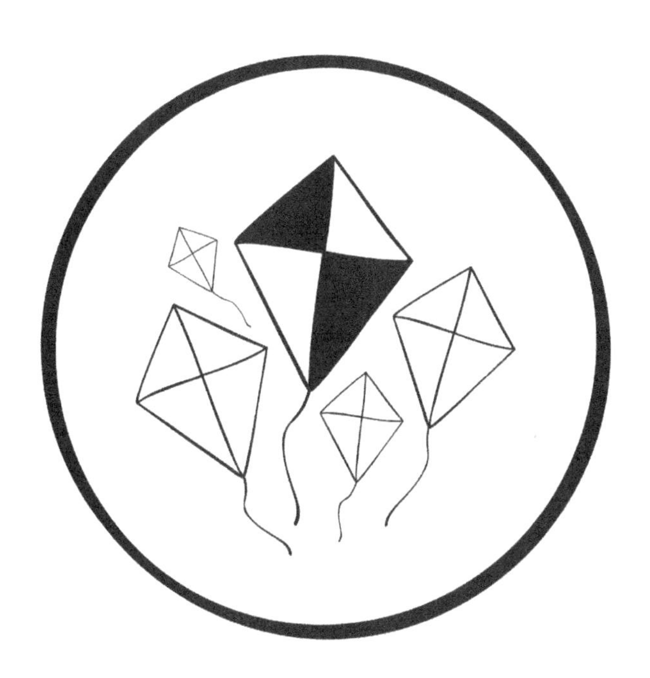

This chapter focuses on agency and autonomy and what independence means for different people. None of us exist alone as we rely on other people who provide for our needs. Independence to some children may mean becoming increasingly self-sufficient or capable in a particular area of life, or being able to self-advocate. For other autistic children, doing things alone may never be the goal, nor should it be, for them. Some children may always require support from others throughout their life, and this is respected. This chapter discusses routine, predictability and structure in life, and explores why change and transition can be challenging for autistic people, to varying extents. It also talks about the impact of other people's expectations of autistic girls and women in relation to independence. In addition, it explores the various changes that take place over the lifespan, describing the challenges that girls and women experience, so that girls, their families, and those working with them can be better prepared and informed.

Be independent – context

Autistic girls are individuals who have different needs, therefore 'being independent' will mean different things to different people. For some, being independent will involve managing an increasing number of situations and making more choices and decisions with less adult support as they grow up. For others, being independent may require the involvement of other people (parents, carers, professionals) due to communication needs, mobility, cognitive ability or because of how being autistic affects them personally.

Some autistic girls find it difficult to think flexibly, whereas others are able to adapt to different people, situations and environments. Some autistic girls need guidance from others because they require a high level of structure and routine and 'rules' to follow. Some autistic girls follow rules rigidly as this provides security and predictability, while others are able to be more flexible, according to the situation.

Autistic girls rely on adults to help them to become independent and confident young women. They need to be supported by others who listen to them and respect their decisions, even when they disagree or say 'no'. If adults are respectful towards them, they will then learn how they should expect to be treated by others and will be able to recognize when they are not. Teaching girls to always be compliant will place them at greater risk of abuse and exploitation, whereas encouraging them to be assertive and teaching them how to use language (and tone) to convey a particular message will help them to be more safe in the company of others. Autistic girls need to develop social skills and manners. However, they also need to know how to assert themselves when necessary and put their own needs first and foremost.

Autistic girls may take longer than their non-autistic peers to become independent but their potential should not be underestimated. Being able to progress at a pace that suits them means that they are less likely to become burnt out or overburdened. If too many demands and expectations are placed on the child, then she will feel pressurized and may feel overwhelmed. Growing up can be difficult because change makes life uncertain, but being able to do things independently can build confidence:

> My child's well-being is improved by achieving things on her own, so for example if she learns to cook something or if she receives praise from school. An iota of recognition goes a very long way with her and we are always trying to praise her for the small things and help her feel her self-worth.

Being independent can start in the home with supervision. Girls can gradually learn to become more independent outside of the home, when ready.

> I feel very independent in my house. I am able to look after myself and

> even cook tea sometimes. I don't spend any time away from the house really but if I do my mum or dad takes me wherever I need to go and picks me up again.

Being self-aware and knowing what barriers there are to achieving goals can help autistic girls to become more independent.

> I am hoping to go to college next year so I think I'll be getting the bus there and back on my own, so that will be good. I'm not very good at telling the time or directions, so it will have to be practised a few times before I'll feel confident doing it on my own.

Growing up involves considerable change (changing expectations, managing emotions, physical changes, greater pressure and responsibility), so helping girls to realize that change is a gradual process can help them to manage the transition from childhood to becoming young adults. Looking at photographs of their younger selves, and discussing what their needs were then and now, will enable girls to reflect on how change is a long and gradual process. At school and in the home, autistic girls should be encouraged to make decisions for themselves but learn that everyone makes mistakes. Listening, being supportive and helping autistic children to consider the impact of their decisions on themselves and others enables them to be more responsible.

Encouraging autistic girls to become increasingly independent will help them in later life, especially if they gain greater awareness of their own needs. Understanding themselves, knowing what causes them stress, knowing what helps them to feel calm, understanding how other people affect them, and being aware of their own sensory needs and sensitivities and how different environments affect them, can help autistic girls become more able to cope when faced with change and transition at different stages of life.

Some autistic girls will want to go on to further study and pursue their strengths and interests; others will want to gain employment. Some will need support to understand how to apply to college or for jobs. If they have not done this previously, they may be unable to imagine what to do. Work experience can help prepare some autistic girls for employment. Advance preparation can reduce uncertainty. Employers, too, can benefit from training so that they understand the needs of the young person and how best to support her. Well-being and quality of life depend on many factors, including economic stability. Being able to eat, keep warm, pay bills and spend time doing things you enjoy all affect quality of life. Helping autistic girls to feel confident in themselves will allow them to have stability in life. Autistic girls should be able to make decisions for themselves about how they want to live their lives, however different or non-conformist this may seem to others. Parents and professionals can help autistic girls to have greater control over their own lives by encouraging them to problem solve and think for themselves rather than being overly reliant on others or being overly compliant. This can be a delicate balance in supporting girls to make their own decisions whilst staying safe.

Life naturally brings constant change, though some changes are more unexpected than others. Being able to think for themselves can help some autistic girls to be more self-sufficient, enable them as young women to have greater choices in life about friendships, relationships and living arrangements, and provide greater freedom and stability, making them better equipped to manage change. As they grow up, some autistic girls and young women can learn to advocate for themselves in a way that works for them; they can also ensure that they are listened to and receive adequate care and services from others, though this is sometimes not easy. Asking for accommodations can be difficult and whether you receive them depends on the knowledge and understanding of the person or people being asked.

Be independent – what can autistic girls benefit from knowing or exploring, and what should parents and professionals be aware of?

Autistic children, parents and professionals may explore or consider what being independent means to different people (for some people this can mean doing things alone, but for others it may involve different levels of support), and that people may need different levels of support at different stages of life. They can also explore why people might have different levels of independence due to a disability or health needs.

Children can learn about decision making, making considered choices, how decisions affect themselves and others, and about dealing with the consequences of decisions. They can learn about what being responsible means (for example, through what they communicate and by their actions online and in day-to-day situations). Girls can learn why they need to balance different aspects of their life (for example, school, work, friendships, recreation) and that adults too have various responsibilities, including looking after their own needs (food, mental and physical health, cleanliness, clothing, recreation, sleep), taking care of the home (shelter, warmth, cleanliness), considering other people's needs, keeping themselves and others safe in the home, employment, taking care of finances and budgeting, making choices and managing the consequences of actions.

Children and others can consider what level of support a child might need from family, friends and professionals, both now and in the future, and how the child might feel if she receives too little or too much support. Children should understand what respect means (both self-respect and respect for others) and learn that other people should treat them with respect and dignity. It is important for girls to explore and understand clearly what disrespectful language and behaviour might 'sound' and 'look' like, how to seek help or reassurance, communicate concerns and report situations where they may not have been treated with respect and understanding. They also need to know when to be assertive if other people behave inappropriately towards them (see Chapter 2).

Children should be aware that people can have different thoughts and opinions, and that as people grow up and become more independent, they will have their own expectations about how they want to live their life (this may be different to how other people live their lives or may not match other people's expectations).

Children can consider what their individual needs are (in addition to the things everyone needs, such as love, support, food, shelter, etc.). They should be aware that the choices they make not only affect themselves but may also affect other people. They should understand that others may have reasons for making certain decisions for reasons that will benefit the child in the future (for example, parent might decide not to spend money on certain things now because they are saving up for something important long-term). Girls can be encouraged to develop financial understanding and consider the consequences of spending impulsively (they should be made aware of advertising and marketing gimmicks and how these might encourage them to spend money).

Girls should be made aware that sometimes life does not go according to plan (for example, they may not get the examination grades/job offer/college place they hoped for) and although this might be disappointing at the time, it might lead to a different (sometimes better) outcome. They may learn that people have different aims in life and that these can change; also that people achieve goals at different stages and may change their living accommodation for financial reasons or support needs.

Change and transition

It can be beneficial for children and other people to know that even small changes, including slight changes to routine, can cause some autistic people distress, whereas others can be more flexible – each person's reactions will be different.

Children, parents and professionals may consider how change can be difficult for some autistic people, and explore their own attitudes towards change. They can discuss how planning ahead (with or without support, depending on the individual) can be helpful in managing change.

They may consider the different types of change that can happen in life as people become more independent and how these affect people differently. Here are just a few examples:

- doing things differently from usual
- eating new food
- buying and wearing new or different clothes
- trying new experiences (new hobbies, going to new places, going on holiday)
- learning new skills
- moving home
- transitions such as moving to the next school year/secondary school/college/university
- physical changes such as puberty, pregnancy and the menopause
- bereavement
- getting a job
- changing job
- friendships and relationships
- marriage and divorce.

Change can affect emotions and actions, and children should be aware of this. Children and others need to understand why some people need sameness, routine and predictability, but that sometimes change can be positive. Children can benefit from learning different ways to cope with change and transition. Practical ways to prepare for change (for example, reading information, looking at images, asking questions) should be considered. It is important for children to know that people are able to do certain things independently at different ages and that they should be allowed to achieve things at their own pace (i.e. some people take longer to achieve something, whereas others achieve things more quickly).

Children should be aware that change can cause stress and anxiety, so learning how to offset this can be beneficial to well-being. Some people find it difficult to imagine what changes will be like until they have experienced them (for example, it may be difficult to understand or predict the lifestyle changes that will occur when a baby is born) and may understand better if these are explained visually.

Transition and travel

Children may learn about where they live (their own address, home phone number, parent/carer contact details, etc.) in relation to their community, country and the wider world. They may be aware of the local area and places further afield. They may learn to be prepared for going out and about (they will need appropriate clothing, money, phone, etc.), and be able to find their way around the immediate area and further afield (they may be supported to do this depending on their age and stage). They might able to plan a route to somewhere nearby (accompanied or unaccompanied, depending on individual need), use public transport (with support from others or independently), pay for travel (if appropriate), be aware of their own needs in relation to travel (for example, they may need space around them, they may prefer to sit in a specific place, or they may be noise/light sensitive). They can learn how to manage situations such as getting lost and think about who to contact if they experience difficulties when out and about.

Leisure skills

When gaining independence, children can consider their own interests and hobbies, and other people's. They may want to know about social/interest groups in the local area or online that appeal to them. They may learn why leisure time is important to well-being, what facilities there are in the local environment and their own social preferences (doing things alone or with others), which should be respected. Children and young people should have opportunities to do things that are meaningful to them. Some may enjoy repetitive activities (for example, going to the same place and saying the same things to familiar people) as this is predictable and safe. Any new activities should be planned for in advance if a child needs this.

Financial understanding

Opportunities to manage money, such as recognizing and managing small/larger amounts of money, should be provided. Role play, games and other resources can also be used to give children practice in shopping and ordering items.

Children need to know about choices and where and how to shop for different things (products, goods and services). They can be taught how to plan ahead for shopping and may be able to estimate the cost in advance. Children should be aware of different ways to order and pay for goods (for example, by using technology). They can also learn about being a consumer (ethical considerations, value for money, what to do if they are overcharged for something).

It can be beneficial for children to be aware that people have different attitudes towards money and that there are various reasons for this. Children might learn about budgeting, lending and borrowing money (and about exploitation), household bills and average wages. They might learn more about living independently, with others or alone, and how they can finance this. They may learn about the consequences of overspending, and that some people are impulsive with money whereas others are cautious. They may learn when it is appropriate to share the cost of items with others and when it is not. They should learn about money and risk (for example, gambling and why for some people this might become a habit), so that they can make choices about how to spend their own money. Some girls might learn about opening and accessing a bank account, saving money in a savings account, why people save, and how to keep money safe. Some children might learn about giving money to charity and choices in relation to donations. They may also learn about debt, benefits, their rights and choices in relation to how their money is spent. Children should learn how to find out what has been spent or saved, what is meant by a scam, and who to ask for support if concerned about money, including organizations.

Work experience and employment

Children can learn about the reasons why people work, what is meant by 'work experience', and what a 'mentor' is. They may learn about the choices people may/may not have in relation to work (for example, work from home or go out to work, work part time or full time, etc.) and why. They can learn about being an employee, including the advantages (for example, having a regular routine and wage) and disadvantages (for example, not being appreciated for the differing range of skills you may have, your sensory needs being misunderstood by an employer working hours being erratic, being hyper-focussed on the job and forgetting to take breaks, having to manage multiple aspects of a business if the person has organisational difficulties.), about being self-employed, including the advantages (for example, being able to choose one's own hours to an extent, not being limited by others) and disadvantages (for example, some autistic people like the routine of a 9-5 job with regular breaks, self employment means that hours can be erratic). They may learn about different types of employment (being aware that there will be different types of companies, services and demographics in different areas) and consider the types of employment that individuals might prefer. They can gain an understanding of wages and what different jobs pay, about employment and responsibility, and the perceived advantages and disadvantages of having a job.

Children may consider their own skills and strengths and think about the qualities employers might look for. They should understand that some jobs involve working to deadlines and consider what job they might like in the future and why. They should be aware of their options (available courses, work experience, apprenticeships, and employment), that people with different skills may be suited to different types of jobs, and that their strengths and capabilities should not be underestimated (for example, intense interests can lead to employment).

Job interviews are not always the best way to determine a person's skills if they are neurodivergent. Girls can consider why some people find job interviews difficult, learn to prepare for them and request adjustments if necessary. They should consider their feelings in relation to job interviews and how to manage them. They should learn about autism disclosure (the advantages and disadvantages, and choice), self-advocacy, reasonable adjustments in the workplace (for example, to accommodate sensory needs), health and safety, discrimination, employment rights, diversity in the workplace, and what is meant by workplace bullying and how to deal with it.

Children can also learn how to deal with success and disappointment, and about job expectations versus reality. They can learn about being assertive in the workplace and why people change jobs (because of low wages, being under-valued, not using skills, difficulties with colleagues, not being fulfilled). They can learn about the social aspects of work (managing lunch breaks and other social occasions) and why people need to balance work, recreation and other responsibilities.

Developing independence at home

Children can learn skills relating to independence at home. They might learn, for example, how to:

- clean the house(safely) and what products to use
- keep themselves safe indoors and outdoors
- recognize when to clean clothing
- use a washing machine and tumble dryer
- iron clothes
- fold and organize/store clothes
- clean and polish shoes
- make a bed
- clean and dry bedding (and how often to do this)
- create a shopping list
- order and buy food
- make hot and cold drinks
- follow a recipe, cook food (using visual sequences if needed)
- understand food hygiene
- clean the dishes
- learn how to balance a variety of tasks and understand why rest and relaxation are also important in life.

Key points

- Autistic girls are unique, so each child may require different levels of support depending on her needs. The support she requires may also vary at different times throughout her life.
- It is important to achieve the right balance when providing support, neither providing too much nor too little.

- Autistic girls should be treated with respect and dignity and
- should be at the centre of any decisions being made that affect their lives and how they want to live them.

Conclusion

In compiling this book, I was fortunate to be provided with a range of perspectives from parents and professionals. Autistic girls and women of different ages contributed their thoughts and opinions. One autistic woman in her fifties says: 'I want to acknowledge the generational gaps. I grew up in a different era.' Interestingly, she wondered if 'the same challenges and issues still ring true across the generations'.

Whilst autistic women who are older are keen to provide younger autistic girls and women with the benefit of their experience to make life easier (which was one of the aims of this book), the younger generations have equally provided much support and insight, helping older autistic women to understand themselves and make sense of their lives, too. The same autistic woman says: 'The younger generation are incredibly clued up and have helped us older people to understand ourselves, especially in relation to sexuality.'

When asked what she would like autistic girls to know, she says:

> If you have a strong sense of yourself and who you are, if you have a sense of self-worth, then you are more likely to have fulfilling relationships with others. It's really important to develop a good sense of self – then other things will be easier. The most important thing I would like to say to autistic girls is that you may be different, but you are **not** deficient. You may think differently, you may do things differently, you

> may feel things differently, you may experience things differently, and the things you may interested in might not be the same things as your peers but that's okay. That's what makes you **you**. You will find your own path. I want to get across to autistic girls that they matter.

Although there can be many challenges to being autistic, it's important that autistic girls realize that they have worth, regardless of their capabilities and needs, and that they each will have strengths and personal qualities that make them an individual.

> Being autistic means you have a different perspective of the world, you may notice the details that other people miss, you can make connections that other people may not and you may have strengths, skills and interests that enrich your life and other people's. Although self-acceptance is key to well-being, it is vital that others understand autistic girls, so that they can make the necessary adjustments and accommodations to include rather than exclude them. Autistic girls should be able to live long, happy, healthy, safe and fulfilled lives.

YOU MATTER. Be yourself.

References

Chapter 1: References

Asperger, H. (1944) 'Die Autistischen Psychopathen im Kindesalter.' ['Autistic psychopathy in childhood.'] *Archive für Psychiatrie und Nervenkrankheiten 117*, 76–136. doi:10.1007/BF01837709

Kenny, L., Hattersly, C., Molins, B., Buckley, C., Povey, C. & Pellicano, E. (2016) 'Which terms should be used to describe autism? Perspectives from the UK autism community.' *Autism 20*(4), 442–462. doi.org/10.1177/1362361315588200

Lawson, W. (2017) 'Women and girls on the autism spectrum.' *Journal of Intellectual Disability – Diagnosis and Treatment 5*(3), 91.

Milton, D. (2012) 'On the ontological status of autism: The "double empathy problem".' *Disability & Society 27*(6), 883–887.

Milton, D. (2014) 'So what exactly are autism interventions intervening with?' *Good Autism Practice 15*(2), 6–14.

NASUWT (2013) Support for Children and Young People with Special Educational Needs

Sinclair, J. (2013) 'Why I dislike "person first" language.' *Autonomy, The Critical Journal of Interdisciplinary Studies 1*(2).

South, M., Costa, A.P., McMorris, C. (2021) 'Death by suicide among people with autism: Beyond zebrafish.' *JAMA Network Open 4*(1). doi:10.1001/jamanetworkopen.2020.34018

Vermeulen, P. (2014) 'The practice of promoting happiness in autism.' Available at www.researchgate.net/publication/269072830_The_practice_of_promoting_happiness_in_autism (accessed 13/05/21).

Wood, R. (2019) *Inclusive Education for Autistic Children: Helping Children and Young People to Learn and Flourish in the Classroom.* London: Jessica Kingsley Publishers.

Further reading

Kanner, L. (1943) 'Autistic disturbances of affective contact.' *Nervous Child* 2, 217–250.

Chapter 2: References

American Psychiatric Association (2013) *Diagnostic and Statistical Manual of Mental Disorders, fifth edition* (*DSM-5*). Arlington, VA: American Psychiatric Association.

Autistic Girls Network (2021) https://autisticgirlsnetwork.org/wp-content/uploads/Autism-Diagnosis-Waiting-Times-for-Girls-Before-the-Pandemic.png

Bargiela, S., Steward, R. & Mandy, W. (2016) 'The Experiences of late diagnosed women with autism spectrum conditions: An investigation of the female autism phenotype.' *Journal of Autism and Developmental Disorders 46*, 3281–3294. doi 10.1007/s10803-016-2872-8

Beardon, L. (2020) *Avoiding Anxiety in Autistic Children.* London: Sheldon Press.

Begeer, S., Mandell, D., Wijnker-Holmes, B., Venderbosch, S. *et al.* (2013) 'Sex differences in the timing of identification among children and adults with autism spectrum disorders.' *Journal of Autism Developmental Disorders* 43, 1151–1156.

Bolis, D., Lahnakoski, J.M., Seidel, D., Tamm, J. & Schilbach, L. (2021) 'Interpersonal similarity of autistic traits predicts friendship quality.' *Social Cognitive and Affective Neuroscience 16*(1–2), 222–231. doi.org/10.1093/scan/nsaa147

Craft, S. (n.d.) 'Recognition that autistic people are unique.' https://the-art-of-autism.com/females-and-aspergers-a-checklist

Crompton, C.J., Ropar, D., Evans-Williams, C.V.M., Flynn, E.G. & Fletcher-Watson, S. (2020) 'Autistic peer-to-peer information transfer is highly effective.' *Autism* 24(7), 1704–1712.

Csikszentmihalyi, M. (1990) *Flow: The Psychology of Optimal Experience.* New York, NY: Harper & Row.

Dean, M., Harwood, R. & Kasari, C. (2017) 'The art of camouflage: Gender differences in the social behaviours of girls and boys with autism spectrum disorder.' *Autism 21*(6), 678–689. doi: 10.1177/1362361316671845

George, R. & Stokes M.A. (2018) 'Gender identity and sexual orientation in autism spectrum disorder.' *Autism: The International Journal of Research and Practice 22*, 970–982.

Goodall, C. (2020) *Understanding the Voices and Educational Experiences of Autistic Young People: From Research to Practice.* Abingdon: Routledge.

Gould, J. (2017) 'Towards understanding the under-recognition of girls and women on the autism spectrum.' *Autism 21*(6), 703–705.

Gould, J. & Ashton-Smith, J. (2011) 'Missed diagnosis or misdiagnosis? Girls and women on the autism spectrum.' *Good Autism Practice 12*(1), 34–41.

Gunn, K. & Delafield-Butt, J. (2016) 'Teaching children with autism spectrum disorder with restricted interests: A review of evidence for best practice.' *Review of Educational Research 86*(2), 408–430.

Halladay, A.K., Bishop, S., Constantino, J.N., Daniels, A.M. *et al.* (2015) 'Sex and gender differences in autism spectrum disorder: Summarizing evidence gaps and identifying emerging areas of priority.' *Molecular Autism 6*(36).

Hebron, J. & Bond, C. (2019) *Education and Girls on the Autism Spectrum: Developing an Integrated Approach*. London: Jessica Kingsley Publishers.

Hesmondhalgh, M. & Breakey, H. (2001) *Access and Inclusion for Children with Autistic Spectrum Disorders: Let Me In*. London: Jessica Kingsley Publishers.

Hirvikoski, T., Mittendorfer-Rutz, E., Boman M., Larsson, H., Lichtenstein P. & Bölte, S. (2015) 'Premature mortality in autism spectrum disorder.' *The British Journal of Psychiatry 208*(3), 1–7. doi: 10.1192/bjp.bp.114.160192

Hodge, N., Rice, E.J. & Reidy, L. (2019) '"They're told all the time they're different": How educators understand development of sense of self for autistic pupils.' *Disability & Society* 34(9–10), 1353–1378. doi: 10.1080/09687599.2019.1594700

Hofvander, B., Delorme, R., Chaste, P., Nyden, A. *et al.* (2009) 'Psychiatric and psychosocial problems in adults with normal-intelligence autism spectrum disorders.' *BMC Psychiatry 9*(35). doi:10.1186/1471-244X-9-35.

Hull, L. & Mandy, W. (2017) 'Protective effect or missed diagnosis? Females with autism spectrum disorder.' *Future Neurology 12*(3), 159–169.

Hull, L., Petrides, V. & Mandy, W. (2020) 'The female autism phenotype and camouflaging: A narrative review.' *Review Journal of Autism and Developmental Disorders 7*, 306–317.

Hussein, A.M., Pellicano, E. & Crane, E. (2019) 'Understanding and awareness of autism among Somali parents living in the United Kingdom.' *Autism: The International Journal of Research and Practice* 23, 1408–1418.

Jones, G., English, A., Guldberg, K., Jordan, R., Richardson, P. & Waltz, M. (2008) *Educational Provision for Children and Young People on the Autism Spectrum Living in England: A Review of Current Practice, Issues and Challenges*. London: Autism Education Trust. Available at www.actcommunity.ca/resource/3448 (accessed 14/05/21).

Kapp, S.K., Gillespie-Lynch, K., Sherman, L.E. & Hutman, T. (2013) 'Deficit, difference, or both? Autism and neurodiversity.' *Developmental Psychology 49*, 59–71.

Kapp, S.K., Steward, R., Crane, L., Elliott, D., Elphick, C. *et al.* (2019) '"People should be able to do what they like": Autistic adults' views and experiences of stimming.' *Autism 23*(7), 1782–1792.

Kirkovski, M., Enticott, P.G. & Fitzgerald, P.B. (2013) 'A review of the role of female gender in autism spectrum disorders.' *Journal of Autism and Developmental Disorders* 43(11), 2584–2603.

Lai, M.C., Baron-Cohen, S. & Buxbaum, J.D. (2015) 'Understanding autism in the light of sex/gender.' *Molecular Autism* 6(24). Available at https://molecularautism.biomedcentral.com/articles/10.1186/s13229-015-0021-4#ref-CR43 (accessed 14/05/21).

Lai, M.C., Lombardo, M.V., Auyeung, B., Chakrabarti, B. & Baron-Cohen S. (2015) 'Sex/gender differences and autism: Setting the scene for future research.' *Journal of the American Academy of Child and Adolescent Psychiatry* 54(1), 11–24. doi: 10.1016/j.jaac.2014.10.003

Leatherland, J. (2018) 'Understanding how autistic pupils experience secondary school: Autism criteria, theory and FAMe™.' Doctoral thesis , Sheffield Hallam University. doi.org/10.7190/shu-thesis-00101

Livingston, L.A., Colvert, E., Bolton, P. & Happé, F. (2019) 'Good social skills despite poor theory of mind: Exploring compensation in autism spectrum disorder.' *Journal of Child Psychology and Psychiatry* 60(1),102–110.

Loomes, R., Hull, L., Mandy, W.P.L. (2017) 'What is the male-to-female ratio in autism spectrum disorder? A systematic review and meta-analysis.' *Journal of the American Academy of Child and Adolescent Psychiatry* 56(6), 466–474.

Maddox, B., Trubanova, A. & White, S.W. (2017) 'Untended wounds: Non-suicidal self-injury in adults with autism spectrum disorder.' *Autism* 21(4), 412–422.

Mandy, W., Chilvers, R., Chowdhury, U., Salter, G., Seigal, A. & Skuse, D. (2012) 'Sex differences in autism spectrum disorder: Evidence from a large sample of children and adolescents.' *Journal of Autism and Developmental Disorders* 7, 1304–13. doi: 10.1007/s10803-011-1356-0.

McDonnell, A. & Milton, D. (2014) 'Going with the Flow: Reconsidering "Repetitive Behaviour" through the Concept of "Flow States".' In G. Jones & E. Hurley (Eds) *Good Autism Practice: Autism, Happiness and Wellbeing*. Birmingham: BILD.

Milton, D.E.M. (2012) 'On the ontological status of autism: The "double empathy problem".' *Disability and Society* 27(6), 883–887. doi 10.1080/09687599.2012.710008

Milton, D.E.M. (2017) *A Mismatch of Salience: Explorations of the Nature of Autism from Theory to Practice*. Shoreham-by-Sea: Pavilion Publishing.

Murray, D., Lesser, M. & Lawson, W. (2005) 'Attention, monotropism and the diagnostic criteria for autism.' *Autism* 9(2), 139–156.

Murray, F. (2021) *Craft, Flow and Cognitive Styles - Conference Paper*. Available at https://www.researchgate.net/publication/353413064_Craft_Flow_and_Cognitive_Styles/link/60faded9169a1a0103b1caa2/download

National Autistic Society (2020) www.autism.org

NHS Digital (2020) 'Autism Statistics 19 November.' Available at https://digital.nhs.uk/data-and-information/publications/statistical/autism-statistics/autism-statistics (accessed 08/08/20).

Parliamentary Office of Science and Technology (2020) UK Parliament, 'Autism', *POST notes 612*.

Public Health England (2019) *Child Health Profiles*. Available at https://fingertips.phe.org.uk

Rain Man (1988) Film directed by Barry Levinson. Distributed by United Artists.

Review Journal of Autism and Developmental Disorders (2020) 7:306–317

Russell, G., Steer, C. & Golding, J. (2011) 'Social and demographic factors that influence the diagnosis of autistic spectrum disorders.' *Social Psychiatry and Psychiatric Epidemiology 46*(12), 1283–1293. doi.org/10.1007/s00127-010-0294-z

Russo, F. (2018) 'The costs of camouflaging autism.' *Spectrum*. Available at www.spectrumnews.org/features/deep-dive/costs-camouflaging-autism (accessed 01/01/21).

Rutherford, M., McKenzie, K., Johnson, T., Catchpole, C. *et al.* (2016) 'Gender ratio in a clinical population sample, age of diagnosis and duration of assessment in children and adults with autism spectrum disorder.' *Autism 20*(5), 628–34. doi: 10.1177/1362361315617879

Sedgewick., F., Hill, V. & Pellicano, E. (2018) 'Parent perspectives on autistic girls' friendships and futures.' *Autism and Developmental Language Impairments* 3(1–12). doi.org/10.1177/2396941518794497

Sedgewick, F., Hill, V. & Pellicano, E. (2019) '"It's different for girls": Gender differences in the friendships and conflict of autistic and neurotypical adolescents.' *Autism 23*(5), 1119–1132.

Simone, R. (2010) *Aspergirls*. London: Jessica Kingsley Publishers.

Singer, J. (1998) 'Odd People In: A personal exploration of a new social movement based on neurological diversity.' Thesis. Sydney: University of Technology Sydney.

Solomon, M., Miller, M., Taylo,r, S.L., Hinshaw, S.P. & Carter, C.S. (2012) 'Autism symptoms and internalizing psychopathology in girls and boys with autism spectrum disorders.' *Journal of Autism and Developmental Disorders 42*(1), 48–59.

Vermeulen, P. (2014)'The Practice of Promoting Happiness in Autism.' In G. Jones & E. Hurley (Eds) *Good Autism Practice: Autism, Happiness and Wellbeing*. Birmingham: BILD.

Winter-Messiers, M., Herr, C., Wood, C., Brooks, A., Gates, M. *et al.* (2007) 'How far can Brian ride the Daylight 4449 Express? A strength-based model of Asperger syndrome based on special interest areas.' *Focus on Autism and Other Developmental Disabilities* 22, 67–79.

Wittemeyer, K., Charman, T., Cusack, J., Guldberg, K. *et al.* (2011) *Educational Provision and Outcomes for People on the Autism Spectrum.* London: Autism Education Trust.

Wood, R. (2019) 'Autism, intense interests and support in school: From wasted efforts to shared understandings. *Educational Review* 73(2),1–21. doi: 10.1080/00131911.2019.1566213

World Health Organization (2004/2020) *ICD-10/11: International Statistical Classification of Diseases and Related Health Problems.* Available at www.who.int/news/item/18-06-2018-who-releases-new-international-classification-of-diseases-(icd-11).

Further reading

Castellon, S. (2020) *The Spectrum Girl's Survival Guide: How to Grow Up Awesome and Autistic.* London: Jessica Kingsley Publishers.

Cook, B. & Garnett, M. (2018) *Spectrum Women. Walking to the Beat of Autism.* London: Jessica Kingsley Publishers.

Pang, C. (2021) *Explaining Humans. What Science Can Teach Us about Life, Love and Relationships.* London: Penguin Books.

Silberman, S. (2016) *NeuroTribes: The Legacy of Autism and How to Think Smarter about People Who Think Differently.* Melbourne: Allen & Unwin.

Steward, R. (2019) *The Autism-Friendly Guide to Periods.* Jessica Kingsley Publishers, London.

Chapter 3: References

Cook, B. & Garnett, M. (2018) *Spectrum Women: Walking to the Beat of Autism.* London: Jessica Kingsley Publishers.

Department for Education. Relationships Education, *Relationships and Sex Education (RSE) and Health Education* 'Statutory guidance for governing bodies, proprietors, head teachers, principals, senior leadership teams, teachers.' https://assets.publishing.service.gov.uk/government/uploads/system/uploads/attachment_data/file/908013/Relationships_Education__Relationships_and_Sex_Education__RSE__and_Health_Education.pdf

Dickerson Mayes, S., Calhoun, S.L., Aggarwal, R., Baker, C. *et al.* (2013) 'Unusual fears in children with autism.' *Research in Autism Spectrum Disorders* 7(1), 151–158.

Edelson, M.G. (2010) 'Sexual abuse of children with autism: Factors that increase risk and interfere with recognition of abuse.' *Disabilities Studies Quarterly* 30(1) Special issue: Autism and Neurodiversity (invited manuscript).

Gaigg, S., Crawford, J. & Cottell, H. (2018) 'An evidence based guide to anxiety.' *Autism Research Group*. City, University of London: Autism and Social Communication Team, West Sussex County Council.

Gray, C. (1994) *Comic Strip Conversations™*. Arlington, TX: Future Horizons Inc.

Krishnarathi, A., William Dharma Raja, B. & Sundaravalli, S.R. (2018) 'Empowerment of girls and women with ASD.' *International Journal of Recent Advances in Multidisciplinary Research* 5(5), 3817–3820.

Lawson, W. (2017) 'Women and girls on the autism spectrum: A profile.' *Journal of Intellectual Disability – Diagnosis and Treatment* 5, 90–95.

Mandy, W. & Tchanturia, K. (2015) 'Do women with eating disorders who have social and flexibility difficulties really have autism? A case series.' *Molecular Autism* 6, 6. Available at www.molecularautism.com/content/6/1/6 (accessed 11/03/21).

Mansell, S., Sobsey, D. & Moskal, R. (1998) 'Clinical findings among sexually abused children with and without developmental disabilities.' *Intellectual and Developmental Disabilities* 36(1), 12–22. doi: 10.1352/0047-6765(1998)036<0012:CFASAC>2.0.CO;2.

Mayes, S.D., Calhoun, S.L., Aggarwal, R., Baker, C. *et al.* (2012) 'Unusual fears in children with autism.' *Research in Autism Spectrum Disorders* 7(1), 151. doi 10.1016/j.rasd.2012.08.002

Sedgewick, F., Hill, V. & Pellicano, E. (2018) 'Parent perspectives on autistic girls' friendships and futures.' *Autism and Developmental Language Impairments* 3(1–12). doi.org/10.1177/2396941518794497

Sedgewick, F., Crane, L., Hill, V. & Pellicano, E. (2019) 'Friends and lovers: The relationships of autistic and neurotypical women.' *Autism in Adulthood* 1(2), 112–123. doi.org/10.1089/aut.2018.0028

Further reading

Gould, J. (2013) 'Towards the under recognition of girls and women on the autism spectrum.' *Autism* 21(6) 703–705.

Holliday Willey, L. (2011) *Safety Skills for Asperger Women: How to Save a Perfectly Good Female Life*. London: Jessica Kingsley Publishers.

Lovegrove, E. (2020) *Autism, Bullying and Me*. London: Jessica Kingsley Publishers.

Nicholls, S. (2009) *Girls Growing up on the Autism Spectrum*. London: Jessica Kingsley Publishers.

Ridout, S. (2020) 'Establishing Neurodivergent Authorship in the Sexual Violence Debate.' In D. Milton (Ed.) *The Neurodiversity Reader*. Shoreham-on-Sea: Pavilion.

Ridout, S. (2021) *Neurodiversity, Autism and Recovery from Sexual Violence*. Shoreham-on-Sea: Pavilion.

Chapter 4: References

American Psychiatric Association (2013) *Diagnostic and Statistical Manual of Mental Disorders, fifth edition (DSM-5)*. Arlington, VA: American Psychiatric Association.

Bargiela, S. Steward, R. & Mandy, W. (2016) 'The experiences of late-diagnosed women with autism spectrum conditions: An investigation of the female autism phenotype.' *Journal of Autism and Developmental Disorders* 46, 3281–3294.

Begeer, S., Mandell, D., Wijnker-Holmes, B., Venderbosch, S. *et al.* (2013) 'Sex differences in the timing of identification among children and adults with autism spectrum disorders.' *Journal of Autism and Developmental Disorders* 43(5), 1151–1156. doi: 10.1007/s10803-012-1656-z

Bethoz, S. & Hill, E.L. (2005) 'The validity of using self-reports to assess emotion regulation abilities in adults with autism spectrum disorder.' *European Psychiatry* 20(3), 291–298.

Camm-Crosbie, L., Bradley, L., Shaw, R., Baron-Cohen, S. & Cassidy, S. (2019) 'People like me don't get support and treatment for mental health difficulties, self-injury and suicidality.' *Autism* 23(6), 1431–1441.

Cook, A., Ogden, J. & Winstone N. (2018) 'Friendship motivations, challenges and the role of masking for girls with autism in contrasting school settings.' *European Journal of Special Needs Education* 33(3), 302–315. doi: 10.1080/08856257.2017.1312797

Crompton, C.J., Hallett, S., Ropar, D., Flynn, E. & Fletcher-Watson, S. (2020a) '"I never realised everybody felt as happy as I do when I am around autistic people": A thematic analysis of autistic adults' relationships with autistic and neurotypical friends and family.' *Autism* 24(6), 1309–1310. doi.org/10.1177/1362361320908976

Crompton, C.J, Ropar, D., Evans-Williams, C.V.M., Flynn, E.G. & Fletcher-Watson, S. (2020b) 'Autistic peer-to-peer information transfer is highly effective.' *Autism* 24(7), 1704–1712. doi.org/10.1177/1362361320919286

Dunn Buron, K. & Curtis, M. (2012) *The Incredible 5 Point Scale. The Significantly Improved and Expanded Second Edition*. Shawnee, KS: AAPC Publishing.

Edey, R., Cook, J., Brewer, R. & Johnson, M. (2016) 'Interaction takes two: Typical adults exhibit mind-blindness towards those with autism spectrum disorder.' *Journal of Abnormal Psychology* 125, 879–885.

Gaigg, S.B., Cornell, A.S.F. & Bird, G. (2018) 'The psychophysiological mechanisms of alexithymia in autism spectrum disorder.' *Autism* 22(2), 227–231. doi.org/10.1177/1362361316667062

Gaigg, S., Crawford, J. & Cottell, H. (2018) 'An evidence based guide to anxiety.' City, University of London & the Autism and Social Communication Team, West Sussex County Council.

Garfinkel, S.N., Seth, A.K., Barrett, A.B., Suzuki, K. & Critchley, H.D. (2015) 'Knowing your own heart: Distinguishing interoceptive accuracy from interoceptive awareness.' *Biological Psychology* 104, 65–74. doi: org/10.1016/j.biopsycho.2014.11.004

Giarelli, E., Wiggins, L.D., Rice, C.E., Levy, S.E. *et al.* (2010) 'Sex differences in the evaluation and diagnosis of autism spectrum disorders among children.' *Disability Health Journal* 3(2), 107–16. doi: 10.1016/j.dhjo.2009.07.001.

Heasman, B. & Gillespie, A. (2018) 'Perspective-taking is two-sided: Misunderstandings between people with Asperger's syndrome and their family members.' *Autism* 22(6), 740–750.

Hill, A. (2018) 'Different for girls: Understanding autism.' The Guardian (28 April). Available at www.theguardian.com/lifeandstyle/2019/apr/28/girls-women-autism-diagnosis-aspbergers#comments (accessed 14/05/21).

Hull, L., Mandy, W., Lai, M.C., Baron-Cohen, S. *et al.* (2018) 'Development and validation of the Camouflaging Autistic Traits Questionnaire (CAT-Q).' *Journal of Autism and Developmental Disorders* 49(3), 819–833. doi.org/10.1007/s10803-018-3792-6

Hull, L., Petrides, K.V., Allison, C., Smith, P. *et al.* (2017) '"Putting on my best normal": Social camouflaging in adults with autism spectrum conditions.' *Journal of Autism and Developmental Disorders* 47(3), 2519–2534. doi: 10.1007/s10803-017-3166-5

Hirvikoski, T., Mittendorfer-Rutz, E., Boman, M., Larsson, H., Lichtenstein, P. & Bölte, S. (2015) 'Premature mortality in autism spectrum disorder.' *The British Journal of Psychiatry* 1–7. doi: 10.1192/bjp.bp.114.160192

Kanner, L. (1943) 'Autistic disturbances of affective contact.' *Nervous Child* 2, 217–250.

Kourti, M. & MacLeod, A. (2019) '"I don't feel like a gender. I feel like myself:" Autistic individuals raised as girls exploring gender identity.' *Autism in Adulthood* 1(1). doi.org/10.1089/aut.2018.0001

Lawson, W. (2017) 'Women and girls on the autism spectrum.' *Journal of Intellectual Disability – Diagnosis and Treatment* 5, 90–95.

Lawson, J. (2010) 'An investigation into behaviours which challenge at university: The impact of neurotypical expectations on autistic students.' *Good Autism Practice (GAP)* 11(1), 45–51.

Maisel, M.E., Stephenson, K.G., South, M., Rodgers, J., Freeston, M.H. & Gaigg, S.B. (2016) 'Modeling the cognitive mechanisms linking autism symptoms and anxiety in adults.' *Journal of Abnormal Psychology* 125(5), 692–703. doi.org/10.1037/abn0000168

McKay, M. (2020) 'The energy accounting system for autism.' Available at https://medium.com/age-of-awareness/the-energy-accounting-activity-for-autism-3a245e34bdfb

Milton, D.E.M. (2012) 'On the ontological status of autism: The "double empathy problem".' *Disability & Society* 27, 883–887.

Milton, D.E.M., Heasman, B. & Sheppard, E. (2018) 'Double Empathy.' In F. Volkmar (Ed.) *Encyclopedia of Autism Spectrum Disorders*. New York, NY: Springer.

Morrison, K.E., DeBrabander, K.M., Jones, D.R., Faso, D.J., Ackerman, R.A. & Sasson, N.J. (2019). 'Outcomes of real-world social interaction for autistic adults paired with autistic compared to typically developing partners.' *Autism* 24(5) 1027–1030. doi.org/10.1177/1362361319892701

Moyse, R. & Porter, J. (2015) 'The experience of the hidden curriculum for autistic girls at mainstream primary schools.' *European Journal of Special Educational Needs* 30(2), 3. doi: 10.1080/08856257.2014.986915

Parish-Morris, J., Liberman, M.Y., Cieri, C., Herrington, J.D *et al.* (2017) 'Linguistic camouflage in girls with autism spectrum disorder.' *Molecular Autism* 8(1), 48. doi.org/10.1186/s1322 9-017-0164-6.

Pelton, M.K. & Cassidy, S. A. (2017) 'Are autistic traits associated with suicidality? A test of the interpersonal-psychological theory of suicide in a non-clinical young adult sample.' *Autism Research, 10(11)*, 1891-1904.

Rynkiewicz, A., Schuller, B., Marchi, E., Piana, S. *et al.* (2016) 'An investigation of the "female camouflage effect" in autism using a computerized ADOS-2 and a test of sex/gender differences.' *Molecular Autism* 7(10), 1. doi.org/10.1186/s1322 9-016-0073-0

Sasson, N.J., Faso, D.J., Nugent, J., Lovell, S., Kennedy, D.P. & Grossman, R.B. (2017) 'Neurotypical peers are less willing to interact with those with autism based on thin slice judgments.' *Scientific Reports* 7, 40700.

Sedgewick, F., Crane, L., Hill, V. & Pellicano, E. (2019) 'Friends and lovers: The relationships of autistic and neurotypical women.' *Autism in Adulthood* 1(2), 112–123. doi.org/10.1089/aut.2018.0028

Shattuck, P.T., Durkin, M., Maenner, M., Newschaffer, C. *et al.* (2009) 'Timing of identification among children with an autism spectrum disorder: findings from a population-based surveillance study.' *Journal of the American Academy of Child and Adolescent Psychiatry* 48(5), 474–483. doi: 10.1097/CHI.0b013e31819b3848

Sheppard, E., Pillai, D., Wong, T.-L., Ropar, D. & Mitchell, P. (2016) 'How easy is it to read the minds of people with autism spectrum disorder?' *Journal of Autism and Developmental Disorders* 46, 1247–1254.

Sifneos, P.E. (1973) 'The prevalence of "alexithymic" characteristics in psychosomatic patients.' *Psychotherapy and Psychosomatics* 22(2–6), 255–262. doi.org/10.1159/000286529

South, M. & Rodgers, J. (2017) 'Sensory, emotional and cognitive contributions to anxiety in autism spectrum disorders.' *Frontiers in Human Neuroscience* 11, 1–7. doi.org/10.3389/fnhum.2017.00020

Van Steensel, F., Bögels, S.M. & Perrin, S. (2011) 'Anxiety disorders in children and adolescents with autistic spectrum disorders: A meta-analysis.' *Clinical Child and Family Psychology Review* 14(3), 302–317.

Wood, R. (2019) *Inclusive Education for Autistic Children: Helping Young People to Flourish and Learn in the Classroom.* London: Jessica Kingsley Publishers.

World Health Organization. (2018). *The International Classification of Diseases, 11th edition (ICD-11)*. Geneva, Switzerland: American College of Physicians.

Chapter 5: References

ARFID (nd) *What is ARFID?* Available at www.arfidawarenessuk.org/what-is-arfid (accessed 14/05/21).

Begeer, S., Mandell, D., Wijnker-Holmes, B., Venderbosch, S. *et al.* (2013) 'Sex differences in the timing of identification among children and adults with autism spectrum disorders.' *Journal of Autism and Developmental Disorders* 43(5), 1151–1156.

Brede, J., Babb, C., Jones, C., Elliott, M., Zanker, C., Tchanturia, K., ... & Mandy, W. (2020). "For me, the anorexia is just a symptom, and the cause is the autism": Investigating restrictive eating disorders in autistic women. *Journal of autism and developmental disorders,* 50(12), 4280-4296.

Casanova, E.L., Sharp, J.L., Edelson, S.M., Kelly, D.P. & Casanova, M.F. (2018) 'A cohort study comparing women with autism spectrum disorder with and without generalized joint hypermobility.' *Behavioural Science* 8(3), 35. doi: 10.3390/bs8030035

East Suffolk and North Essex NHS Foundation, Leeds and York Partnership NHS Foundation Trust (nd) 'Postnatal Care Information' and 'Pregnancy Passport'. Visuals ©LYPFT. Available at www.easyonthei-leeds.nhs.uk.

Geelhand, P., Bernard, P., Klein, O., Van Tiel, B. & Kissine, M. (2019) 'The role of gender in the perception of autism symptom severity and future behavioral development.' *Molecular Autism* 10(1), 16.

Gray, C. (2015) *The New Social Story Book, Revised and Expanded 15th Anniversary Edition.* Arlington, TX: Future Horizons.

Green, J. (nd) 'Understanding hypermobility disorders/syndromes in schools.' NASEN. Available at www.sussexeds.com/post/understanding-hypermobility-disorders-syndromes-in-schools (accessed 15/03/21).

Hakim, A. and Graham, R. (2003) 'Joint hypermobility.' *Best Practice & Research Clinical Rheumatology* 17(6) 989–1004. doi:10.1016/S1521-6942(03)00108-6

Hirvikoski, T., Mittendorfer-Rutz, E., Boman, M., Larsson, H., Lichtenstein, P. & Bölte, S. (2016) 'Premature mortality in autism spectrum disorder.' *British Journal of Psychiatry* 208(3), 232–238. doi:10.1192/bjp.bp.114.160192

Karim, K. & Baines, S. (2016) 'Deliberate self-harm in autistic children and young people. National Autistic Society.' Available at www.autism.org.uk/advice-and-guidance/topics/mental-health/self-harm/professionals (accessed 15/03/21).

Kerr-Gaffney, J., Halls, D., Harrison, A., & Tchanturia, K. (2020). Exploring relationships between autism spectrum disorder symptoms and eating disorder symptoms in adults with anorexia nervosa: A network approach. *Frontiers in psychiatry, 11*, 401.

Kinnaird, E., Norton, C., Pimblett, C., Stewart, C., & Tchanturia, K. (2019). Eating as an autistic adult: An exploratory qualitative study. *PloS One, 14*(8), e0221937.

Lockwood Estrin, G., Milner, V., Spain, D., Happé, F. & Colvert, E. (2020) 'Barriers to autism spectrum disorder diagnosis for young women and girls: A systematic review.' *Review Journal of Autism and Developmental Disorders*. https://doi.org/10.1007/s40489-020-00225-8

Mandy, W., Chilvers, R., Chowdhury, U., Salter, G., Seigal, A. & Skuse, D. (2012) 'Sex differences in autism spectrum disorder: Evidence from a large sample of children and adolescents.' *Journal of Autism and Developmental Disorders 42*, 1304–13.

Mandy, W. & Tchanturia, K. (2015) 'Do women with eating disorders who have social and flexibility difficulties really have autism? A case series.' *Molecular Autism 6*(1), 6. https://doi.org/10.1186/2040-2392-6-6

Matheson, B. E., & Douglas, J. M. (2017). Overweight and obesity in children with autism spectrum disorder (ASD): a critical review investigating the etiology, development, and maintenance of this relationship. *Review Journal of Autism and Developmental Disorders, 4*(2), 142-156.

Matthews, A., Kramer, R. A., & Mitan, L. (2021). Eating disorder severity and psychological morbidity in adolescents with anorexia nervosa or atypical anorexia nervosa and premorbid overweight/obesity. *Eating and Weight Disorders-Studies on Anorexia, Bulimia and Obesity*, 1-10.

Meierer, K., Hudon, A., Sznajder, M., Leduc, M. F., Taddeo, D., Jamoulle, O., ... & Stheneur, C. (2019). Anorexia nervosa in adolescents: evolution of weight history and impact of excess premorbid weight. *European journal of pediatrics, 178*(2), 213-219.

Moseley, R. L., Druce, T., & Turner-Cobb, J. M. (2020). `When my autism broke': A qualitative study spotlighting autistic voices on menopause. *Autism, 24*(6), 1423-1437.

Moseley, R. L., Druce, T., & Turner-Cobb, J. M. (2020). Autism research is `all about the blokes and the kids': Autistic women breaking the silence on menopause. *British Journal of Health Psychology*.

Muskens, J.B., Velders, F.P. & Staal, W.G. (2017) 'Medical comorbidities in children and adolescents with autism spectrum disorders and attention deficit hyperactivity disorders: A systematic review.' *European Child and Adolescent Psychiatry 26*, 1093–1103. https://doi.org/10.1007/s00787-017-1020-0

Pavlopoulou, G. (2020) 'A good night's sleep: Learning about sleep from autistic adolescents' personal accounts.' *Frontiers in Psychology*. https://doi.org/10.3389/fpsyg.2020.583868

Reinoso, G., Carsone, B., Weldon, S., Powers, J., & Bellare, N. (2018). Food selectivity and sensitivity in children with autism spectrum disorder: A systematic review defining the issue and evaluating interventions. *New Zealand Journal of Occupational Therapy, 65*(1), 36-42.

Russell, G., Steer, C. & Golding, J. (2011) 'Social and demographic factors that influence the diagnosis of autistic spectrum disorders.' *Social Psychiatry and Psychiatric Epidemiology 46*(12), 1283–1293.

Siklos, S. & Kerns, K.A. (2007) 'Assessing the diagnostic experiences of a small sample of parents of children with autism spectrum disorders.' *Research in Developmental Disabilities 28*(1), 9–22.

Smink, F.R.E., van Hoeken, D., Oldehinkel. A.J. & Hoek, H.W. (2014) 'Prevalence and severity of DSM-5 eating disorders in a community cohort of adolescents.' *International Journal of Eating Disorders* 47, 610–619.

Steward, R., Crane, L., Roy, E. M., Remington, A., & Pellicano, E. (2020). "Life is much more difficult to manage during periods": autistic experiences of menstruation. *The Palgrave Handbook of Critical Menstruation Studies*, 751-761.

Sundelin, H. Stephansson, O. Hultman, C. & Ludvigsson, J.F. (2018) 'Pregnancy outcomes in women with autism: A nationwide population-based cohort study.' *Clinical Epidemiology* 10, 1817–1826. Available at www.ncbi.nlm.nih.gov/pmc/articles/PMC6280895/pdf/clep-10-1817.pdf (accessed 14/05/21).

Toloza, C. and Tchanturia, K. (n.d.) *Common comorbidities with eating disorders*. Available at https://peacepathway.org/blog/common-comorbidities-with-eating-disorders

Valicenti-McDermott, M., McVicar, K., Rapin, I., Wershil, B.K., Cohen, H. & Shinnar, S. (2006) 'Frequency of gastrointestinal symptoms in children with autistic spectrum disorders and association with family history of autoimmune disease.' *Journal of Developmental and Behavioral Pediatrics* 27(2 Suppl.), S128–S136.

Virgo, H.(2019) *Stand Tall Little Girl*. Newark: Trigger.

Vuillier, L., Carter, Z., Teixeira, A.R. & Moseley, R.L. (2020) 'Alexithymia may explain the relationship between autistic traits and eating disorder psychopathology.' *Molecular Autism* 11, 63. https://doi.org/10.1186/s13229020-00364-z

Wilson, C.E., Murphy, C.M., McAlonan, G., Robertson, D.M. *et al.* (2016) 'Does sex influence the diagnostic evaluation of autism spectrum disorder in adults?' *Autism* 20(7), 808–819.

Further reading

Hendrickx, S. & Tinsley, M (2008) *Asperger Syndrome and Alcohol: Drinking to Cope?* London: Jessica Kingsley Publishers.

Kunreuther, E. & Palmer, A. (2017) *Drinking, Drug Use, and Addiction in the Autism Community.* London: Jessica Kingsley Publishers.

Chapter 6: References

Allen, R. & and Heaton, P. (2010) 'Autism, music, and the therapeutic potential of music in alexithymia.' *Music Perception* 27, 251–261. doi: 10.1525/mp.2010.27.4.251

Bojner Horwitz, E., Lennartsson, A.-K., Theorell, T.P.G. & Ullén, F. (2015) 'Engagement in dance is associated with emotional competence in interplay with others.' *Frontiers in Psychology* 6, 1096. doi: 10.3389/fpsyg.2015.01096

Loomes, G. (nd) Voicespaces. Available at https://voicespaces.co.uk/about (accessed 15/03/21).

Malkina-Pykh, I.G. (2013) 'Effectiveness of rhythmic movement therapy: Case study of alexithymia.' *Body, Movement and Dance in Psychotherapy* 8, 141–159. doi: 10.1080/17432979.2013.804435

Meijer-Degen, F. & and Lansen, J. (2006) 'Alexithymia – a challenge to art therapy.' *The Arts in Psychotherapy* 33, 167–179. doi: 10.1016/j.aip.2005.10.002

Neckar, M. & and Bob, P. (2017) 'Synesthetic associations and psychopathological symptoms: Preliminary evidence in young women.' *Activitas Nervosa Superior* 58, 78–83. doi: 10.1007/bf03379738

Poquérusse, J., Pastore, L., Dellantonio, S. & Esposito, G. (2018) 'Alexithymia and autism spectrum disorder: A complex relationship.' *Frontiers in Psychology*, 17 July. https://doi.org/10.3389/fpsyg.2018.01196

Zangwill, N. (2013) 'Music, autism, and emotion.' *Frontiers in Psychology* 4, 890. doi: 10.3389/fpsyg.2013.00890s

Subject Index

Author Index